PLENTY

Good, uncomplicated food for
the sustainable kitchen

DIANA HENRY

MITCHELL BEAZLEY

Contents

Introduction

I started to write this book just before the current global recession. As soon as the downturn hit, publishers and newspaper and magazine editors went into recession overdrive; they all wanted books and articles about inexpensive food. I thought this was missing the point. Before the recession, a sea change in our attitude towards food was already taking place. We had known for ages—though we hadn't fully faced it—that we were not using what we have in the best way. In the developed world we were over-fishing, using too many of the world's resources to produce meat, and totally disconnected from the agricultural practices that put the food on our plates. Many of us were eating a dangerously unhealthy diet. Perhaps worst of all, we were wasting tons of food; literally throwing it out.

My response to the cry for articles on inexpensive food was that a desire for this had already brought about a tragic state of affairs: not only mad cow disease, but also a world full of unhealthy, processed junk food that comes with a low price tag but at a high cost in other ways. And when people bemoaned how little we had, all I could think was how very much we had.

This book is about a thoughtful approach to food, one that is better for you in terms of money saved and pleasure gained, and for the world around you. By that I don't just mean the planet, but the people who produce our food.

I am not here to preach, though. The last thing I want to do is make you don a hair shirt before you go shopping. I am a food writer. I am essentially in the business of giving pleasure. But I believe that approaching food in a caring, thoughtful way will increase the pleasure you get from it. Knowing what to do with the leftover chicken in your refrigerator, how to deal with a glut of apples by making chutney, how to turn a load of inexpensive potatoes and winter greens into the most delicious, olive oil–rich supper (the dish is from Greece and it's on page 85) will bring you more joy than buying overprocessed food, and make for a healthier, happier life.

A shift in emphasis

We are much more concerned, post–mad cow disease, about where our food comes from and how it has been produced. We go to farmers' markets, we demand information about provenance, and we have even taken to growing our own vegetables. We want good food. But good food can come with a higher price tag. Intensively farmed meat is cheaper than meat from animals reared with care on a small farm. Artisan bread is more expensive than factory-made loaves.

I am not asking you to triple your food spending. The key to good eating is to buy better food and use it well. This means balancing the cost of good food by, for example, using all of a roast—making more meals from the leftovers and stock from the bones—and eating cheaper cuts of meat and inexpensive dried beans, vegetables, and grains at other times. The food that offers terrible value for money is that which is prepared for us: supermarket ready meals and the like. It lasts for only one meal and contains cheaper ingredients (such as meat produced under conditions–often in other countries–that we know nothing about).

The remains of the day

As I was growing up I learned the art of dovetailing meals: always using up leftovers. This was not out of poverty, but because a philosophy of using every bit of an animal and not throwing out food prevailed. This is good for the household budget, but it's also a sane way to think about the world's resources. The word "leftovers" does not sound great. The French, more charmingly, call them *les delicieux petits restes*. They have the right approach: leftovers can produce some of the most imaginative and delicious dishes.

My favorite kind of cooking is not the showy-off sort, which takes days of planning and shopping, but the pottering, "I-wonder-what's-in-the-fridge" kind. There's no grand plan: you just go where serendipity and improvisation take you. Monday, when there's a bit of weekend roast left, is the best day for this musing kind of approach. Chicken–if you can get your hands on it–is perfect (though we fight over cold roast chicken in our house). Fry the leftover nuggets with bacon, a couple of tablespoons of cream, and a handful of frozen peas and you have a sauce for pasta. (Even half a cup of gravy, fried mushrooms, and a dollop of cream are delicious on pasta.) You can toss shredded chicken with rice, strips of omelet and chile to make a perfect hangover cure, too.

Cold roast lamb, cooked nice and pink so that a bit more heat won't harm it, can form the basis of a Middle Eastern pilaf that will be just as enjoyable as yesterday's roast. If you have some preserved lemon to throw in, or a few dried apricots, so much the better. What of leftover vegetables? Potatoes are easy. Sauté slowly–maybe with some mushrooms–until the pan is covered with golden flakes, finish with garlic and parsley, and you have a dish that is perfect with duck or chicken.

And then there is stock. Get those bones into a pot. There is so much flavor still to be extracted, it is a shame to throw them away. It takes next to no effort, and you can reduce the result by boiling, then freeze it in tubs. Soups and sauces are then yours for the making (and although it's great that you can now buy fresh stock, just look at its price; much better to make your own).

The art of using food up even goes as far as finding something to do with a bag of overly-soft plums. They can easily be transformed into a pot of jam. You don't have to get out a preserving pan and go into full-scale production–it's very easy to make just one small pot and keep it in the refrigerator for eating on toast or with yogurt at breakfast.

What to do with "*les restes*" is a primary feature of my opening chapter, and one of the cornerstones of this book. But throughout the chapters you will find tips about what to do with leftovers. For me the path to contentment definitely wends its way past the stove, but it's always a good idea to go via the remains in the refrigerator.

Seasonal sustenance

Seasonality is the modern cook's mantra, so you hardly need me to repeat it, but eating food in season saves you money and makes you feel better. Why pay $3.50 for a package of tastleless strawberries in February? They'll be delicious in June, and by July they'll be relatively inexpensive too.

The mad practices employed to give us out-of-season produce are also bad for the planet. (I do make an exception for exotic fruit and vegetables; they're not cultivated here, and I'm glad to eat mangoes and pineapples when they are in season in the countries in which they are grown.)

To market, to market...

You have a lot of power. With every supermarket purchase you tell them how much you're prepared to pay for pork from a well-cared-for pig, you can save a great heritage apple variety, you can choose to support local food producers, and you can have an impact on whether a particular fish is fished to extinction.

I don't want the day to come when I tell my grandchildren about the fish we used to eat, or look at countryside that has been turned into a theme park and reminisce about the agriculture we once had. And I think it's brilliant that we have bakers and cheesemakers who are so passionate about their products that they make it their life's work.

So buy local, support good farmers and artisan food producers, and have a thought for sustainability. It doesn't have to cost the earth. With a bit of care, you can buy good food that will take you through the week for less than it costs to buy a weekful of ready meals.

Caring about ourselves

We are more anxious these days about what food is doing to our bodies. This is laudable, but has also led to a kind of craziness. Shopping for my children, I realized I felt guilty about not buying them food with added "bonuses". You know the kind of thing: drinks with extra vitamins, spreads that reduce cholesterol, bio yogurt that balances gut bacteria. Then two things happened. I saw that Coca–Cola appeared to be boasting about its healthiness (an 8oz serving of Diet Coke Plus provides, according to their website, 15 per cent of your RDA for niacin and vitamins B6 and B12). Then I interviewed the journalist Michael Pollan. Pollan had written a book called *In Defence of Food*, and it put my thinking straight. The book is about getting back to real food, forgetting about what nutritionists and marketeers tell us we should eat (as they so often get it wrong) and instead enjoying food with nothing added or taken out. As Pollan says, this food has no information on it and doesn't make extra money for those who sell it. A simple carrot cannot be labelled. But a carton of vegetable juice can, so you go for that option for the misguided sense of security it gives you. Pollan's mantra, and I urge you to follow it, is this: eat food, not too much, mostly plants. If you buy as much fresh and unprocessed stuff as possible, increase your intake of vegetables, grains, and beans, and don't overeat, you're going in the right direction. Happily, it will also save you money and treat the planet in a more responsible way.

Making life easier and more enjoyable

Where it seems appropriate, I have suggested cooking some ingredients—especially dried beans—in larger quantities than you immediately need, so you can use them later in the week. Cooking for the week ahead makes sense economically and also makes life easier (you've expended both effort and fuel, so you might as well get the most out of it). Look out for tips on ingredients that you can cook and adapt to see you through several days.

There are also recipes for what I call "long–term cooking": chutneys, jams, and other preserves. For years I was a bit embarrassed about doing this kind of thing. Although it gave me enormous pleasure (there's a real thrill in stashing jars of food away), preserving was seen as the domain of old ladies or frumpy aunts. Now we're realizing that it saves you money and allows you to create a bit of luxury. French cherry wine, anyone? It's on page 256....

The recipes

This is a book for home cooks. None of the recipes requires a high level of skill. It also reflects a do-able approach to food. I'd love to be able to buy a whole animal from the butcher (it does save money) or cure my own ham (ditto), but I don't have a big enough freezer or, as I live in a city, the space or environment for doing these things. But most of us have room for a few jars of chutney in the kitchen cupboard, and the time occasionally to make our own pizzas or a loaf of bread. You don't have to move to the country or go part-time to get the most out of *Plenty*.

All of the dishes are homely; and some are, in fact, humble, but that doesn't mean dull. There are dishes here from all over the world—from Sicily to Sweden, Ireland to Iran—all of them economical but indulgent, too.

What it boils down to is taking more care. We need to value our planet, our bodies, the people who produce our food, the animals who provide it, and those we feed every day. It makes for a much happier life.

The roast and "*les restes*"

A roast, juicy, sweet, and burnished from the oven, isn't just about good food, it's a way of living. It is a grand gesture, the pinnacle of home cooking, honoring both the animal and those you are feeding. It's also one of the most sensible meals you can cook, providing food that keeps on nourishing you in the coming days.

The art of looking in the refrigerator and pondering what you can do with bits of cooked meat (which the French, poetically, term *les restes*) used to be something we learned as children. Now we live in a "one meal, one dish" culture. Food is finished and cleared (even scraped into the garbage) on a daily basis. But this is a more expensive and less enjoyable way to cook and eat. If you begin the week with a roast, make stock from the bones for soup, then use the leftover meat for a pie or pilaf, the meat more than earns its place.

Even so, though I've given information on what to look for in the priciest cuts of beef– such as sirloin–below, I haven't covered it in the recipes. I just find it too expensive.

What to buy

Scares about meat have had an upside: we are now more concerned about where our meat comes from, how it has been raised, and what it has been fed.

Even if you don't care how animals are treated, your palate will benefit from taking it into consideration. A stressed animal means tougher meat. An animal reared at a normal rate (not fast-grown) and allowed to roam outdoors, foraging for whatever it fancies, will taste better than one that has undergone a standardized feeding regime and been fattened quickly. Also, slow-grown animals that are not densely stocked are more resistant to illness, so don't need regular antibiotics. And after slaughter, they are more likely to be properly hung. The problem is that this meat costs more. I am not telling you always to buy the expensive option; I don't. Even going for the "least bad" makes a difference. I just want you to know how to eat better, and in a way that is caring.

The supermarkets have smartened up their act lately. They now sell meat that is organic or free-range, but read the labels carefully and be aware that you could get more information from a butcher or farmer.

There is better meat available, beef that has been reared on small farms rather than a CAFO (confined animal feeding operation); cattle that has eaten grass for most of its life rather than a diet of corn; chickens that have been alowed to roam outside instead of crammed into houses. Think about where your meat has come from when you go shopping and be aware when reading labels. You can get more information from a good butcher, or, even better, a farmer from whom you buy directly.

Where to buy it

It's getting harder to find a good butcher. Many have gone out of business because they cannot compete with supermarkets. But faced with plastic-wrapped packs in a supermarket, whom do you ask for advice? A butcher can tell you where your meat comes from, what breed it is, and how it lived. He will source unusual cuts, bone a shoulder of lamb or cut up a chicken. A good butcher will hang meat properly, and he is unlikely to sell you poor meat, as he'll have to face you over the counter and apologize when you complain. An alternative is to buy from farm stores and farmers' markets. This cuts out the middle man and supports small farmers. Lastly, you can have home-delivery from a high-quality meat company or farm. But there's no point in me being holier-than-thou. I know that, because of time and cost, your only option may be the supermarket. If so, go for the best you can afford.

What to look for

PORK Pork is the meat on which I will not compromise. Pigs can be farmed so cruelly that I buy only outdoor reared pork. Apart from welfare, it's the flavor of properly reared pork that has compelled me to spend more money. There's a world of difference between pork from an old-fashioned breed that has grazed outside, eating windfall apples and roots, and pork that has been intensively farmed. Do yourself a favor and experience that difference.

BEEF Great beef comes from beef cattle that have fed on grass and natural forage, grown slowly on small farms. You should be able to get information from your butcher, or the farmer himself, on how the animal has lived and died.

Good beef should not be "aged" in vacuum packs, but dry-aged (hung). This breaks down the fibers, making it more tender and flavorful. It also dries the meat–making it better for cooking–and darkens the flesh. Beef should have a good covering of creamy white fat and clear marbling–threads of fat running through it.

LAMB The concerns here are pretty much the same as for beef. Lambs that have been reared on small farms, grown slowly and allowed to graze on natural forage will taste better, and have lived better, than those that are intensively farmed. In countries where lamb is prized, such as France, consumers are even aware of the different type of land on which lamb has foraged (salt marsh lamb, for example) and wants and expects this to be reflected in the flavor. In Britain, too, the area in which a lamb has been farmed will affect the taste and texture of the meat.

Lamb needs a good covering of white fat, something that can only be properly developed through slow growing, and the flesh should be pink.

New Zealand lamb is a good product in terms of taste, but it is harder to ascertain how it has been farmed. And why buy meat from the other side of the world when there is plenty of other stuff to eat? Certainly if your region has good lamb farmers, I would support them before buying lamb from abroad.

CHICKEN I am agog when I see a chicken for less than you'd pay for a bag of spuds. But high-profile campaigning has had an impact. Many shoppers are willing to pay more for chickens reared with care, and many poultry farmers are happy to make changes as long as supermarkets don't try to drive down prices.

Be very careful about reading the labels when buying poultry. The word "natural", though it sounds good, neither means "free-range" nor "organic". The best way to buy a tasty, healthy bird is to buy direct from a farmer a farmers' market. If you are buying from a supermarket look for the words "free-range" or "free roaming". You will also be getting a better product if you go for a chicken with the USDA organic label, though it wont mean that the chicken is free-range. Avoid chicken that is labeled "basted" or "self-basted" as it can contain flavor enhancers as well as edible fat, and water (although these are allowed by the USDA on chickens that are thus labeled).

I buy less, but better, chicken than I used to, usually a whole bird (much more economical) and I use it well, making good meals from the leftovers and stock for soup from the bones. I can see the benefits in terms of flavor and I feel better about the animal's welfare. Buy the best you can.

How to roast

We have become nervous about roasting. I myself have been in tears over lamb (when it wasn't cooked to the required pinkness), but experience has taught me two things: roast red meat for less time than you imagine it needs, and anybody can roast a chicken.

With all roasts, allow them to rest for 15–25 minutes after cooking, insulated well (I cover with foil, then a few thick towels kept for this purpose). It's better to undercook than overcook meat. Undercooked meat can be thrown back in the oven. If it's overcooked, all you can do is pretend it was deliberate....

You need to know your oven and how you like your meat, but here are my guidelines. Like Hugh Fearnley-Whittingstall, I believe in roasting prime cuts at a high heat for the first 15–30 minutes (what Hugh calls "the sizzle"), though there are variations in this chapter.

After the initial sizzle:

For pink lamb, cook for 12 minutes per pound at 350°F.

For rare beef, cook for 10 minutes per pound at 325°F.

For pork (which should be thoroughly cooked, though not to dryness), cook for 25 minutes per pound at 350°F.

Chickens are different. I don't do an initial "sizzle." Cook a chicken at 375°F for 20 minutes per pound, plus an extra 10 minutes.

Simple roast chicken with herbs

There's nothing like roast chicken to make you feel hungry, happy, and cared for. You can vary the herbs, though rosemary and sage are pretty powerful so use them carefully, and chervil (if you can find it) is lovely in spring. My only rule is to roast for 20 minutes at 375°F for each pound, plus an extra 10 minutes.

Serves 6

leaves from 4 thyme sprigs	**5 lb chicken**
1 tbsp chopped fresh flat-leaf parsley	**1 glass (⅔ cup) dry white wine**
2 tbsp butter, softened	**or water**
salt and pepper	

1 Preheat the oven to 375°F. Mash the herbs with the butter and season. Carefully lift the skin of the breast of the bird, starting from the neck end, so that you have a pocket into which to stuff the butter. Ease the skin from the legs in the same way. Push in as much butter as you can without tearing the skin, then set the chicken in a roasting pan and smear the remaining butter on the outside. Season.

2 Roast for about 1 hour 50 minutes, pouring the wine or water into the pan halfway through. To check if it's cooked, plunge a skewer between the leg and the body; the juices that run out should be clear, with no trace of pink.

3 Cover the bird with foil, then insulate it (I keep old towels for this) and leave to rest for 15–20 minutes. Put the bird on a heated platter (or just take it to the table in the roasting pan) and serve.

GRAVY

I must admit I hardly ever make gravy, preferring instead simply to spoon out the wonderful cooking juices, but if you want to make it properly, let the bird rest, insulated, and put the roasting pan on the burner. Skim off the excess fat. Add chicken stock or water (about 1¾ cups) to the tin and bring to a boil, scraping up all the juices and sediment from the bottom as you do so. Boil until you have a flavor and texture you like. You don't need to use a thickener; there's nothing wrong with thin gravy. Just make sure you don't reduce it so much that it is unpalatably salty.

ALSO TRY...

Leave out the herbs used above and mix the butter with torn basil and chopped sunblushed (semi-dried) tomatoes, or chopped black olives and anchovies, or grated Parmesan cheese and crushed garlic. These butters should be stuffed under the skin, or their ingredients will burn, so use plain butter to smear on the outside.

MORE WAYS TO ROAST CHICKEN

Corfu roast chicken with sweet potatoes and cayenne Season the chicken inside and out and place a lemon half and 2 bay leaves in the cavity, sprinkle with 1½ tsp cayenne and drizzle with olive oil and lemon juice. Cook as for Simple Roast Chicken (see page 16). Cut 2 red onions into wedges and cut 2 lb sweet potatoes (no need to peel) into chunks. Toss with another 1½ tsp cayenne, salt, pepper, and 2 tbsp olive oil. Put these around the chicken when there's 45 minutes cooking time left. Turn the vegetables a couple of times and sprinkle with chopped parsley and mint before serving.

Roast chicken with autumn fruits Cook as for Simple Roast Chicken (see page 16), but use only thyme in the butter and put the bird into a pan large enough for the fruit as well. You'll need 2 pears, quartered; 2 apples, cut into wedges; 4 plums, halved and pitted; 2 red onions cut into wedges; and ¼ cup dried cranberries or dried sour cherries (soaked in boiling water for 15 minutes and drained). Add 6 thyme sprigs. Sprinkle with 2 tbsp light brown sugar, season, and dot with butter. Toss in the fruit 45 minutes before the end of the cooking time and stir a couple of times for even browning.

Smoked paprika roast chicken with aioli Mix 6 tbsp olive oil, salt, pepper, and 2½ tbsp smoked paprika. Paint this on the chicken. Cook as for Simple Roast Chicken (see page 16). Meanwhile, crush 2 garlic cloves with a little salt in a large mortar and pestle or bowl. Stir in 2 egg yolks. Add 1¼ cup olive oil drop by drop, very slowly at first, beating as you do so. Only add more oil once the previous lot has been incorporated and the mixture has thickened. (If it splits, add the curdled mixture to a new yolk a little at a time, beating as before, but go easy this time) Taste and season with more salt, pepper, and lemon juice or white wine vinegar or both. Keep in the refrigerator, covered, until ready to serve with the chicken.

Roast chicken with preserved lemon and bay An idea from my friend, chef Matt Tebbutt. Put a whole preserved lemon (drained), a handful of cilantro sprigs, 6 bay leaves, and 2 heads of garlic, halved horizontally, inside the chicken. Season inside and out, put into a roasting tin and drizzle with olive oil. Roast as for Simple Roast Chicken (see page 16). Toast sourdough or French bread, then squeeze the softened garlic from inside the bird onto the toasts with some of the preserved lemon, diced. Carve at the table and moisten the toasts with the cooking juices.

Greek lemon roast chicken with potatoes and oregano Season the chicken inside and out and put into a very large roasting pan (you'll be adding vegetables later). Put half a lemon and a few bay leaves inside. Drizzle on some olive oil, squeeze on the other half of the lemon, and roast as for Simple Roast Chicken (see page 16). Cut 2 large, peeled red onions into wedges (you should get 5 wedges from each half), halve 2¼ lb of small waxy potatoes, cut 2 lemons into wedges, and break 2 heads of garlic into separate cloves (no need to peel). Toss with olive oil, salt and pepper, 1½ tsp dried oregano, and the juice of ½ lemon. When the chicken still has 45 minutes roasting to go, put the vegetables around the chicken, sprinkle 2 tsp dried oregano on top, and return to the oven. By the time the chicken is ready, the vegetables will be cooked.

Buttermilk-dressed roasted chicken with pickled rhubarb, potatoes and greens
Smear butter all over the chicken and season inside and out. Cook as for Simple Roast Chicken (see page 16). Meanwhile, prepare the rhubarb. Put ¾ cup cider vinegar and ¾ cup sugar in a pan and bring to a boil, stirring every so often to help the sugar dissolve. Turn the heat down and simmer for 10 minutes. Add 1 red onion, very thinly sliced, and simmer, uncovered, for 10 minutes. The onions will get soft in this time and the mixture will become thicker. Now add 12 oz rhubarb, cut into 2½ in lengths, and simmer gently for about 4 minutes more, or enough time for the rhubarb to become just tender. Don't overcook as you want the rhubarb to remain pink and the shape of the pieces to stay intact. Leave to cool. The mixture will thicken slightly as it cools down. To make a dressing, combine 1½ cups buttermilk with 6 tbsp whipping cream, 1 garlic clove, crushed, salt and pepper, a pinch of sugar, and a small bunch of mint leaves, chopped. Once the chicken is cooked, cover it with foil, insulate, and leave to rest for 15–20 minutes. Boil 1⅛ lb waxy potatoes and toss them in the pan with a little butter, salt, and pepper. Put the potatoes and the leaves of 3 baby Little Gem lettuce or hearts of romaine, in a bowl and drizzle over some of the dressing. Serve the salad with the chicken, offering the rhubarb sauce and the rest of the dressing on the side.

Malaysian roast chicken Prick the skin of the chicken all over with a fork so that the flavorings can penetrate the flesh. Mix together 6 tbsp oyster sauce, 4 tbsp soy sauce, 4 tbsp light brown sugar, 4 garlic cloves, crushed, 2 tsp chili paste (such as Chinese chili paste with garlic or harissa), and ¾ in square piece of fresh ginger, peeled and very finely chopped. Taste for the balance of hot, sour, salty, and sweet. Paint this all over the chicken, and rub it inside as well. Cover with foil and refrigerate for a couple of hours, or overnight if you can. Put into a roasting pan lined with fresh foil (to save your roasting pan) and roast as for Simple Roast Chicken (see page 16). After 15 minutes, pull the foil up around the chicken, then uncover the bird again in the last 15 minutes of cooking time—this stops the sugars in the marinade burning. Cover and insulate the chicken with fresh foil for 15–20 minutes so that it can rest before serving. Serve with the cooking juices. Rice and stir-fried green vegetables are good on the side.

Cherry and goat cheese–stuffed chicken

In the summer you can use fresh cherries, pitted, instead of dried ones.

Serves 6

4 lb chicken

salt and pepper

1 tbsp butter, softened

FOR THE STUFFING

2 tbsp butter

1 onion, finely chopped

3 garlic cloves, crushed

2 cups fresh white breadcrumbs

6 oz creamy goat cheese, in chunks

¼ cup chopped fresh dill

⅔ cup dried sour cherries, soaked in hot water for 15 minutes, then drained

1 Preheat the oven to 375°F. Wash the chicken inside and out and pat dry with paper towels. Season inside and out.

2 Melt the butter for the stuffing in a frying pan and cook the onion until soft but not colored. Add the garlic and cook for another minute. Spoon into a bowl and add the other stuffing ingredients. Gently mix (don't squash the cheese) and season well. Stuff the bird, place in a roasting pan and smear the butter on the outside. Roast for 1½ hours or until cooked through.

3 Spoon the stuffing into a serving bowl. Serve the chicken with the stuffing, lemon wedges, a cucumber salad, and a big bowl of bulgur.

ALSO TRY…

Pelopponese chicken with bread, feta, and tomato stuffing Sauté 1 onion, finely chopped, in ¼ cup olive oil until soft. Add 4 garlic cloves, finely chopped, for 2 more minutes. Add 8 oz cherry tomatoes, chopped, and sauté until soft. In a bowl put 10 slices of bread (such as ciabatta) torn into chunks, ½ cup crumbled feta cheese, and ⅓ cup chopped dill, parsley, or mint. Add 1 tbsp tomato paste mixed with 2 tsp olive oil, a small beaten egg, the onion, and tomatoes and seasoning. Mix well, then use to stuff the chicken. Season the outside of the bird, drizzle with olive oil, and roast as above.

Saffron roast chicken with Azerbaijani stuffing Adapted from a Margaret Shaida recipe. Preheat the oven as above. Rinse 6 tbsp basmati rice. Parboil in lightly salted water for 10 minutes. Drain. Chop ⅓ cup each dried figs and apricots and mix with 3 tbsp dried cranberries and 6 tbsp dried cherries. Put in a bowl and cover with just-boiled water. Leave for 15 minutes, then drain. Sauté an onion, chopped, in 2 tbsp butter until soft, then add the rice and stir to coat. Add the fruit with ½ cup walnuts or almonds, chopped. Season and cook for 2 minutes, stirring. Dissolve ½ tsp saffron threads in hot water and add 7 tbsp melted butter and the juice of 1 lemon. Season the chicken and stuff with the rice mixture. Put a piece of foil, big enough to tent the chicken, into a roasting pan. Place the chicken on top and pour over the saffron mixture. Pull the foil together and scrunch the edges to make a good seal. Roast for 1 hour. Open the foil and cook for another 30 minutes. Serve with the juices, green salad, and a bowl of chopped cucumber mixed with yogurt and mint.

Restorative chicken and parsley risotto

Sometimes I long to have leftover chicken just so that I can make this risotto. It isn't authentically Italian but seems to me to be the Italian equivalent of that great Jewish penicillin, chicken soup. You can make the risotto without the chicken–a lemon and parsley risotto is lovely–and you don't have to add the embellishment of the egg yolk or, indeed, the cream. But there's nothing wrong with making the most of your leftovers; life's too short to make them into the kind of food that feels puritan and austere.

Serves 4

5 cups chicken or vegetable stock
⅓ cup butter
1 tbsp olive oil
1 small onion, finely chopped
1½ cups risotto rice
½ unwaxed lemon
1¾ cups leftover cooked chicken,
    cut into chunks

1 egg yolk
5 tbsp freshly grated Parmesan cheese, plus
    more to serve
2 tbsp finely chopped fresh flat-leaf parsley
salt and pepper
½ cup heavy cream

1 Heat the stock to a simmer and keep it simmering throughout the cooking time. Heat half the butter and all the oil in a heavy saucepan and add the onion. Cook over a medium heat until soft but not colored. Add the rice and turn it around in the fat and juices until translucent.

2 Start to add the stock, a ladle at a time, stirring continuously. Don't add any new stock until the last addition has been absorbed. You are aiming for rice with the faintest hint of bite in the center of the grains. This should take about 20 minutes.

3 Finely grate the lemon zest and stir it in two-thirds of the way through the cooking. Add the chicken for the last 5–10 minutes, making sure it is heated through thoroughly. Squeeze the juice from the lemon half and mix it in a small bowl with the egg yolk, Parmesan, parsley, salt and pepper, and cream.

4 When the risotto is ready, take it off the heat, add the lemon juice mixture and the rest of the butter, and stir gently but thoroughly. Taste for seasoning. Cover and leave to rest for 2 minutes, then serve immediately. Offer extra grated Parmesan, if you want.

Vietnamese chicken with Nuoc Cham

This is a quite ordinary dish in itself, basically an Eastern pilaf, the rice absorbing the stock in which it is cooked. But it is the accompaniment that makes it special. Hot, sour, salty, sweet, this dish ends up being much more than the sort of food you expect to throw together with leftovers. It is literally a blast for the tastebuds. I do add other ingredients I have on hand, perhaps mushrooms, green beans, or julienned carrot. But no corn, please!

Serves 4

FOR THE NUOC CHAM
4 garlic cloves, chopped
2 fresh red chiles, halved, seeded
   and chopped
good pinch of salt flakes
juice of 1 lime
2 tbsp fish sauce
4 tsp superfine sugar

FOR THE CHICKEN AND RICE
2 cups long-grain rice
3 cups chicken stock

4 slices fresh ginger
salt and pepper
1 tbsp peanut oil
3 shallots, very thinly sliced
2¾ cups leftover cooked chicken, shredded
   or in small chunks
6 scallions, chopped on the diagonal
generous handful of mint leaves, torn

1 To make the Nuoc Cham, put the garlic and chiles in a mortar and pestle with the salt and grind until you almost have a paste. (It doesn't have to be perfectly smooth.) Add everything else and mix. Taste and adjust the balance of hot, sour, salty, and sweet to taste. It's very powerful, so dilute with a little water if you like, but remember it's going to be eaten with something starchy.

2 Put the rice into a saucepan and pour on the stock. Bring to a boil. Add the ginger and season. Boil until the rice starts to look "pitted" (about 4 minutes), then cover the pan and reduce the heat to very low. There will still be liquid left underneath the rice; it will be absorbed—and the steam will cook the rice—in about 15 minutes. Don't stir because this makes the rice sticky, but make sure it isn't sticking at the bottom (check gently with a fork) and add a little more boiling water if it is. The rice should be tender, light, and fluffy. Remove the bits of ginger. Keep the rice warm.

3 Heat the oil in a frying pan and quickly fry the shallots until pale gold. Add the chicken and cook until hot through. Carefully fork these into the rice with the scallions and mint. Serve with the Nuoc Cham—either drizzle it on top or let people help themselves.

Chiang Mai chicken noodles

A great change from Thai chicken curry, which I seem to make rather a lot. You can also make this with leftover pork.

Serves 4

FOR THE NOODLES
peanut oil
1 onion, sliced into crescent moon-shapes,
   or 6 shallots, sliced
4 garlic cloves, sliced
1 tsp ground turmeric
2 tbsp red Thai curry paste
14 oz can coconut milk
1 cup chicken stock
2½ cups leftover cooked chicken,
   in chunks

½ tsp light brown sugar, or to taste
2 tsp fish sauce, or to taste
juice of ½ lime, or to taste
12 oz Chinese wheat noodles

TO SERVE
2 scallions, chopped on the diagonal
1 fresh red chile, halved, seeded and
   shredded
2 tbsp chopped fresh cilantro
wedges of lime

1 Put 1 tbsp of the oil into a saucepan and sauté the onion or shallots until golden. Add the garlic and cook for 2 minutes, then add the turmeric and curry paste. Stir for 1 minute until the spices become fragrant. Add the coconut milk and stock and bring to a simmer. Cook for 15 minutes. Add the chicken and heat through thoroughly. Season with the sugar and fish sauce and adjust it to your taste; you may want lime or more sugar.

2 Cook the noodles according to the packet instructions. Divide them between four bowls, spoon over the chicken curry and sprinkle over the scallions, chile and cilantro. Offer wedges of lime to serve.

Chicken and ham pie

This is a perfect post-Thanksgiving dish when you have left over turkey and ham.

Serves 4

¼ cup butter	1 cup cooked ham, cut into chunks
3 leeks, cleaned and sliced	2 tbsp chopped fresh flat-leaf parsley
½ cup flour, plus more to dust	freshly grated nutmeg
1¾ cups milk	2 x 17 oz boxes puff pastry (thawed
salt and pepper	if frozen)
1 tsp English mustard (available online, or	1 egg yolk, mixed with a little water
substitute Dijon mustard)	and salt
2 cups leftover cooked chicken, cut in chunks	

1 Melt the butter in a heavy pan and add the leeks. Cook gently for 5 minutes, add a splash of water, reduce the heat, cover the pan and sweat for 10 minutes. Add the flour and stir for 1 minute. Take the pan off the heat and gradually add the milk. Return to the heat and bring to a boil, stirring; reduce the heat and simmer for 5 minutes. Season, and add the mustard, chicken, and ham. Heat through, then add the parsley and nutmeg to taste. Cool.

2 Preheat the oven to 400°F. Spoon the chicken into an enamel pie dish (measuring about 8 x 9 in). On a floured surface, pinch together two sheets of pastry and roll out to the thickness of a quarter. Cut off a strip, wet it, and place it on the lip of the pie dish. Lay the rest of the pastry on top, pressing down firmly. Trim off the excess. Crimp the edges and use pastry scraps to decorate. Make 3 cuts in the middle to let the steam escape.

3 Brush with the egg yolk and bake for 30–40 minutes, or until golden.

ALSO TRY...

Russian chicken, mushroom, sour cream, and dill pie Cook ⅔ cup rice until *al dente*. Set aside. Sauté 8 oz white mushrooms and 6 oz oyster mushrooms, both coarsely chopped, with 1 onion, chopped, in 3½ tbsp butter until golden. Season, add 2 garlic cloves, finely chopped, and cook for 2 minutes. Stir in 5 tbsp flour and cook for 1 minute. Remove from the heat and gradually add 1¼ cups milk. Return to the heat, bring to the boil and stir until thickened. Stir in 3 cups cooked chicken, cut into chunks, the juice of ½ lemon, ⅔ cup sour cream, and ¼ cup finely chopped dill, and heat through. Spread the rice in a buttered dish (measuring roughly 10½ x 8½ in and 2½ in deep), then pour on the sauce. Leave to cool. Roll out 17 oz puff pastry, wet the edges of the dish and press it down. Trim off the excess and crimp the edges. Make a few little slits in the pie to let steam escape, then brush with beaten egg yolk. Bake in a preheated oven at 400°F for 10 minutes, then reduce the heat to 350°F for another 20–25 minutes, until golden.

Greek chicken, pumpkin, and feta pie

You can make this in advance if you butter the top well and cook it at the very last minute.

Serves 8

2¾ lb well-flavored pumpkin or butternut squash

6 tbsp olive oil

¾ tsp ground cinnamon

salt and pepper

1¾ lb spinach, washed and tough stems removed

2 onions, finely chopped

2 garlic cloves, finely chopped

generous grating of nutmeg

¾ cup grated Parmesan cheese, grated

8 oz ricotta cheese

2 eggs, lightly beaten

16 oz feta cheese, crumbled

1½ tbsp chopped fresh parsley

3 tbsp butter

9 oz filo pastry

2½ cups leftover cooked chicken, cut into chunks

1 Preheat the oven to 400°F. Cut the pumpkin into slices, discard the seeds and fibers, and put in a roasting pan. Brush with oil. Sprinkle with the cinnamon and season. Roast for 20–25 minutes, or until tender. Remove the skin.

2 Put the spinach into a large saucepan with the water clinging to it after washing. Cover and set over a low heat. Let it wilt for 5 minutes, turning. Leave to cool. Squeeze out all the water, using your hands.

3 Heat the remaining oil in a frying pan and sauté the onions until soft and golden, then add the garlic and cook for another 2 minutes. Add the spinach. Season; add the nutmeg and half the Parmesan. Set aside. In a bowl mix the remaining Parmesan, the ricotta, eggs, feta, and parsley. Season.

4 Take an 8½ in springform pan. Melt the butter. Keep the filo under a slightly damp cloth towel as you work, otherwise it will become brittle and break. Brush the pan with butter and line with two-thirds of the filo. Lay overlapping sheets on the bottom first, then place sheets like the spokes of a wheel, radiating from the center of the bottom with each hanging over the edge. Brush with butter as you go.

5 Lay in the spinach, then half the pumpkin and all the chicken. Put the cheese and egg layer on and top with the remaining pumpkin. Pull the overhanging filo over the filling, brushing with butter as you go. Use the remaining filo to cover the top, overlapping the sheets and tucking them down the sides. Brush liberally with butter. Don't worry about the pie looking neat–filo is very forgiving.

6 Bake in the oven for 45–50 minutes, until golden. If the pastry is getting too dark, cover it with foil, as it takes this amount of time for the egg layer to set. After baking, leave for 10 minutes, then carefully remove the side of the pan and slide the pie onto a hot serving dish.

Chicken and toasted bread salad with raisins, pine nuts, and capers

This is based on a dish I had in Sicily, and on Californian chef Judy Rodger's famous roast chicken with bread.

Serves 4

FOR THE SALAD
½ cup raisins
about 5 tbsp olive oil
8 oz rustic white bread, coarsely torn
3 cups leftover cooked chicken, torn
  into pieces
5 tbsp pine nuts
2 tbsp capers, rinsed
4½ oz salad greens (baby spinach and
  arugula are good)

FOR THE DRESSING
2 tbsp medium-dry sherry
1 garlic clove, finely chopped
1½ tbsp sherry vinegar
½ tsp Dijon mustard
salt and pepper
good pinch of sugar
5 tbsp extra-virgin olive oil

1 Pour boiling water over the raisins and leave them to plump up for 15 minutes or so. Mix together all the ingredients for the dressing, except the oil. Using a fork, whisk these while steadily pouring in the oil. Set aside.

2 Heat half the oil for the salad in a frying pan and sauté the bread pieces all over until golden and crisp. Throw these into a broad shallow bowl. Heat the remaining oil in the pan, season the chicken pieces, and heat through thoroughly. Toss on top of the bread.

3 Toast the pine nuts in the frying pan: they don't need oil—just cook them while agitating the pan a little, until golden (it takes about 30 seconds, so watch they don't burn). Put these into the salad bowl and add the drained raisins and the capers. Throw in the salad greens, add the dressing, and toss. Serve immediately.

ALSO TRY...

Chicken, watercress, and potato salad with herb and preserved lemon dressing To make the dressing, put 5 canned anchovy fillets; 10 basil leaves; 15 mint leaves; the leaves of a small bunch of parsley; 2 garlic cloves; 1 tbsp capers, rinsed; 2 tbsp preserved lemon juice; and some pepper into a blender. Pulse to mix, adding ⅔ cup extra-virgin olive oil as you do so. Discard the fleshy bit from a preserved lemon. Chop a quarter of the rind and add to the dressing. Shred the rest and set aside. Boil 12 oz small waxy potatoes until tender, drain, add a pat of butter and keep warm. Cook 16 oz green beans until *al dente*. Toss the potatoes, beans, and 8 oz watercress with a little of the dressing, fresh lemon juice, and 2 tbsp extra-virgin olive oil. Add 3½ cups cooked chicken, torn into pieces, on top and drizzle over more dressing. Scatter the preserved lemon shreds over. Serve, providing the remaining dressing in a bowl.

Chicken, wild rice, and blueberry salad

A mixture of wild and brown or basmati rice is fine, or you can buy a bag with wild, brown basmati, and Camargue red rice all in one, which looks great.

Serves 6–8

1⅔ cups wild, red, and basmati
   rice mixture
2½ cups chicken stock
salt and pepper
5⅓ cups leftover cooked chicken,
   cut into broad strips
½ cup toasted, flaked almonds, or
   chopped, unsalted pistachios
¼ cup chopped fresh flat-leaf parsley

8 oz arugula, watercress, or baby
   spinach
4 handfuls blueberries
FOR THE DRESSING
1 tbsp cider vinegar
½ tbsp Dijon mustard
1 tbsp honey
¼ cup peanut oil
¼ cup extra-virgin olive oil

1 Put the rice into a saucepan and cover with the stock. Bring to a boil, season, then reduce the heat to a simmer. Cook until all the stock has been absorbed and the rice is tender. If it gets too dry, add a little water. It will take 25–30 minutes. Remember, wild rice never gets soft; it remains firm and nutty. Meanwhile, make the dressing by simply whisking everything together. Taste for seasoning.

2 As soon as the rice is ready, pour on half the dressing and mix well so it absorbs the dressing while still warm. Let cool to room temperature.

3 Toss in everything else, together with the rice and the remaining dressing. Taste for seasoning; rice dishes need a lot. This is also good the next day, but let it come up to room temperature once you've taken it out of the refrigerator.

ALSO TRY...

You can make a version of this salad with dried apricots and pistachios (it's very pretty) or dried cranberries and chopped pecans instead of fresh blueberries.

Roast lamb with sherry, thyme, and red onions

Time accompanying dishes to be ready when you carve, not when the lamb comes from the oven.

Serves 8

FOR THE LAMB
6 garlic cloves
salt and pepper
leaves from 8 thyme sprigs
olive oil
6½ lb leg of lamb
1¼ cups medium sherry

FOR THE ONIONS
8 small red onions, halved
3 tbsp olive oil
6 tbsp sherry vinegar
1 cup sweet sherry
about a dozen thyme
   sprigs

1 Preheat the oven to 425°F. Crush the garlic with the salt, pepper, and thyme leaves in a mortar and pestle. Add enough oil to make a loose paste. Rub over the lamb, place in a roasting pan and roast for 20 minutes, then reduce the heat to 350°F for another 70 minutes. Halfway through cooking, add half the medium sherry. Now baste the lamb at intervals, adding the remaining medium sherry and ⅔ cup water, watching that the pan does not dry out or the juices will burn.

2 Meanwhile, put the onions in a heatproof gratin dish or small roasting pan, where they fit snugly in a single layer. Drizzle with the oil, season, then add the vinegar and sweet sherry. Scatter the thyme sprigs on top. When the lamb has 30 minutes cooking time left, put the onions in the oven for 50 minutes, basting occasionally. The sweet sherry should be absorbed by the onions. If they become too dry, add another good slug.

3 Take the lamb out of the oven, insulate with foil and towels and rest for 20–25 minutes. Put on a heated platter, surrounded by the onions. Serve immediately with the juices.

4 If you want gravy, pour the cooking juices into a pitcher and spoon off the fat. Set the roasting pan over a medium heat and add 1 cup water or white wine. Bring to a boil, scraping up the bits stuck to the pan, and taste. Adjust with more wine, sherry, even a splash of balsamic vinegar, if you like.

ALSO TRY...

Roast lamb, Castilian style Make incisions all over the lamb and stuff with slivers of garlic. Rub with olive oil, salt, pepper, and 2 tsp paprika. Roast as above. Put 1¼ cups water in a saucepan with the juice of 1 lemon, 2 tbsp sherry vinegar, 2 bay leaves, ½ tsp each ground cumin and dried oregano, 2 rosemary sprigs, and 3 whole peeled garlic cloves and bring to a boil. When the lamb has roasted for 20 minutes, ladle half the liquid over. Add the remainder at intervals during the cooking time. Rest as above, then serve with the juices.

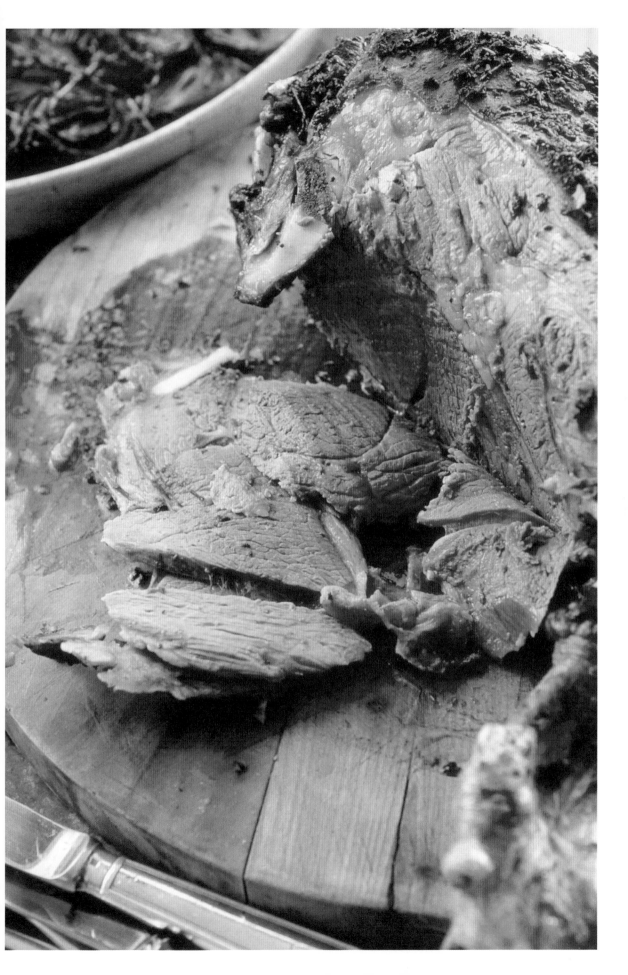

Lamb with caper, parsley, and preserved lemon stuffing

A great way to stretch a leg of lamb.

Serves 6

2 onions, finely chopped
2 garlic cloves, crushed
5 tbsp butter
1 cup fresh white bread crumbs
5 tbsp capers, rinsed
⅔ cup finely chopped fresh flat-leaf parsley
2 tsp preserved lemon juice

¾ large homemade or 2 small commercial
  preserved lemons
2 tbsp olive oil, plus more for the roast
flaked sea salt and pepper
3¼ lb boneless leg of lamb
5 tbsp white wine
1¼ cups lamb or chicken stock

1 Preheat the oven to 425°F. Put the onions, garlic, and 3 tbsp of the butter in a pan and cook for 4 minutes, until the onions are soft. Put the bread crumbs, capers, parsley, and lemon juice in a bowl and add the onions. Discard the lemon flesh. Cut the rind into slivers and add, with the oil and pepper. The mixture should be neither soggy nor dry; add oil or bread crumbs as needed.

2 Spread out the lamb and season. Pat on the stuffing. Roll up and tie at intervals with kitchen string. Dribble over a little oil and season. Place in a roasting pan and roast for 15 minutes, then reduce the temperature to 350°F. Cook for 40 minutes for pink lamb.

3 Put the lamb on a platter, cover, and rest for 20 minutes. Deglaze the pan with the wine, scraping up the juices. Add the stock, boil, and reduce until thickened slightly. Strain into a clean saucepan, heat, and whisk in the remaining butter. Serve with the lamb.

ALSO TRY...

Pack these stuffings into a boned leg and cook as above:

Orange, mint, and watercress Add 6 oz watercress, chopped, to wilt with the sautéed onions. Mix with the bread crumbs, the grated zest of 1 orange, 2 tbsp orange juice, 4 tbsp chopped fresh mint, and ¼ cup chopped almonds. Add 1 tbsp butter, in chunks, and season. Make the gravy with a little added orange juice.

Eggplant and date Fry 1 eggplant, cubed, in 4 tbsp olive oil until soft. Separately soften ½ onion, chopped, in 1 tbsp oil. To the onion, add 2 garlic cloves, chopped; 1½ tsp ground cumin; 1 tsp ground cinnamon and cook for 2 minutes. Add 2 oz dates, chopped, and 1½ tbsp pistachios. Add a handful of chopped fresh mint and some grated lemon zest, then mix with the eggplant. Eat with tahini dressing (see page 82).

Spanish Chorizo and olive Sauté 1 onion, chopped, 6 oz chorizo, chopped, and 6 oz waxy potatoes, diced, in 2 tbsp olive oil. When the onion is soft, add 6 tbsp pitted black olives, 3 tbsp chopped fresh parsley, the grated zest of 1 lemon, finely chopped and ½ tsp cayenne. Season and cook for 1 minute.

Lamb and roast pepper salad with garlic and anchovy cream

Cooked lamb loves strong flavors, but it needs to be cooked rare to work in salads, and the fat must be trimmed.

Serves 4

FOR THE SALAD
3 red bell peppers
salt and pepper
olive oil
12 oz small waxy potatoes
3 oz watercress and baby spinach
2 tbsp extra-virgin olive oil
good squeeze of lemon juice
1⅓ lb rare-cooked lamb, sliced

FOR THE CREAM
2 oz can anchovies in olive oil
2 garlic cloves
6 tbsp pine nuts
½ cup extra-virgin olive oil
lemon juice, to taste
1 tbsp very finely chopped fresh
   flat-leaf parsley

1 Preheat the oven to 400°F. Halve and seed the peppers and put them into a small roasting pan. Rub with oil, season, and roast for 30 minutes. Slice and leave them in their juices. Steam or boil the potatoes until tender.

2 To make the cream, put the anchovies with their oil, garlic, and pine nuts into a food processor. Turn it on and add the oil in a steady stream. Add the lemon juice and parsley.

3 Put the greens, potatoes, and peppers (with their juices) into a bowl. Add the extra-virgin olive oil and lemon juice, and season. Toss. Put on a platter. Arrange the lamb on top and spoon over the garlic and anchovy cream.

ALSO TRY...

Use the same amount of sliced, rare lamb in these salads:

...with roast peppers, labneh, chickpeas, and sumac To make the labneh, put 9 oz Greek yogurt in a sieve lined with muslin. Pull the cloth up around the yogurt to make a bag and gently squeeze. Place over a bowl and refrigerate for 4–24 hours, squeezing every so often. When firm, peel off the cloth and break into walnut-sized chunks. Roast 4 red bell peppers as above and slice. Mix with 4 oz watercress or baby spinach; a handful of cilantro leaves; the lamb, and a 14 oz can of chickpeas, drained and rinsed. Whisk 2¼ tsp white wine vinegar with ¼ cup extra-virgin olive oil and seasoning; toss most of this with the salad. Dot in the labneh and drizzle on the remaining dressing. Sprinkle with sumac and serve.

...with white and green beans and anchovies Cook 8 oz green beans until tender. Toss with a 14 oz can white beans, drained and rinsed, and 4 tbsp extra-virgin olive oil. Add the juice of half a lemon; half a 2 oz can anchovies, drained and finely chopped; a garlic clove, crushed; and 3 tbsp chopped fresh flat-leaf parsley. Arrange the lamb on top and drizzle with more oil and grind on salt and black pepper.

Lamb pilaf with figs, pomegranate, feta, and pistachios

Pilafs are great for using up leftover meat. This works well with chicken, too. Just stick to the same quantities for rice and stock. You don't need homemade stock for this: a good commercial one is fine.

Serves 4

1 onion, coarsely chopped
olive oil
1 fresh red chile, seeded and thinly sliced
½ tsp ground allspice
2 garlic cloves, crushed
2 cups basmati rice
2½ cups chicken or lamb stock
salt and pepper
⅓ cup dried cherries or cranberries soaked in hot water for 15 minutes and drained

6 dried figs, quartered
¼ lb leftover cooked lamb, cut into chunks
3 oz feta cheese, crumbled
2 tbsp chopped fresh flat-leaf parsley or mint, or a mixture
¼ cup unsalted pistachios or toasted almonds, chopped
seeds from ½ pomegranate
Greek yogurt, to serve (optional)

1 Cook the onion in a little oil in a saucepan until soft and golden. Stir in the chile, allspice, and garlic and sauté for another minute. Add the rice and stir briefly to coat in the oily juices. Now add the stock, seasoning, and dried fruit. Bring to a boil, then immediately reduce the heat to a simmer. Cover the pan and cook for 20 minutes until the liquid has been absorbed and the rice is tender. Don't stir the rice while it's cooking. If the rice isn't yet tender, pour in a little boiling water, replace the lid, and cook for another 4–5 minutes. If the stock hasn't been completely absorbed, turn the heat up and quickly boil off whatever remains.

2 Heat 1 tbsp oil in a frying pan and quickly cook the lamb until heated through. Season and gently fork through the rice along with the feta, herbs, and nuts. Shower with pomegranate seeds at the last minute and serve immediately. Plain Greek yogurt is good on the side.

ALSO TRY…

You can make an everyday version of the rather jewelled dish above with lamb, regular or golden raisins and dried apricots, or with chunks of sautéed eggplant and chopped dates. In both cases, you can bulk out the pilaf with canned chickpeas (drained and rinsed) or lentils. The spices also can be changed according to what you have around: ground cinnamon is good, as is cumin.

Middle Eastern shepherd's pie with spiced parsnip crust

Don't be put off by the long ingredients list. This is very simple.

Serves 6

FOR THE MEAT
5 tbsp olive oil
1¾ lb leftover cooked lamb,
   cut in small chunks
2 onions, coarsely chopped
2 celery stalks, finely chopped
2 carrots, diced
6 garlic cloves, crushed
2 tsp ground cumin
2 tsp ground pumpkin pie spice
1 tbsp ground cinnamon
2 tbsp all purpose flour
1¼ cups chicken or lamb stock
grated zest and juice of 1 orange
½ cup raisins, soaked in boiling
   water for 15 minutes and drained
6 tbsp tomato paste
½ cup pine nuts, toasted

FOR THE PARSNIP CRUST
1 lb floury potatoes, cut into
   even chunks
2 lb parsnips, chopped
3 tbsp butter
1 tsp ground cinnamon
2 tsp cayenne pepper
¼ cup whipping cream
salt and pepper

FOR THE SPICED ONION TOPPING
2 onions, very thinly sliced
1 tbsp butter
1½ tsp olive oil
½ tsp ground cinnamon
1 fresh red chile, seeded and thinly sliced
1 tbsp dark brown sugar
good squeeze of lemon juice
small bunch cilantro or mint, coarsely
   chopped (optional)

1 Heat the oil in a large skillet and brown the lamb. Transfer the lamb to a bowl. In the same pan cook the onions, celery, and carrots until golden. Add the garlic and spices and cook for 1 minute. Put the lamb back and add the flour. Stir for 1 minute, then add the stock, zest, juice, raisins, and tomato paste. Bring to a boil, reduce the heat, and simmer for 45 minutes, stirring. The mix should be thick but not dry – add a little more stock if you need to. Add the pine nuts.

2 Meanwhile, preheat the oven to 350°F. Boil the potatoes and the parsnips separately until soft. Drain the potatoes and keep them in the saucepan in which they were cooked. Put a cloth towel on top, then cover with a lid. Let these sit for a few minutes over a very low heat to dry out. Drain the parsnips and add to the potatoes. Heat the butter in a large saucepan with the spices. Add the potatoes, parsnips, and mash, adding the cream and seasoning.

3 Spoon the lamb into a pie dish, spread the mash on top, and put into the oven for 20–25 minutes until golden. Meanwhile, fry the onions for the topping in the butter and oil until golden. Increase the heat and allow some to become crisp. Add the cinnamon, chile, salt, pepper, and sugar. Cook until slightly caramelized. Squeeze on some lemon juice and mix in the herbs, if using. Pile the onions on the pie and serve.

Roast pork loin, porchetta style

Get your butcher to remove the skin from the pork and leave about ½ in fat.

Serves 6

4½ lb boneless pork loin
6 garlic cloves, sliced
1 tbsp fennel seeds, crushed
4 rosemary sprigs, leaves chopped, plus
   more for the roasting pan

olive oil
salt and black pepper
about 8 bay leaves

1 Lay the pork on a board, flesh side up. Make incisions all over with a sharp knife and fill with the slivers of garlic. Rub the fennel and rosemary all over the flesh, along with olive oil to lubricate, pushing bits down inside the slits, and season generously. Make a bed in a roasting pan with rosemary sprigs and the bay leaves and lay on the pork, fat side down. Cover and refrigerate overnight. Bring to room temperature before cooking.

2 Preheat the oven to 425°F. Tie the loin at intervals with kitchen string (not too tightly; it should hold its shape but not look like a sausage). Put into the roasting pan fat-side up on top of the herbs (make sure these are under the pork or they will scorch) and cook for 25 minutes. Reduce the oven temperature to 350°F and cook for 1 hour 40 minutes, basting every so often.

3 Check to make sure it is properly cooked; the juices should run clear with no trace of pink when the flesh is pierced. Because I worry about pork, I also cut into the underside (so I don't ruin the appearance) to check the flesh is white. Take the pork out of the oven, cover with foil, insulate, and allow to rest for 15–20 minutes. Serve hot or at room temperature.

ALSO TRY...

Honey and mustard roast pork loin Lay the same-sized cut of pork as above on a board, flesh side up. Make incisions all over with a sharp knife. Stuff the chopped leaves from 3 rosemary sprigs into the incisions and season. Mix ¼ cup Dijon mustard, ½ cup honey, and the juice of ½ lemon and pour three-quarters of it over the roast, making sure it goes down into the incisions. Refrigerate for a few hours, but bring to room temperature before cooking. Preheat the oven to 425°F. Tie the loin with kitchen string as above. Put into a roasting pan with it's marinade. Cook as above, basting. Add the remaining honey and mustard mix 10 minutes before the end of the cooking time. If the roast is becoming too dark (if the honey begins to burn), cover with foil. When it is cooked, take it from the oven and cover with foil, insulate, and rest for 15 minutes. Serve hot or at room temperature.

Pork, roasted squash, apple, and chestnut salad

This shows what you can make out of leftover roast: earthy, spicy, and very more-ish.

Serves 4

FOR THE SALAD

3½ tbsp butter

¼ cup olive oil

½ tsp ground cinnamon

½ tsp ground ginger

2¼ lb squash or pumpkin, in peeled
  wedges

salt and pepper

2 tsp superfine sugar

2 apples, halved, cored, and cut into wedges

4 oz cooked chestnuts (vacuum-
  packed are fine)

4 oz spicy pork sausage (or hot Italian
  sausage), cut into chunks

8 oz leftover cooked pork, cut into chunks

2 tbsp hazelnuts, toasted

6 oz watercress or baby spinach,
  or a mixture

FOR THE DRESSING

1½ tbsp balsamic vinegar

smidgen of Dijon mustard

¼ cup olive oil

3 tbsp hazelnut oil

1 Preheat the oven to 375°F. Melt 2 tbsp of the butter in a saucepan. Add 3 tbsp of the olive oil, the cinnamon, and ginger. Put the squash in a roasting pan, pour the spicy mixture over, and toss to coat. Season, then sprinkle on half the sugar. Roast for 25 minutes, until tender and slightly caramelized.

2 Make the dressing by simply whisking everything together and season.

3 Melt the remaining butter in a large frying pan and sauté the apples until golden. Add the chestnuts to heat through, then set aside. Add the remaining oil to the pan and sauté the sausage until cooked and brown, then add the pork and heat through. Season. Toss the warm squash with all the salad ingredients and the dressing.

ALSO TRY...

Pork, squash, and mushroom salad with caramelized peanut and chile sauce
Roast the squash (or pumpkin) as above. Sauté a 1½ in chunk of fresh ginger, a fresh red chile, and a garlic clove, all finely chopped, in 2 tbsp peanut oil until pale gold. Add 2 tsp light brown sugar and 4 shallots, finely chopped, and cook for 2 minutes. Add 3 tbsp peanuts and cook for 4 minutes; the sugar and shallots should caramelize. Pour it all into a mortar and pound to a coarse paste. Stir in 2 tbsp peanut oil, 1 tbsp sesame oil, 1 tbsp soy sauce, the juice of 1 lime, and a generous handful of finely chopped cilantro. Dilute with water, to taste. Season the same amount of leftover pork and sausage as above and fry in 1 tbsp peanut oil. Set aside and sauté 4 oz mushrooms in another 1 tbsp oil. Toss the meat and mushrooms with the squash, 4 oz baby spinach, 2 tbsp light olive oil, the juice of ½ lime, and seasoning. Drizzle a little sauce over the salad and serve the rest on the side. Use this sauce with roast pork belly and stir-fried greens, too.

Saigon crêpes

Vietnamese street food: there they use ground pork, but this is a perfect vehicle for leftover roast meat. It's a good party dish; there's something celebratory about street food when it's cooked at home, and it's perfect for a casual supper for friends.

Serves 4–6

FOR THE BATTER
¾ cup rice flour
1 tbsp ground turmeric
4 tsp curry powder
2 tsp light brown sugar
good pinch of salt
1¼ cups coconut cream
4 scallions, finely chopped
peanut oil, for frying

FOR THE TOPPING
3 tbsp peanut oil
6 oz mushrooms (button, chestnut, oyster, or shiitake), sliced
salt and pepper
1 onion, thinly sliced

2 garlic cloves, crushed
2 fresh red chiles, seeded and thinly sliced
4 oz raw or cooked shrimp (optional)
10 oz leftover cooked pork, in little chunks
8 oz bean sprouts
1½ tbsp fish sauce

TO SERVE
juice of 1 lime
leaves from a small bunch of cilantro, coarsely chopped
Nuoc Cham (see page 23) if you have it, or wedges of lime

1 To make the batter, put all the dry ingredients into a bowl, make a well in the center and gradually pour in the coconut cream and 1½ cups water, mixing in the dry ingredients as you go. Add the scallions. Leave to stand for about 30 minutes.

2 For the topping, heat half the oil in a frying pan and fry the mushrooms until dark gold. Season and set aside. Heat the remaining oil in a large frying pan or wok and cook the onion over a medium heat until soft and golden, about 10 minutes. Add the garlic and chiles and cook for another 2 minutes. Add the raw shrimp now if you are using them, with the pork. Toss everything together, then add the bean sprouts (and the cooked shrimp if you are using those) and mushrooms. Season, add the fish sauce, and make sure everything is well mixed. Cover to keep warm.

3 To make the crêpes, heat 1½ tsp oil in a large nonstick frying pan. Add a scant ½ cup of the batter and swish it around to the edges. In Vietnam they add the filling now and cook it with the batter but I think the crêpes taste better if they are made the French way, so cook each crêpe on both sides until golden. Keep in a low oven (300°F) until you have cooked all the crêpes. To serve, spoon the filling on to the top, squeeze over some lime, and sprinkle on cilantro. Provide a bowl of Nuoc Cham if you have it.

Nasi goreng

This is a wonderful Indonesian dish. It can be made with fresh meat–pork, chicken or beef–but is a great for leftovers. It is basically a simple fried rice and it's best not to fancy it up too much, but you can adapt the main idea: leave out the shrimp, for example, or add mushrooms or sugar snap peas.

Serves 4

2 tbsp peanut oil

1 onion, cut into crescent moon-shapes about ½ in thick at their widest

3 garlic cloves, thinly sliced

2 fresh red chiles, halved, seeded, and cut into slivers

10 oz (2½ cups) leftover cooked pork, in little chunks or shreds

2½ cups cooked rice

4 scallions, sliced on the diagonal

3 eggs, beaten

4 oz cooked, peeled shrimp

¼ cup dark soy sauce, or to taste

salt and pepper

1 Heat 1½ tbsp of the oil in a large frying pan, sauté pan, or wok. Add the onion and cook over medium-high heat until softer (though still with bite) and golden, even slightly singed at the tips. Add the garlic, chiles and pork and cook for another couple of minutes (it's good to get a bit of color on the pork). Toss in the rice and scallions and mix everything together lightly–it's important not to press the rice or it will become starchy–and cook until the rice is heated through.

2 Meanwhile, quickly heat the remaining oil in a nonstick frying pan and add the eggs. Cook as if you are making an omelet, rather than scrambled eggs: don't stir the egg but drag the bits which are set around the side into the center, then tilt the pan to allow runny egg to set around the outside. Continue until it is all cooked. With a sharp knife, cut the egg into ribbons.

3 Add the egg to the rice along with the shrimp, soy sauce, salt and pepper. Continue cooking for 2 minutes until heated through. Even though the soy sauce is salty you may still want to add a bit of salt, as starchy dishes always need a lot of seasoning.

Pork and apple pie

Pies made using a béchamel sauce to bind the filling can be heavy, so it's good to have a recipe in your repertoire without it. This filling is chunky, and thickened with bread crumbs (great thickeners for braises and stews, but you do need to season again after you've added them). To make this slightly more luxurious, add ¼ cup heavy cream to the filling. You can vary the filling, using mushrooms instead of apples, or cooked pumpkin instead of leeks. Try it, too, with cooked chicken instead of pork.

Serves 6
2 leeks
2 tbsp unsalted butter
1 onion, coarsely chopped
6 slices bacon, chopped
2 small or 1 medium apple (I like Cox for this)
1 lb (3¼ cups) leftover cooked pork, in chunks
¾ cup apple juice or cider

1¼ cups chicken stock
2 tsp Dijon mustard (or more, to taste)
salt and pepper
3 tbsp fresh flat-leaf parsley, chopped
½ cup whole-wheat or white bread crumbs
17 oz package puff pastry (thawed if frozen)
all-purpose flour, to dust
1 egg, lightly beaten

1 Remove and discard any of the tough outer leaves from the leeks and trim the root end. Cut the leeks into 1 in lengths. Melt the butter in a sauté pan and add the leeks, onion, and bacon. Cook over a medium heat until there's some color on the onion and bacon. Halve and core the apple(s) and slice. Add to the pan and cook until they are also coloring a little.

2 Toss in the pork, juice or cider, stock and mustard. Season and bring to a boil. Reduce the heat, add the parsley and bread crumbs, and stir it all together. Preheat the oven to 400°F.

3 Put the mixture into a pie dish and leave to cool a little. Roll out the pastry on a lightly floured surface. Cut strips that you can stick all the way around the edge of the pie dish (so the pastry lid has something to stick to). Lightly wet one side and press down all the way round. Now lay the remaining pastry on top and press down. Trim off the excess and crimp the edges. Use the leftover pastry to make decorations for the top. Make a few little slits in the center through which the steam can escape. Using a blunt knife, tap the sides of the pastry all the way around; this helps it to rise. Brush with egg and bake for 20 minutes, or until golden and puffy.

4 Serve hot. This is pretty much a meal in itself. I tend not to serve potatoes on the side (more starch) but offer watercress or spinach salad, or a big bowl of buttery cabbage.

Vegetable love

The weather, as I write, has changed dramatically. Yesterday we were enduring a long, harsh winter, today we have a bright blue-skied spring. Last week's vegetable dishes– a gratin of potatoes, parsnips, and onions with dried cranberries and chestnuts, a cauliflower and blue cheese risotto, and a Vietnamese pumpkin curry–won't get another outing until fall. Now I'm planning Greek olive oil–braised leeks with dill and daydreaming about what I'll do with fava beans when they arrive.

Cooking more vegetables has been the biggest change in my kitchen during the last five years. I now eat meat or fish only three times a week. This wasn't deliberate, and I'm not alone. Friends who used to bring chocolates or wine now offer gifts of asparagus, bearing them like bunches of flowers, or squashes from the garden. Is this vegetable love due to straitened finances? Health concerns? I think there's another reason. My theory is that the popularity of farmers' markets and growing your own is about connecting. Cooking vegetables is very grounding (some, after all, arrive covered in soil). I love even walking past my greengrocer's. There's always something to fit into the week's food: crimson globes of beets, wild heads of frisée, slender stems of purple-headed broccoli. And they have produce I wouldn't find in the supermarket, such as ruby chard. Just looking at vegetables makes you feel healthy, gladdened by the colors, amazed at the abundance.

It's lucky that our increasing interest in vegetables has coincided with a need to take them more seriously. We know they're good for our health, but they're also a better way of using the planet's resources as it takes much more energy to produce meat. Eat more vegetables and you're in a win-win situation.

So, what to buy? Eat seasonally. Vegetables in season taste better, cost less, and won't have been flown halfway round the world. Of course, I also buy what we can't grow well here (eggplant, for example) but try to find Mediterranean ones that have benefited from the sun.

Going on flavor alone, I buy organic when I can and *always* organic carrots, green beans, and potatoes (they taste so different). Avoid packaging–apart from its being wasteful, most vegetables suffer, sweating under plastic rather than breathing–and bags of prepared salad. Even if they haven't been washed in chlorine, they're no bargain; better to buy whole lettuces and use them up (cooked as well as in salads). Anything you have to wash yourself will be cheaper.

Vote with your purse and give business to those who care about flavor. Don't buy tomatoes that taste of cotton. Be demanding. And, to ensure particular vegetables don't disappear, buy a broad range. Kale may be "in" at the moment but if its popularity dwindles, it will become harder to find. Support greengrocers (they are disappearing at an alarming rate), farm stores, and farmers' markets; that way you can talk to people who actually know about what they're selling.

Go cultivate some vegetable love. It will improve your life immeasurably.

Pinzimonio

Oh, the Italians do things with style. This starter is both simple and very chic. Don't offer the clumsy, faded crudités supermarkets sell to dip in tubs of bad guacamole. You need fresh stuff. Use an extra-virgin olive oil you particularly like: Tuscan will be bitter and grassy; Ligurian sweet and buttery.... There's no "right" choice. Offer good bread and flaked sea salt as well.

Serves 4

12 oz French breakfast radishes, with leaves

8 oz young carrots

1 fennel bulb

juice of ½ lemon

12 oz young peas in the pod

6 oz (1 cup) shelled fava beans

6 oz cherry tomatoes

¾ cup extra-virgin olive oil

sea salt flakes and crushed black pepper

firm-textured rustic bread, to serve

1 Wash the radishes, keeping the leaves attached if really fresh. Wash the carrots and trim the tails if long. Remove the tough outer leaves from the fennel and cut into thin wedges (keep the core, or the slices fall apart). Squeeze over some lemon to stop it discoloring.

2 Take some peas from their pods and leave the rest. There's no need to cook either peas or beans if young and sweet. Divide the vegetables among four plates, or put them all on a platter. Provide each diner with a small tumbler of oil. Serve with salt, pepper, and good bread.

ALSO TRY...

Cold-weather vegetables with bagna cauda A more hearty, Piedmontese starter that also showcases the loveliness of good, simple things: vegetables with a warm bath of anchovy-flavored oil. Prepare a selection of vegetables–whatever's in season –and put on a platter. Cut carrots and celery into thin sticks (keep the celery leaves if possible) and cauliflower into florets. Trim purple-sprouting broccoli shoots, cut fennel into thin wedges, and separate radicchio or chicory into leaves. Melt ¼ cup butter in a small, heavy saucepan over the lowest heat. Add 6 garlic cloves, thinly sliced, and sauté very gently until soft, not colored. Add 15 canned anchovies and pour in 1¼ cups olive oil very gradually, stirring and pressing the anchovies and garlic with the back of a wooden spoon. Both the heat and the pressure help the anchovies "melt". Cook for 7 minutes, on the lowest heat, stirring constantly, until well mixed and smooth. Keep it hot over a spirit lamp or candle, or just get it to the table as quickly as possible and let diners dip their vegetables into the bagna. Serve bread on the side. Serves 8.

LEFTOVERS...

...Bagna cauda is also great on toast. Top–or not–with mozzarella.

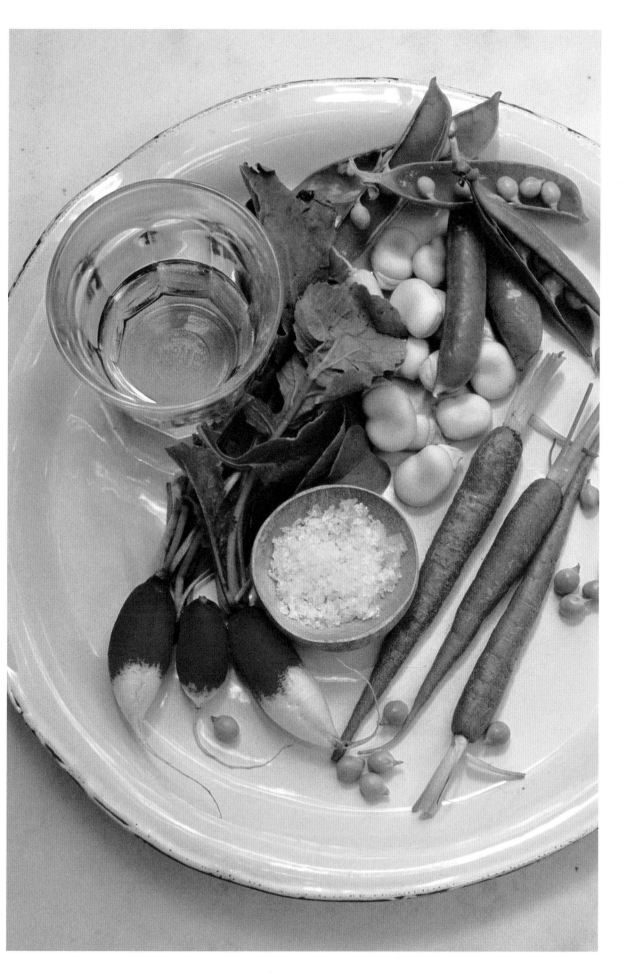

Herbed ricotta with summer veg

Another variation on the theme of plain, raw vegetables. Fresh ricotta can be hard to get but the stuff sold in tubs in the supermarket just doesn't cut it here. Go to a good Italian deli or cheese shop to seek out the fresh version. It is milky, sweet-smelling, and almost crumbly.

Serves 4–6 as a starter or light lunch dish

FOR THE RICOTTA

1 lb fresh ricotta cheese
1 garlic clove, crushed or grated
1 tbsp fresh chives, snipped
2 tbsp fresh flat-leaf parsley, chopped
1 tbsp fresh mint leaves, chopped
finely grated zest of 1 lemon, plus a good
  squeeze of lemon juice
3 tbsp extra-virgin olive oil, plus more
  to serve
salt and pepper

FOR THE VEGETABLES

A selection from:
raw peas
raw fava beans
French breakfast radishes with fresh,
  perky leaves, trimmed
baby carrots, trimmed
cherry tomatoes
high-quality black olives
toasted ciabatta, to serve

1 Mash the ricotta together with all the other ingredients, cover with plastic wrap and put in the refrigerator to allow the flavors to mingle (it needs at least an hour). Bring it out before you want to serve it to allow it to get to room temperature.

2 Divide the ricotta among four to six plates (or put in a bowl or mound on a wooden board and surround with the vegetables and olives).

3 If it's early in the season and the fava beans are young, serve them shelled but not cooked. If it's a little later, cook the shelled beans until tender and slip them out of their skins so you can see their beautiful color. Arrange the vegetables and olives beside the ricotta and drizzle olive oil over everything. Serve with toasted ciabatta.

ALSO TRY...

Lou cachat An old French dish created to use up bits of leftover cheese. Deliciously strong, it is lovely with toasted croûtes, radishes, and black olives. Just mash together 8 oz goat cheese and 4 oz Roquefort with 5 tbsp crème fraîche and 3 tbsp brandy. Add pepper; it should be salty enough because of the Roquefort. The mixture should be slightly chunky. Leave, covered, in the refrigerator overnight, or even for a few days, so that the alcohol can infuse the cheese.

Claqueret Another French cheese dish—this one is light and herby rather than strong and boozy—that goes with all sorts of spring and summer vegetables. You can also add crumbled goat cheese. Mix 2 cups crème fraîche; 3 shallots finely chopped; 3 garlic cloves, crushed; 1 tbsp white wine vinegar; 1 tbsp extra-virgin olive oil; 2 tbsp dry white wine; 3 tbsp each finely chopped chives, parsley, and chervil; and some salt and pepper.

Purple-sprouting broccoli with mozzarella, chile, and anchovies

Purple-sprouting broccoli tastes sweet and is so good for you. It arrives when we really need it—at the brighter end of winter when we're dying for new ingredients. I steam it as I do asparagus, standing with the heads out of the water. You may need to trim the stalks (they dry out quickly) but don't remove the leaves.

Serves 4 as a starter or 2 as a main course

1 lb purple-sprouting broccoli or brocollini
12 oz fresh mozzarella cheese
2 x 2 oz cans anchovies in oil
6 tbsp extra-virgin olive oil, plus more
   to drizzle
4 garlic cloves, thinly sliced

1 fresh red chile, seeded and thinly sliced
juice of 1 lemon
freshly ground black pepper
1 tbsp fresh flat-leaf parsley or
   torn basil, chopped

1 Trim the broccoli and steam until just tender (4–5 minutes). Slice the mozzarella into rounds, or tear into chunks.

2 Drain the anchovies. Gently heat the oil in a small frying pan. Add the garlic and chile and cook for a few minutes until the garlic is very pale gold. Add the anchovies and press with the back of a wooden spoon to break them up (they melt into a sauce).

3 Put the hot broccoli on plates and top with the mozzarella. Add the lemon juice, pepper, and parsley to the anchovy oil and spoon over. Drizzle with more oil, grind on more pepper, and serve.

ALSO TRY...

As a side dish Omit the mozzarella and halve the amount of anchovies. Very good with roast lamb.

With cumin, chile, mint, and yogurt Heat 6 tbsp peanut oil in a wok. Add 1½ lb trimmed broccoli. Stir-fry for a few minutes. Add 1 tbsp cumin seeds; 2 fresh red chiles, seeded and very thinly sliced, and 3 garlic cloves, thinly sliced. Cook for 2 minutes, tossing. Splash in some water, season, cover, and cook on low heat for a minute, until just tender. Drizzle with plain yogurt and chopped fresh mint.

With ginger, chile, and soy sauce Stir-fry as above, but add fresh ginger, peeled and grated, to the chiles and garlic and omit the cumin. Replace the water with sherry. Splash on soy sauce at the end and let it bubble away to glaze.

With ricotta, lemon, olive oil, and Parmesan Steam 1 lb broccoli until just tender. Divide among plates and quickly top with 4 oz ricotta cheese, broken into chunks, the finely grated zest of 1 lemon and the juice of ½, salt and pepper, a really generous slug of extra-virgin olive oil and 1¾–2½ oz Parmesan cheese, shaved.

Lebanese runner beans with tomatoes

I wasn't brought up with runner beans—I have no idea why they never seemed to be around in Ireland—and when I came to live in England I found most people scorned them. Fresh from someone's garden, though, they are delicious. If you don't have runner beans, green beans are just as good. And this is definitely a dish to use up a glut of ripe tomatoes.

Serves 4

6 tbsp olive oil

1 onion, coarsely chopped

4 garlic cloves, thinly sliced

4 tsp ground cumin

1¾ lb tomatoes, coarsely chopped

salt and pepper

1½ tsp tomato paste

1½ tsp light brown sugar

good squeeze of lemon juice or slug of
  white wine vinegar

1 lb runner beans, cut into strips lengthwise
  or in 2 in lengths

extra-virgin olive oil, to serve

2–3 sprigs of mint (optional)

1 Heat the olive oil in a heavy pan and sauté the onion until soft and golden. Add the garlic and cook for another couple of minutes, until soft; then add the cumin, tomatoes, salt, and pepper. Stir everything around so that the tomatoes get coated in the oil.

2 Add ⅓ cup water and the tomato paste, sugar, and lemon juice or vinegar. Keep over a medium heat, cover, and let the tomatoes sweat. You need to turn them over every so often, pressing them to help them disintegrate as they cook. The sauce shouldn't be too wet.

3 After about 15 minutes, stir in the beans and allow them to cook for about 12 minutes. They will become really soft but you can cook them for a shorter time if you prefer. Add more water or olive oil if you find the mixture becomes too dry. Taste for seasoning and add the extra-virgin olive oil and some mint leaves, if you like.

ALSO TRY...

Runner beans are lovely just stewed in olive oil, so cook as above without the cumin, tomatoes, or sugar—just add more olive oil and about ¼ cup water and cook until tender. The water will evaporate (but don't let the pan boil dry), and the beans will become rich with the oil. They need good seasoning, too.

Green beans with feta, chile, and tarator sauce

Mediterranean and Middle Eastern people cook green beans for longer than we do. While that mutes their color, it does wonders for flavor. You don't have to cook them to death, just make sure they're not undercooked.

Serves 4–6 as a side dish

FOR THE TARATOR SAUCE

1 small slice coarse country bread
¼ cup milk
⅓ cup blanched almonds or hazelnuts
1 fat garlic clove
6 tbsp extra-virgin olive oil
juice of ½ lemon, or to taste

FOR THE BEANS

1 lb green beans
6 oz feta cheese, crumbled
2 tbsp chopped fresh flat-leaf parsley,
   cilantro or mint
1 fresh red chile, seeded and shredded
salt and pepper
generous squeeze of lemon juice
3 tbsp extra-virgin olive oil
finely grated zest of 1 lemon

1 To make the tarator, soak the bread in the milk for 30 minutes. Purée in a food processor with the nuts and garlic, adding the oil and lemon juice. Add water if you want it thinner. Season to taste with salt and pepper.

2 Trim the beans. Steam or boil until just tender. Toss in a shallow bowl with the feta, half the herbs, half the chile, salt, pepper, lemon juice, and olive oil. Drizzle with the tarator and sprinkle with the lemon zest, remaining herbs, and chile.

ALSO TRY…

Green and flageolet beans with mustard and herb crumbs These crumbs are also good on courgettes, broccoli, and cauliflower. Preheat the oven to 350°F. Melt 2 tbsp butter with 1½ tbsp olive oil. Mix with 1½ tbsp Dijon mustard, 2 tsp thyme leaves, 1½ tsp finely chopped fresh parsley and the finely grated zest of 1 lemon. Put 1¾ cups coarse fresh white bread crumbs into a roasting pan and stir in the butter-mustard mixture. Cook in the oven for 10–12 minutes, until toasted, shaking occasionally. Cook 8 oz green beans, trimmed, in boiling, lightly salted water until just tender. Rinse. Drain a 14 oz can flageolet (or any white) beans and rinse. Heat 2 tbsp olive oil and sauté 4 chopped scallions until soft. Add both kinds of beans, season, and heat through. Sprinkle with the toasted crumbs and serve.

Potatoes, beans, and pesto Put 2½ cups basil, 6 tbsp pine nuts, ¼ cup grated Parmesan cheese, 1 garlic clove, ½ cup extra-virgin olive oil, and salt and pepper into a food processor. Process. Check the seasoning. Scrape into a bowl and stir in 3 tbsp grated Parmesan. Cook about 20 waxy potatoes in boiling salted water until almost tender; then add 8 oz French beans, trimmed, and cook for 4 minutes. Drain (add 2 tbsp of the water to the pesto) and season. Carefully toss the potatoes and beans with the pesto. Serve immediately. Serves 4 as a side dish.

Peas, fava beans, and chorizo with mint

A Spanish combination very good with fish (toss in quickly fried squid for a delicious supper), rabbit, and chicken (see the recipes below). Chopped scallions—cooked with the chorizo—are a good addition.

Serves 4–6

1¾ cups fresh or frozen peas

salt and pepper

9 oz (1½ cups) fresh or frozen shelled
  baby fava beans

2 tbsp olive oil

6 oz Spanish chorizo, cut into chunks

good squeeze of lemon juice

leaves from 5 mint sprigs, torn

1 Cook the peas in boiling salted water until tender. Do the same with the beans. Drain. If the beans aren't young, slip off the skins so the lovely emerald color is revealed.

2 Heat the oil in a frying pan and fry the chorizo until golden. Add the peas and beans and heat through. Season, add the lemon juice, and put into a warm, broad shallow bowl. Add the mint and serve.

ALSO TRY...

Adding the above to a sauté of rabbit or chicken. Brown seasoned bone-in chicken thighs or rabbit parts, add 2 cups chicken stock, and cook until tender and cooked through (about 40 minutes). Remove the meat and reduce the cooking liquid by half. Make the above dish and add it to the liquid with the meat, heat through, and serve.

Peas and beans with dill Cook beans and peas until tender, then add a slosh of heavy cream, a squeeze of lemon juice, chopped dill, and a smidgen of Dijon mustard, if you like. Beautiful with salmon, trout, roast lamb, or chicken.

French peas with lettuce Sauté shredded lettuce—I like slightly bitter, milky baby Gems or hearts of romaine—and chopped scallions in abundant butter until just soft; then throw in cooked peas, salt, and pepper. Toss. Add mint, parsley, or chervil.

Raw fava beans with cured ham or cheese Serve young, raw beans with prosciutto, Serrano, or even an expensive Spanish ham (worthwhile a couple of times a year when beans are in their prime). The young, green freshness of fava beans goes exceptionally well with sweet, salty pork. Slices of hard goat or sheep cheese are also good accompaniments.

Toasts with crushed fava beans Coarsely mash cooked fava beans (slip off the skins first) with plenty of extra-virgin olive oil, salt, and pepper, and a bit of lemon juice. Add chopped dill, parsley, mint, or chervil. Pile on bits of toasted ciabatta, baguette or sourdough bread and top with shaved Parmesan or hard goat cheese. Alternatively top with cooked white crab meat or shrimp. Great for a lunch or an informal starter.

Beet, fennel, and radish salad

This is great with salmon, trout, or mackerel (both fresh and smoked), or with a hunk of cheese (goat cheese works well). I even like it the next day, when the salad is soft and stained with beet juice.

Serves 4

FOR THE DRESSING

½ tsp wholegrain mustard

1 tsp honey

salt and pepper

2½ tsp cider vinegar

¼ cup extra-virgin olive oil

½ globe of preserved ginger, very finely chopped, plus 1 tsp syrup (available online or in Asian markets)

1 garlic clove, crushed

1 fresh small red chile (not too hot), seeded and finely shredded

FOR THE SALAD

10 radishes, trimmed

1 fennel bulb

lemon juice

½ red onion

½ green apple

2–3 small raw beets

handful of fresh mint leaves, chopped

1 To make the dressing, put the mustard, honey, salt, pepper, and vinegar into a small pitcher or cup and, using a fork, whisk in the olive oil in a steady stream. Add all the other ingredients.

2 Slice the radishes thinly, lengthwise, to get teardrop-shaped slices and toss in a bowl.

3 Halve and quarter the fennel and trim the tops (discard the dried-out tips, but reserve the tufty fronds for tossing with the salad). Core each quarter. Using a very sharp knife, cut into wafer-thin slices, lengthwise. Add to the bowl and squeeze on some lemon juice to keep the fennel from discoloring.

4 Cut the onion so thinly that it's almost shaved. Halve the apple and remove the core. Cut each piece into matchstick-like lengths. Add these to the bowl, too, and toss in more lemon juice. Peel the beets and, using a mandolin or a very fine, sharp knife, cut the flesh into wafer-thin slices. Toss these into the bowl, too, along with the mint. Add any fennel fronds. Pour on the dressing, toss, and serve.

ALSO TRY...

Indian spiced carrot and beets salad This is the most spectacular color. It's worth making for that alone but its sweetness is lovely against the starchiness of hummus or the subtlety of sliced avocado. It's good, too, with spicy roast chicken. Peel 1 carrot and 1 small beet and grate coarsely into a bowl. Add 1 tsp ground cumin, a drop of hot pepper sauce, 2 tbsp canola oil, 1 tsp red wine vinegar, a couple of good squeezes of lemon juice, 2 tbsp chopped blanched almonds, 1½ tsp sesame seeds, 1½ tsp pumpkin seeds, 1½ tbsp raisins, plumped up in boiling water and drained, and 2 tbsp chopped fresh cilantro. Mix carefully and check the seasoning.

Spanish tomato and bread salad

I like *panzanella*, the Tuscan bread and tomato salad, but, in truth, usually find it a bit soggy. The bread chunks are made as Spanish *migas*, soft in the middle but crunchy outside. I like them warm, so there's a contrast of temperatures in the salad. Use a range of tomatoes: little yellow ones, round ones, oval ones, baby plums, and so on, to look as lovely as possible. This salad is good with *bocconcini* or, if you leave out the anchovies, little chunks of ricotta salata dropped in at the last minute. It looks best in a shallow bowl where you can see the array of tomato colors and shapes.

Serves 4

6 slices bread (such as ciabatta)
5 tbsp milk
1½ lb mixed tomatoes
20 canned anchovies
2 tbsp tiny capers, rinsed
5 tbsp extra-virgin olive oil

1½ tbsp balsamic vinegar
salt and pepper
1 tsp superfine sugar
leaves from 1 bunch basil (about ½ oz), torn
3 tbsp olive oil, for frying

1 Tear the bread into chunks and put into a bowl with the milk. Turn the bread over in the milk and leave for 15 minutes or so. Halve the small tomatoes and cut the large ones into quarters or eighths; you may want to leave some of the tomatoes whole if they are really tiny; you just need a good selection of color and shape. Put into a broad, shallow serving bowl with all the other ingredients, except the basil (which is better tossed in at the last moment) and the oil for frying.

2 Squeeze the milk out of the bread. It doesn't matter if some chunks seem to be falling apart: just reform them by squeezing with your hand. Heat the olive oil for frying and cook the bread pieces in batches, so that they become a lovely golden color all over the outside.

3 Add the basil to the salad along with the bread, toss well, and serve.

ALSO TRY...

Pa amb tomàque A great Catalan snack. Toast a piece of sourdough or good country bread on both sides (if you do it under a broiler, fine; if you do it on a grill, you're in for a big treat). Immediately rub with garlic–this is much easier if you use half a head, halved horizontally–mucking about with a clove will only make you cross. Now cut a ripe, well-flavored tomato in half and rub that on, squeezing out the juices and squishing the flesh so it soaks into the bread. Drizzle with your favorite extra-virgin olive oil and sprinkle with sea salt and black pepper.

Tomato and basil tart

Large, scarlet, fragrant with basil, this is a gorgeous tart and, in terms of cooking, is not much more than an assembly job. Do make sure your tomatoes are thinly sliced or they won't become cooked through and slightly caramelized in the cooking time.

Serves 6

2¾ lb plum tomatoes
8 oz mascarpone
1 garlic clove, crushed
1¼ cups grated Parmesan cheese
⅔ cup grated Gruyère cheese

1½ oz basil leaves, torn, plus more
 to serve
salt and pepper
17 oz ready-made puff pastry

1 Preheat the oven to 400°F. Slice the tomatoes about ¼ in thick. Discard the slice that has the core (you can use this and the other end piece for a tomato sauce); you need only the clean slices for this. Mash the mascarpone with a fork and add the garlic, cheeses, and basil. Season.

2 Roll the pastry out to make a 13 in circle and put it on a floured baking sheet. Spread the mascarpone mix over this, leaving a 2 in rim around the outside. Place the tomatoes on the pastry, starting from the outside edge. Place them in overlapping concentric circles, ending up with one slice in the middle of the tart. Season the tomatoes with salt and pepper.

3 Bake for 30 minutes. Reduce the heat to 300°F and bake for another 35 minutes. The tomatoes should be slightly caramelized. Sprinkle with some basil leaves and serve immediately.

ALSO TRY...

Tomato, thyme, and aged cheddar tart Make the tart as above, but replace the Parmesan with really strong cheddar cheese and leave out the basil. Sprinkle the tomatoes with the leaves from about 5 thyme sprigs before baking.

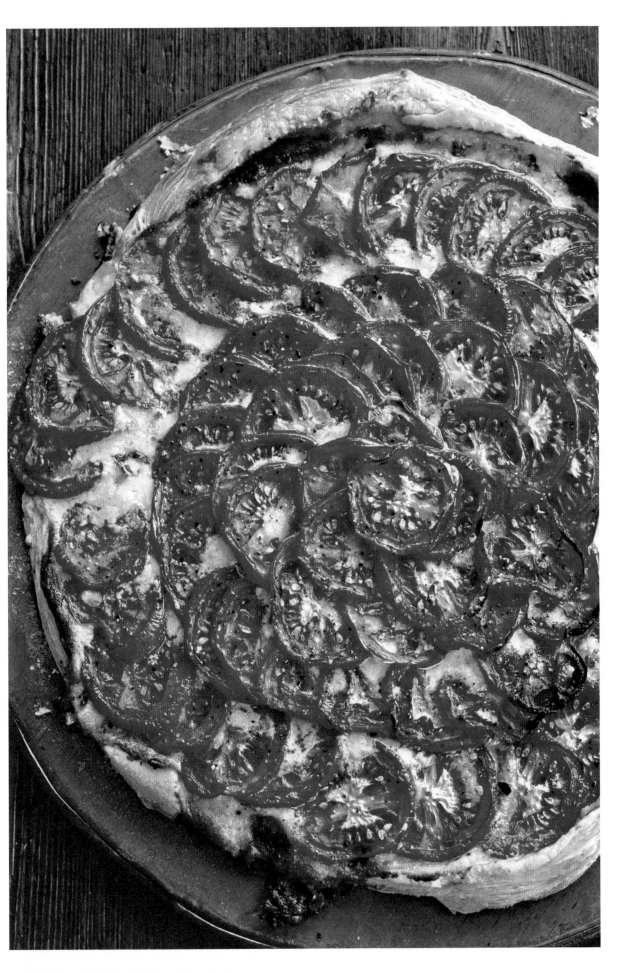

Caramelized onion, pear, and blue cheese tarts with walnuts and rosemary

Tarts are very comforting—the buttery pastry and the faint rustle as you cut a slice—and look as though they take more effort than they do.

Serves 4

5 tbsp unsalted butter

¼ cup olive oil

3 large onions, very thinly sliced

salt and pepper

leaves from 1 rosemary sprig, chopped

all-purpose flour, to dust

2¼ lb puff pastry

3 pears, peeled, cored, and sliced
  lengthwise

2 tsp superfine sugar

10 oz gorgonzola cheese, in chunks

½ cup walnut pieces, toasted

1 Preheat the oven to 425°F and put in two baking sheets.

2 Heat 3 tbsp of the butter and the oil in a large saucepan. Add the onions and turn to coat. Add 1 tbsp water, cover, and sweat over a very low heat, stirring occasionally. After 30 minutes, uncover and cook for a further 30 minutes, stirring. The onions will darken and caramelize. Season and add the rosemary. Set aside.

3 On a lightly floured surface, roll the pastry into four 9 in rounds. Top with the onions, leaving a rim. Transfer to the baking sheets, putting a sheet of parchment paper under each tart. Bake for 8 minutes. Melt the remaining butter and quickly sauté the pears. Sprinkle with the sugar and cook for 30 seconds, until golden.

4 Sprinkle the tarts with cheese and pears and bake for 3–4 minutes. Sprinkle with the walnuts and serve with a green salad.

ALSO TRY...

Goat cheese, onion, and spinach tart with pine nuts and raisins Preheat the oven to 375°F. Heat 6 tbsp oil in a pan and add 4 onions, thinly sliced. Add 2 tbsp water and sweat for 25 minutes. Wilt 2¾ lb spinach, drain, and squeeze out the water. Chop and mix with the onions. Season and add grated nutmeg. Roll out 17 oz puff pastry very thinly. Put onto a floured baking sheet, prick with a fork and bake for 20 minutes. Remove and gently flatten. Turn the heat up to 400°F. Spoon on the spinach, leaving a rim. Top with 8 oz goat cheese, crumbled; 2 tbsp pine nuts; and 3 tbsp raisins (plumped in boiling water, then drained). Bake for 10–15 minutes. Serves 4 as a starter.

Bacon, potato, and onion galette Roll out and bake 17 oz puff pastry as above. Slice 1 lb cooked potatoes thinly. Sauté 1 large onion, sliced, in 1 tbsp butter over a low heat. Lay the potatoes and onions on the pastry, brush with melted butter and season, leaving a rim. Bake for 15 minutes. Sauté 1 lb bacon, chopped, until crisp. Sprinkle on the tart when it has 5 minutes cooking time left. Serves 4 as a starter.

Zucchini with raisins, pine nuts, and mint

This is based on a recipe in Claudia Roden's *Book of Middle Eastern Cookery*. I've been making it for years as it behaves very well (it's good the day after, and hot, warm, or at room temperature). Leave out the onions if you prefer a more purely zucchini dish. Lovely with lamb or as part of a Middle Eastern mezze.

Serves 4 as a side dish

1 lb zucchini

olive oil

1 small red onion, in crescent
  moon-shaped slices

2 garlic cloves, thinly sliced

⅓ cup raisins, soaked in boiling water
  for 15 minutes and drained

1½ tbsp pine nuts or chopped blanched
  almonds, toasted

juice of ½ lemon

torn leaves from 8 mint sprigs

1 Slice the zucchini to about the thickness of a quarter. Heat 2 tbsp olive oil in a large frying pan and cook the zucchini in batches until golden on both sides and soft. Season as you go and add more oil as you need it (zucchini soak up quite a lot but that only makes them more delicious). Put each batch into a shallow bowl as they finish cooking.

2 Now add another 1 tbsp oil and cook the onion until completely soft and golden (even slightly singed at the tips). Add the garlic and cook for another 2 minutes, until pale gold and soft. Toss the onion and garlic with the zucchini, raisins, nuts, lemon juice, and mint. Taste and adjust the seasoning. You may find you want more lemon; there should be a balance of sweetness from the raisins and sourness from the lemon.

ALSO TRY...

Zucchini with hazelnut tarator Sauté the courgettes in olive oil as above–with the onion, if preferred–and, once they are soft, drizzle with tarator (see page 58). Sprinkle with fresh chopped parsley, mint, or cilantro and grated lemon zest.

Slow-cooked garlic zucchini Deliciously rich. Heat 1 tbsp unsalted butter and 3 tbsp olive oil in a very large frying pan and gently cook 6 garlic cloves, very thinly sliced, until soft but not colored. Add 1 lb zucchini sliced to the thickness of a quarter, and turn over to coat. Increase the heat a bit so the zucchini get a little bit of color, then reduce the heat, season, and cook slowly (you almost "stew" them in the butter and oil) until completely soft, almost collapsing. This tastes purely of zucchini and doesn't need anything else. I can eat a plateful on their own.

Radish, olive, anchovy, and parsley salad

Lovely with a chunk of goat cheese and absolutely fantastic with cold roast beef or lamb: the strong flavors go so well with meat. You don't have to use white balsamic vinegar—I know not everyone has it—but it means the lovely white and pink radishes aren't tainted.

Serves 4

12 oz radishes, preferably with really fresh leaves attached

1 cup black olives

½ cup fresh flat-leaf parsley, coarsely chopped

10 salt-cured anchovies, drained and finely chopped

1 small garlic clove, crushed

½ fresh red chile, seeded and shredded (optional)

¼ cup extra-virgin olive oil

1 tbsp white balsamic vinegar (or dark if white isn't available)

freshly ground black pepper

1 Wash the radishes, trim, and, if they have good leaves, carefully pat these dry and set aside to go into the salad. Cut the radishes into thin slices (if you have French breakfast radishes, cut them lengthwise; this makes lovely teardrop shapes).

2 Pit the olives, or slice the flesh off the stones if they are hard to pit, and chop. Toss everything together in a shallow bowl along with any reserved leaves and serve immediately. Don't be tempted to add salt—the ingredients are salty enough.

Turkish carrots and lentils with herbs

This shows just how delicious frugality can be.

Serves 4–6 as a side dish, 3 as a main course

¼ cup olive oil

1 onion, in thin crescent moon shapes

4 garlic cloves, thinly chopped

1½ tsp coriander seeds, crushed

¼–½ tsp dried red pepper flakes

½ cup green or Puy lentils

6 large carrots, sliced

2 tbsp tomato paste

2 tsp superfine sugar

1¼ cups vegetable stock or water

salt and pepper

2 tbsp chopped fresh mint, parsley, or dill

good squeeze of lemon juice

extra-virgin olive oil, to serve

1 Heat the oil in a saucepan and sauté the onion until soft and pale gold. Add the garlic and spices and cook for 2 minutes. Now add everything else except the herbs, lemon juice, and extra-virgin olive oil.

2 Bring to a boil and cook until tender and the liquid has been absorbed. It should take 30 minutes.

3 Taste, add the herbs and lemon juice, then adjust the seasoning. Add a generous slug of extra-virgin olive oil. Serve hot, warm, or at room temperature.

ALSO TRY...

Moroccan spiced carrots Heat 1½ tbsp olive oil in a heavy saucepan and sauté 2 garlic cloves, finely chopped, and 1 fresh red chile, seeded and shredded, until the garlic is pale gold. Add 2 tsp ground cumin and 1 tsp cayenne and cook for another minute, then add 1 lb carrots, in batons, and turn to coat. Add ⅓ cup orange juice, a pinch of light brown sugar, seasoning, and water to cover. Bring to a boil, reduce the heat, and cook until tender. The carrots should absorb the liquid. Stir in 2 tbsp chopped fresh cilantro. Serve hot, warm, or at room temperature as a side dish or part of a Middle Eastern mezze. Serves 4 as a side dish.

Uzbeki carrots Cook 1 lb carrots (in batons or chunks) in water until tender, then drain. Heat 1 tbsp olive oil and 1 tbsp butter in a frying pan and add 2 tsp caraway seeds, 2 tsp sweet paprika, and ½ tsp dried red pepper flakes. Cook for 30 seconds, then toss in the carrots. Stir them around, season, and serve. Serves 4 as a side dish.

The recipes above are quite exotic, but also consider: Cook 1 lb carrots (in batons or slices) in chicken stock or water with a pat of butter, seasoning, and a little sugar until the liquid has been absorbed and the carrots are tender and glazed. Or add chunks of fried bacon and parsley or mint. A slug of heavy cream is lovely, too. Or go luxurious and toss the cooked carrots with butter-fried wild (or cultivated) mushrooms, adding a dollop of cream and a generous grating of nutmeg or sprinkling of parsley.

Kaye korma curry

Use this as a blueprint for a mild vegetable curry, with whatever is abundant. I sometimes make it with eggplant, zucchini, or summer squash, and don't always add beans or peas. It is very good-tempered and reheats well.

Serves 4

2 tbsp sunflower or peanut oil

1½ tsp black mustard seeds

2 onions, finely chopped

4 garlic cloves, crushed

1½ in fresh ginger, peeled and finely chopped

1 fresh red chile, seeded and finely chopped

½ tsp ground turmeric

1 tsp ground coriander

8 oz tomatoes, cut into chunks

9 oz carrots, cut into chunks

8 oz potatoes (waxy or baking; if waxy, there's no need to peel), cut into chunks

1 cup coconut milk

salt and pepper

4 oz thin green beans, trimmed and halved

¾ cup frozen peas

juice of ½–1 lime, to taste

1 tbsp chopped fresh cilantro

1 Heat the oil in a flameproof Dutch oven and add the mustard seeds. As soon as they pop, add the onions. Fry over a medium heat until the onions are good and brown, but not burnt. Add the garlic, ginger, and chile and cook for 5 minutes, then add the ground spices and cook for another minute to release their fragrance.

2 Add the tomatoes, carrots, and potatoes. Stir and cook for 4 minutes to soften the tomatoes, then add enough water just to cover, followed by the coconut milk. Season and bring to just under a boil. Reduce to a steady simmer and cook until almost tender (add more water if it looks dry). The sauce should just coat the vegetables.

3 The beans and peas need to cook for only about 3–4 minutes, so add them towards the end of cooking. Taste and add half the lime juice, then taste again, adjust the seasoning and decide whether you want to add more. Stir in the chopped cilantro just before you serve the curry.

ALSO TRY...

Vietnamese sweet potato curry On the table in about 20 minutes. Heat 1 tbsp peanut oil in a saucepan and cook 2 onions, cut into crescent moon-shaped slices, over a medium heat until golden. Add 1 fresh red chile, seeded and shredded, 1 tbsp ground coriander and 1½ tsp ground turmeric and cook for another minute, stirring. Add a 14 oz can coconut milk, 1½ tbsp light brown sugar and 2¾ lb sweet potatoes, peeled and cubed. Bring to just under a boil, reduce the heat, and cook until the sweet potato is tender. To thicken, press some of the potato with the back of a spoon so it disintegrates. Add 2 tbsp fish sauce and the juice of 1 lime, then taste for seasoning and a balance of hot, sour, salty, and sweet flavors. Stir in a generous handful of torn basil. Serve with boiled rice.

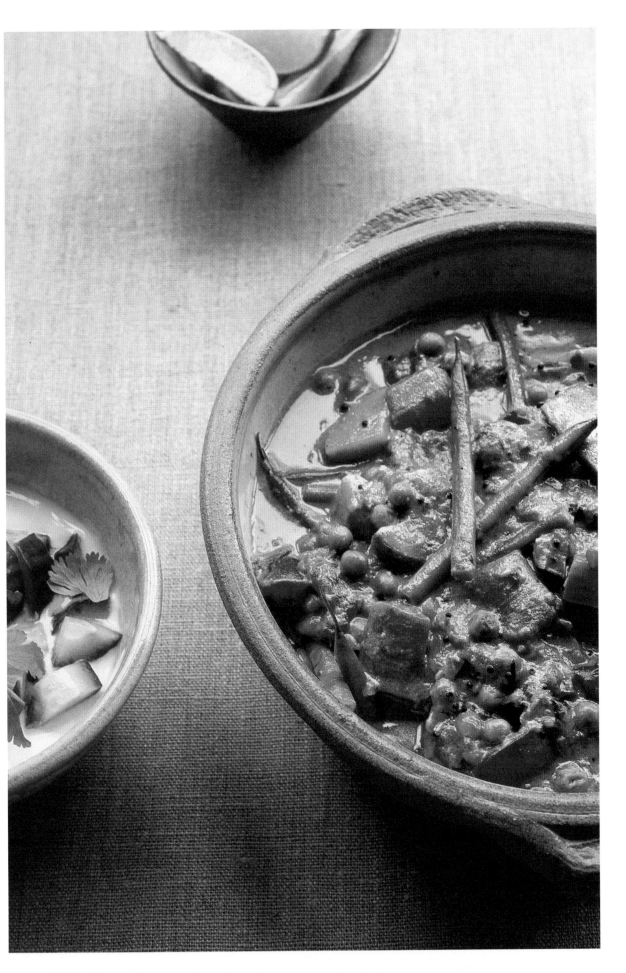

Moroccan seven-vegetable couscous

This is a great dish for a crowd. Use whatever vegetables are in season—just make sure you add each at the right time so it doesn't overcook.

Serves 8

6 tbsp olive oil

2 onions, halved and cut into wedges

1 in fresh ginger, peeled and chopped

3 garlic cloves, finely chopped

¾ tsp ground turmeric

1 lb butternut squash, seeded, peeled and cut into chunks

3 potatoes, sliced

3 large carrots, cut into chunks

6 cups chicken stock or water

good pinch of saffron threads

1 cinnamon stick

2 generous handfuls raisins

salt and pepper

2 small fennel bulbs

4 zucchini, thickly sliced

3 tomatoes, quartered

1 bunch cilantro, stems chopped, leaves coarsely chopped

14 oz can chickpeas, drained and rinsed

2 cups couscous, to serve

1 tbsp harissa, or to taste

1 Heat 2 tbsp olive oil in a large saucepan and add the onions. Cook until softening and slightly singed. Reduce the heat, add the ginger, garlic, and turmeric and cook for 2 minutes. Add the squash, potatoes, carrots, and stock or water. Once it heats, crumble in the saffron and add the cinnamon and raisins. Season and bring to a boil.

2 Remove any tough outer leaves from the fennel, trim the tips (keep any fronds to serve), quarter, and core. Once the vegetables in the pot have cooked for 10 minutes, add the fennel, courgettes, tomatoes, and cilantro stems. Cook for 15 minutes, stirring, until completely soft. Add the chickpeas for the last 5 minutes.

3 Pour 1¾ cups boiling water or stock over the cous cous plus 4 tbsp olive oil. Cover and leave for 15 minutes, then fork through to separate the grains.

4 Remove a ladleful of broth and mix with the harissa in a warmed pitcher so people can help themselves. Sprinkle with the cilantro leaves and serve.

ALSO TRY...

Cauliflower, eggplant, chickpea, and date tajine Heat 1½ tbsp olive oil in a large, heavy saucepan and sauté 1 onion, cut into wedges, until it softens and browns. Heat 1 tbsp olive oil in a large frying pan and sauté 2 eggplants, cut into chunks, until colored on all sides. To the onions add ½ tsp ground ginger, ½ tsp dried red pepper flakes, 1½ tsp ground cumin, ½ cinnamon stick, and 3 garlic cloves, finely chopped, and cook for 1½ minutes over a medium heat. Add the eggplants to the onions with 4 cups stock or water, a good pinch of saffron, 2 stoned dates, halved, and a 14 oz can chickpeas, drained and rinsed. Bring to a boil, then cover and simmer for 10 minutes. Stir in the florets from 1 small cauliflower and cook until tender (10–15 minutes). Mix in the chopped zest of 1 preserved lemon, taste for seasoning, add ¼ cup chopped fresh cilantro, and serve with couscous.

Mediterranean potato, tomato, and goat cheese gratin

This recipe shows gratins can be light and fresh. You can simplify it—you don't have to include eggplants or olives—but if you leave out something substantial, increase the amount of potatoes. Perfect with roast lamb.

Serves 4 as a main course with salad, 6 as a side dish

2 eggplants, thinly sliced	4 large tomatoes, very thinly sliced
olive oil	leaves from 6 thyme sprigs
salt and pepper	6 tbsp finely chopped fresh flat-leaf parsley
2 red onions, very thinly sliced	grated zest of ½ lemon
2 garlic cloves, crushed	¾ cup black olives (preferably Niçoise),
1 lb waxy potatoes, very, very	chopped
thinly sliced	6 oz goat cheese, crumbled

1 Preheat the oven to 375°F. Brush the eggplants with olive oil, put on baking sheets, and roast for 15 minutes. They should be soft, colored, and cooked through. Season well.

2 Using a little more oil, sauté the onions in a frying pan until soft but not colored. Add the garlic and cook for a minute.

3 Brush a gratin dish with a little oil. Arrange a layer of potatoes, then a layer of eggplant, one of onions, one of tomatoes, and then begin again with the eggplant. Sprinkle on the herbs, lemon zest, olives, and goat cheese and season as you go. End with a layer of potatoes, arranged in neat slices. Brush with olive oil and cook in the oven for 45 minutes, or until the potatoes are cooked through. Cover with foil if the gratin is getting too dark. Serve immediately.

ALSO TRY...

Gratin savoyard Preheat the oven to 400°F. Authentic Savoie gratin does not contain leeks, but I don't think it pays to be too purist. Do use Beaufort, though, if you can get it. Wash 10 oz trimmed leeks really well and slice thinly. Melt 2 tbsp butter in a heavy pan and sweat the leeks, covered, until soft. It will take about 15 minutes. Add a tiny splash of water every so often to make sure they don't stick and burn. Butter a gratin dish and sprinkle with 1 garlic clove, chopped. Slice 1¾ lb potatoes very thinly, using a mandolin or very sharp knife. Lay these in the dish in layers, alternating with the leeks and 8 oz Gruyère or Beaufort cheese, grated. Season well as you go along. Finish with a layer of potatoes in neat overlapping slices, sprinkled with cheese. Heat 1¾ cups chicken stock and pour over the vegetables. Bake for 1 hour, or until the potatoes are tender and the liquid has evaporated.

Creamy white vegetable, chestnut, and cranberry gratin

A dish from an inspiring American cook called Jody Adams (it really is worth tracking down her book, *In the Hands of a Chef*). It seems festive because of the cranberries, but I start making it in October.

Serves 4 as a main course, 6 as a side dish

1 lb potatoes	2 garlic cloves, very thinly sliced
12 oz parsnips	leaves from 2 thyme sprigs
12 oz celery root	salt and pepper
2 cups heavy cream	butter, for the dish
½ cup sour cream	6 tbsp dried cranberries
⅓ cup whole milk	4 oz (about ¾ cup) cooked chestnuts, sliced

1 Preheat the oven to 350°F. Slice the potatoes, parsnips and celery root very thinly–a mandolin is the best tool for this. In a large saucepan, mix together the creams and milk and bring to just under a boil. Add the sliced vegetables, garlic, and thyme and cook gently for 5 minutes.

2 Season really well and spoon half the vegetables into a buttered gratin dish. Sprinkle the cranberries and chestnuts on top, then add another layer of the vegetables. Bake for 1 hour, or until completely tender. You may need to cover with foil after 45 minutes to stop the gratin becoming too dark in color.

ALSO TRY...

The recipe above is one of the most useful in the book as it lends itself to so many variations. Stick to the basic quantities of root vegetables or potatoes, cream, and milk and you can improvise to your heart's content. If you end up with a stash of wild mushrooms, they are delicious sautéed, then layered in a gratin of potatoes and parsnips, or potatoes and Jerusalem artichokes. Cheese can be sprinkled between the layers (Parmesan, Gruyère, or cheddar are all good) and sautéed onions, bacon, or ham are good too.

Potato and horseradish gratin Wonderful with roast beef. Make as above but use only potatoes and omit the garlic. Spread a third of the potatoes in a gratin dish and dot 3 tbsp creamed horseradish on top. Repeat to make another layer, then top with the remaining potatoes. Bake as above.

Beet and potato gratin Make as above but use 1 lb each of potatoes and cooked beets. You can also add horseradish (great with salmon or beef). Another good addition is flaked smoked mackerel (layer between the slices and bake).

Cauliflower, bacon, and Cashel blue gratin

This makes a lovely main course. The main recipe shows a gratin with cheese sauce, the winter squash recipe below a gratin with cream (more expensive but less time-consuming). Make sure your vegetables aren't too wet; it produces a watery gratin.

Serves 4 as a side dish

FOR THE GRATIN
1 large cauliflower, in florets
salt and pepper
4 oz bacon, chopped
1¾ oz Cashel or other soft blue cheese, in small chunks
2 tbsp coarse fresh white bread crumbs

FOR THE CHEESE SAUCE
¼ cup butter
¼ cup all-purpose flour
2 cups milk
⅔ cup grated aged cheddar cheese
1 tbsp English mustard (available online)
squeeze of lemon juice

1 Preheat the oven to 400°F. Cook the florets in lightly salted boiling water until just tender, then drain really well (water collects easily in cauliflower).

2 To make the sauce, melt the butter in a heavy saucepan and add the flour. Over low heat, stir for a couple of minutes. Remove from the heat. Gradually add the milk, beating well after each addition, and adding more only when the mixture is completely smooth. Return to the heat and bring to a boil, stirring, until thickened. Reduce the heat and cook for 4 minutes. Add the cheddar and mustard and stir to melt the cheese. Add a squeeze of lemon juice and taste for seasoning.

3 Fry the bacon in its own fat. You want a pale golden color but do not cook it through. Put the cauliflower into a gratin dish, season, and sprinkle with the bacon. Pour on the sauce, then dot with the blue cheese. Sprinkle with the bread crumbs. Bake for 20 minutes, or until golden, bubbling, and toasted. Serve immediately.

LEFTOVERS...

This makes a gorgeous soup. Just add chicken stock and milk (in a 2:1 ratio) and heat gently. Purée. Check the seasoning and bring to the boil again before serving.

ALSO TRY...

Make the gratin above with leeks or broccoli (cook until tender and drain very well), or add a layer of leeks, cooked Savoy cabbage, or spinach to the cauliflower.

Winter squash, tomato, and Gruyère gratin Preheat the oven to 400°F. Peel, seed and cut 2¼ lb squash into wedges. Put into a large roasting pan with 1¾ lb plum tomatoes, halved. Add 6 tbsp olive oil and season. Turn to coat. The tomatoes should end cut-side-up. Roast for 40 minutes. Put into a gratin dish, season, and pour over ⅔ cup heavy cream. Sprinkle on ¼ cup of both Parmesan and Gruyère or cheddar cheese, grated, and some dry bread crumbs. Bake for 20–25 minutes, until golden and bubbling.

Roasted squash and spinach lasagna

Everybody loves lasagna—you can almost hear the sighs of satisfaction as you place it on the table—and you can adapt this at will, adding roasted mushrooms (roasted to drive off the moisture), or sautéed fennel.

Serves 8

FOR THE LASAGNA

5 lb butternut squash, peeled and seeded

¼ cup olive oil

salt and pepper

2¼ lb spinach, washed

3 tbsp butter

generous grating of nutmeg

8 to 12 fresh lasagna noodles

4 oz Parmesan cheese, grated

FOR THE TOMATO SAUCE

2 x 14 oz cans tomatoes in thick juice

1 large onion, finely chopped

4 garlic cloves, finely chopped

2 tbsp olive oil

4 tsp light brown sugar

FOR THE BÉCHAMEL SAUCE

6 cups whole milk

10 peppercorns

½ onion

1 bay leaf

⅔ cup butter

⅔ cup all-purpose flour

grated nutmeg

1 Preheat the oven to 375°F. Slice the squash, put into a roasting pan, drizzle on the oil, and season. Toss and roast until tender and slightly charred. It can take 40 minutes. Increase the oven temperature to 400°F.

2 Meanwhile, make the tomato sauce. Put all the ingredients in a saucepan, bring to a boil, reduce the heat, and simmer, uncovered, for 30 minutes. Season to taste.

3 For the béchamel, put the milk in a saucepan with the peppercorns, onion, and bay leaf and bring to a boil. Remove from the heat and leave for 45 minutes to infuse. Strain. Melt the butter in a heavy saucepan and add the flour. Over a low heat, stir for 2 minutes. Remove from the heat. Gradually add the milk, beating well after each addition and adding more only when completely smooth. Bring to a boil, stirring, until thick. Reduce the heat and cook for 4 minutes, then season well, adding the nutmeg.

4 Put the spinach in a saucepan with the water that clings to it after washing. Cover and put over medium heat. Wilt for about 4 minutes, turning. Squeeze out the water, chop the spinach, and put it in a frying pan with 1 tbsp of the butter. Heat gently, tossing, season, and add the nutmeg.

5 Use the remaining butter to grease a pie or gratin dish (about 1½ qt capacity). Add a layer of squash, then a layer of tomato sauce. Lay lasagna noodles on top, cut so they don't overlap. Add a layer of béchamel, half the spinach, and half the cheese. Now put in another layer of lasagna and the remaining spinach. Add a layer of squash, a layer of tomato sauce and a final layer of béchamel. Sprinkle on the remaining cheese. Bake for 35–40 minutes, or until golden and bubbling.

Moroccan spiced roasted squash and chickpeas with minted onions

It's probably obvious that I'm a big fan of roasted squash and pumpkin. It's partly because I used to yearn for them—they have those lovely fairy-tale connections and look as if they would be sweet and velvety—but they were difficult to get hold of so I'm making up for lost time. This particular recipe is splendid-looking, especially if the tomatoes are on the vine.

Serves 6

4½ lb well-flavored winter squash
  or pumpkin
salt and pepper
olive oil
2 x 14 oz cans chickpeas, drained
6 oz cherry tomatoes
2 fresh red chiles, seeded and very
  thinly sliced

4 star anise
1¼ in fresh ginger, peeled and grated
4 garlic cloves, very thinly sliced
3 onions, very thinly sliced
juice of ½ lemon
leaves from 5 mint sprigs, torn

1 Preheat the oven to 375°F. Seed and peel the squash and cut into wedges. Put it into a roasting pan where the pieces can lie in a single layer with room for the tomatoes later. Season and drizzle with 5 tbsp olive oil. Turn with your hands to coat. Roast for 20–30 minutes.

2 Add the chickpeas, tomatoes, chile, star anise, ginger, and garlic. Toss to distribute the flavorings evenly. Roast for 15–20 minutes, or until tender and slightly singed.

3 Add 3 tbsp oil to a frying pan and cook the onions over a medium heat until soft. Season and increase the heat to brown the onions. Add the lemon juice and the mint. Serve the dish with the onions strewn on top. Couscous is great on the side. For those who want the dish hotter, offer a little bowl of harissa diluted with boiling water.

ALSO TRY...

Roasted pumpkin with spinach and tahini dressing Preheat the oven to 375°F. Slice 2¼ lb pumpkin or winter squash about ¾ in thick. Put into a roasting pan. Mix 7 tbsp olive oil with 2 tsp ground ginger, ½ tsp ground cinnamon, and 1½ tsp superfine sugar. Pour over the wedges, season, and toss. Roast for 20–30 minutes, until tender and slightly caramelized. Beat ⅔ cup Greek yogurt with ⅔ cup tahini, then add the juice of 2 lemons, ¼ cup extra-virgin olive oil, and 4 garlic cloves, crushed. Add enough water to make a sauce a bit thicker than heavy cream. Taste and season; it needs quite a lot of salt. You may also want more oil to thin it out. Toss some baby spinach with enough extra-virgin olive oil and lemon juice to make them glossy. Season, put in a broad, shallow bowl, and set the squash on top. Squeeze over some lemon juice, drizzle on the tahini dressing, and serve.

Sicilian braised vegetables with saffron, pine nuts, raisins, and capers

I have played fast and lose with Italian influences here, but the dish is delicious nevertheless. You can serve it without the gremolata or olives. Lovely with roast lamb or veal, and a main course in it's own right.

Serves 4

FOR THE VEGETABLES

3 tbsp olive oil

1 lb small waxy potatoes, halved lengthwise

8 oz baby onions

3 garlic cloves, crushed

½ tsp dried red pepper flakes

1⅓ cups dry white wine

good pinch of saffron threads

salt and pepper

2 small fennel bulbs, halved

1 small cauliflower, in florets (keep any good, fresh leaves)

⅓ cup raisins, soaked in boiling water and drained

2½ cups vegetable or chicken stock

1½ tbsp capers, rinsed

1½ tbsp pine nuts, toasted

2 tbsp chopped fresh mint

good drizzle of extra-virgin olive oil

FOR THE GREMOLATA (OPTIONAL)

25 good-quality green olives in oil

1 small orange

2 garlic cloves, very finely chopped

2 tbsp chopped fresh mint

1 Heat the oil and gently brown the potatoes and the onions until pale gold. Add the garlic and pepper flakes and sauté for another minute, then add the wine. Bring to a boil, add the saffron, salt, and pepper and reduce to a simmer. Cook until the potatoes are starting to become tender, about 10 minutes. You'll find that a lot of the liquid has evaporated.

2 Add the fennel and cauliflower (including any cauliflower leaves), the raisins, and stock. Stir well and bring to a boil. Reduce the heat and cook until everything is tender, another 12–15 minutes. Carefully stir every so often to make sure everything is well coated in the juices.

3 Add the capers and pine nuts and stir gently; be careful not to break up the vegetables. Taste for seasoning. Sprinkle on the mint and drizzle with extra-virgin olive oil.

4 For the gremolata, pit the olives and chop the flesh coarsely. Remove the orange zest with a zester and mix with everything else. Sprinkle on top of the vegetables, then drizzle with extra-virgin olive oil.

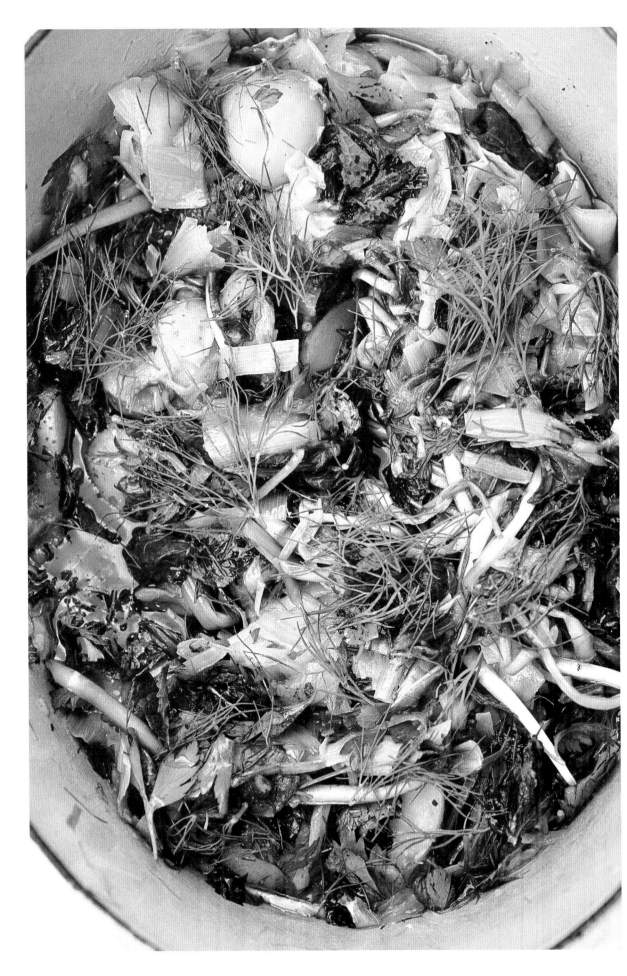

Greek potatoes, frisée, spinach, and leeks with dill, mint, and garlic yogurt

Greece truly makes the most of vegetables. This is a complete, delicious one-pot meal; you won't miss meat. Curly endive cooks to softness and the bitterness is pacified. Arugula can also be used.

Serves 6 as a side dish

¼ cup olive oil

5 leeks, cut into chunks

1¼ lb small waxy potatoes, halved

salt and pepper

10 oz spinach

6 oz frisée (curly endive) leaves, torn

3 tbsp chopped fresh dill

leaves from 6 mint sprigs, torn

good squeeze of lemon juice

extra-virgin olive oil, to serve (optional)

2 garlic cloves, crushed

1 cup Greek yogurt

1 Put half the oil into a heavy saucepan and add the leeks and potatoes. Season, add a splash of water, cover, and sweat for 20 minutes. Add a bit of water every so often and stir.

2 Once the potatoes are almost tender, add the spinach, endive, and remaining oil and turn gently. Add another splash of water, season, cover, and cook until the leaves have wilted—about 4–5 minutes. Add the herbs and lemon juice, put into a serving dish, and drizzle with the extra-virgin olive oil, if you want.

3 Mix the garlic into the yogurt and serve with the vegetables.

LEFTOVERS...

Make these into soup. Add chicken stock, heat, mash to break down the potatoes and leave chunky or purée. Top with Greek yogurt and a drizzle of olive oil.

ALSO TRY...

Turkish potatoes with tomatoes and black olives Heat ¼ cup olive oil in a large, heavy pan and sauté 1 large onion, sliced, until soft and golden. Add 4 garlic cloves, crushed; 2 green chiles, seeded and chopped; and ½ tbsp ground cumin. Cook for 2 minutes, then add 1½ lb waxy potatoes, cubed. Stir to coat in the spices and add 28 oz can tomatoes in thick juice; 1 tbsp tomato paste; ½ tbsp light brown sugar; 1 tbsp red wine vinegar, 1 cup water; 1½ tsp dried oregano; and 2 tbsp coarsely chopped fresh parsley. Stir and bring to a boil. Season. Reduce to a simmer and cook, uncovered, until the vegetables are tender and the sauce is thick. Add ¾ cup good-quality black olives (in oil, not brine), pitted, 4 minutes before the potatoes are ready. If the sauce isn't thick enough, turn up the heat; if it is too thick, add water. Taste for seasoning (add harissa if you want it hotter). Stir in 2 tbsp chopped fresh flat-leaf parsley and serve drizzled with olive oil. Serves 6–8 as a side dish.

Niçoise vegetable stew with rouille

This is like a Provençal fish soup without the fish. It has a really gutsy flavor. If you want to make it fishy, you can poach some fish in the soup at the end; or you can cook fish separately and put some on top of each serving. If you dont like rouille you can serve this stew with aioli (garlic mayonnaise, see page 18) instead.

Serves 4 as a main course, 6 as a side dish

FOR THE STEW
¼ cup olive oil
1 lb small waxy potatoes, halved
  lengthwise
6 oz baby onions
3 leeks, trimmed, washed and cut
  into chunks
2 garlic cloves, crushed
¼ tsp dried red pepper flakes
3 cups vegetable or chicken stock
good pinch of saffron threads
1 strip of orange zest
3 thyme sprigs

salt and pepper
2 small fennel bulbs, sliced lengthwise
6 plum tomatoes, quartered
grated Gruyère cheese and baguette
  croûtes, to serve (optional)

FOR THE ROUILLE
3 garlic cloves, coarsely chopped
2 egg yolks
⅔ cup olive oil
4 tsp tomato paste
lemon juice
½ tsp cayenne pepper

1 Heat the oil and gently sauté the potatoes, onions, and leeks for about 15 minutes. It's nice if the potatoes get a little golden. Stir from time to time to make sure nothing is sticking. Add the garlic and red pepper flakes and sauté for another minute, then add half the stock.

2 Bring to a boil, add the saffron, orange zest, 2 of the thyme sprigs, salt, and pepper and reduce to a simmer. Cook until the potatoes are just becoming tender, about 10 minutes.

3 Add the fennel and the tomatoes. Stir well and cook until the vegetables are tender, another 10 minutes or so. Stir carefully every so often to make sure everything's well coated in the saffron juices, but try not to break up the potatoes.

4 For the rouille, put the garlic and a little salt into a mortar and grind to a purée. (Or crush the garlic and put into a bowl with some seasoning.) Mix in the yolks, then add the oil drop by drop, beating all the time (with a wooden spoon or electric hand beater). The mixture should thicken. Don't add the next drop of oil until the previous drop has been incorporated fully and the mixture has thickened. Add the tomato purée, lemon juice to taste, and the cayenne, then adjust the seasoning.

5 Strip the leaves from the remaining thyme sprig and add to the stew. Serve in soup plates with rouille spooned on top. I sometimes also serve grated Gruyère and croûtes, as you would with Provençal fish soup.

Fried kale and turnip with bacon bits and black pepper

Kale has made a comeback. It's slightly chewy and a bit bitter–both in a good way–and you can feel it making you healthier as you eat it. It's also a joy to handle: those big leaves spring back when squeezed, they're so full of life.

Serves 4

1½ lb turnips or rutabaga, cut into
   chunks
salt and pepper

1 lb kale
2 tbsp butter
6 oz bacon, in chunks or cubes

1 Boil the turnips in lightly salted water until tender, then drain. It can take 45 minutes.

2 Remove the ribs from the kale and tear or shred the leaves. Put into a large saucepan, cover with boiling water. Add salt and cook for about 4 minutes, then drain.

3 Melt the butter in a pan and fry the bacon until colored, then add the turnips. Increase the heat, and fry until golden. Add the kale to heat through. Season, adding lots of pepper, and serve.

ALSO TRY…

Stir-fried kale with ginger, garlic, and chile Prepare, cook and drain 1 lb kale as above. Heat 2 tbsp oil in a wok and fry 1 fresh red chile, seeded and sliced; 2 garlic cloves, sliced; ¾ in fresh ginger, peeled and chopped; and 4 scallions, chopped for 2 minutes (don't let the garlic burn). Add the kale. Cook for 1½ minutes, turning to absorb the flavors. Season, squeeze over fresh lime juice, and serve.

Warm salad of bacon, egg, and kale with fried potatoes and mustard dressing Prepare, cook, and drain 1 lb kale as above. Whisk together ¼ cup extra-virgin olive oil, 1½ tsp balsamic vinegar, 1 tsp wholegrain mustard, ½ tsp honey, and seasoning. Cut 2 medium cooked potatoes into ¼ in slices. Heat 3 tbsp olive oil and fry 12 oz bacon, chopped, and the potatoes. When they are golden, add the kale. Season and carefully toss with most of the mustard dressing. Fry 4 eggs in a little oil. Divide the salad among four plates, then top with a fried egg, and the remaining dressing.

Penne with kale, roasted onions and Gorgonzola Preheat the oven to 375°F. Prepare, cook, and drain 8 oz kale as above. Toss 3 large onions, cut into wedges, into a roasting pan with 6 tbsp olive oil, 2 tbsp balsamic vinegar, salt, and pepper. Roast for 30–35 minutes, until tender and slightly charred. Meanwhile, cook 12 oz penne until *al dente*. Drain and return to the saucepan. Add the kale, 2 tbsp olive oil, and seasoning and cook until everything is warmed through. Stir in the onions and 4 oz Gorgonzola cheese, crumbled, to melt.

Savoy bubble and squeak with aged cheddar and fried egg

This traditional British dish gives leftovers a good name. You can obviously use leftover cabbage but I never seem to have any (leftover mashed potatoes is another matter). Make four smaller cakes if you prefer. Grated Gruyère, in place of cheddar, produces long, melting strings which add to the yum factor.

Serves 4

12 oz Savoy cabbage

3 tbsp butter

salt and pepper

peanut oil, for frying

2 cups cooked mashed potato

1 onion, coarsely chopped

6 oz aged cheddar cheese, grated

4 eggs

1 Trim the cabbage and take out the coarse ribs. Cut into broad strips. Melt 1 tbsp of the butter in a saucepan and add the cabbage, seasoning, and a splash of water. Cover and cook for 3 minutes, shaking a couple of times, or until wilted.

2 Heat the remaining butter and 1½ tsp peanut oil in a large frying pan. Add in the potato and onion and fry, turning and seasoning well. As you turn, bits will brown and almost char. Break it up so you get brown bits mixed in. Stir in the cabbage, then the cheese. When the cheese starts to melt, leave it fairly undisturbed—just press it down every so often with a palette knife—and cook on low heat until golden. Flip it over if you can manage (I find it too heavy) or slide it on to a board, turn over, and slide back into the pan.

3 In a separate frying pan, heat 2 tbsp oil and fry the eggs. Serve them on top of the bubble and squeak. If you really want to make a silk purse out of a sow's ear, make some creamy mustard sauce (see page 155) and pour it over the egg. Delicious.

ALSO TRY...

Savoy and leek Irish colcannon Cook 1¾ lb baking potatoes in boiling salted water. Meanwhile, trim 4 leeks and slice thinly. Melt ⅛ cup butter in a heavy saucepan. Stir in the leeks, add a splash of water, season and cover the pan. Let them sweat for 10 minutes, stirring occasionally, then stir in 8 oz Savoy cabbage, shredded, add another splash of water, and cover. Leave to sweat for 5 minutes until soft and buttery. Drain the potatoes, return them to the saucepan, and set a clean cloth towel on top. Cover and set over low heat for 4 minutes to "dry out" the potatoes and give a better mash. Mash. Heat ⅔ cup milk and gradually add it to the potatoes, mashing until there are no lumps. Finally add the cabbage and leeks with their juices, plus another 2 tbsp butter. Season really well. Serve immediately.

Stuffed baked potatoes

You can make two kinds of baked potato. The simpler way is just to bake them. The second, learned years ago at school, is to bake the potatoes, scoop out the flesh, and mash it with other ingredients before returning to the skins and baking a little more. The second type needs a recipe, so here it is.

Serves 2

2 baking potatoes
sea salt flakes and pepper
2 tbsp butter
4 bacon slices, 2 chopped
¼ onion, finely chopped

1 oz blue cheese, such as Roquefort, crumbled
1 small egg, beaten
1½ tsp chopped fresh parsley (optional)
freshly ground black pepper

1 Preheat the oven to 400°F. Wash the potatoes and pat with salt flakes, then bake for 50 minutes. Test with a knife to check they're tender. They will have lovely crisp skin.

2 Meanwhile, melt the butter in a frying pan until foaming, then add the chopped bacon and onion. Cook until the onion is soft but not colored.

3 Halve the potatoes, scoop out the flesh, and mash with the fried onion and bacon, cheese, egg, parsley (if using), and pepper (the cheese and bacon make this salty so you shouldn't need to add any more). Pile into the potato skins, top with the 2 uncooked bacon slices and bake for 10–15 minutes, until golden and bubbling.

ALSO TRY...

Bacon and egg baked potatoes Make 2 stuffed baked potatoes as above, but omit the beaten egg and use cheddar, grated, instead of blue cheese. When you have returned the mash to the potato skins, make a hollow in each and break in a small egg. Season, add a pat of butter, and bake for 15 minutes to set the egg.

Smoked haddock and aged cheddar baked potatoes Bake 2 potatoes as above. Put 1¾ oz smoked haddock (3 in piece) into a small pan and pour over some milk. Bring to a boil, reduce the heat, cover, and poach for 4 minutes. Break the haddock into large flakes (discard any skin). Halve the potatoes and scoop out the flesh. Mash with 1 tbsp butter, 1 egg, ⅓ cup grated aged cheddar cheese, and seasoning. Loosely fold in the haddock. Pile into the potato skins, sprinkle with more cheese, and return to the oven for 10–15 minutes.

Baked sweet potato with goat cheese and olive-hazelnut salsa Bake 1 sweet potato as above for 40 minutes or until cooked. Meanwhile, put 3 tbsp blanched hazelnuts, 1 garlic clove, and 1½ tsp parsley into a mortar and pestle and pound, gradually adding 1 tbsp extra-virgin olive oil. Add ½ cup pitted black olives, chopped, and pound again. Stir in a good squeeze of lemon juice and season. Split the potatoes, spoon the relish inside, and sprinkle on 2 oz goat cheese. Serves 1.

Criques de Gramat

These are from southern France. Add chopped onion (sauté before mixing with the potatoes) if you fancy, or use bacon instead of ham.

Serves 3 as a main course, 6 as a side dish

1½ lb baking potatoes

8 oz Gruyère cheese, grated

4 oz cooked or cured ham,
  in little chunks

4 garlic cloves, very finely chopped

3 tbsp finely chopped fresh flat-leaf parsley

2 large eggs

salt and pepper

all-purpose flour, to coat

oil, for frying (peanut or light olive)

1 Grate the potatoes coarsely and put into a clean cloth towel. Squeeze the excess moisture out really well. Put the potatoes into a bowl and mix in all the other ingredients except the flour and oil. Season well.

2 Cover a plate with flour. Take a fistful of the mixture and shape it into a cake (about 3½ in across). Press into the flour on both sides. Shake off the excess (too much flour spoils both taste and texture). Put on a baking sheet.

3 Heat 2 tbsp oil in a large frying pan and cook 2–3 cakes at a time over a medium heat. The outside should be golden and crisp. Reduce the heat and cook until meltingly soft within (taste one to check). It takes 15 minutes. Keep them warm while you make the rest. If serving as a main course, offer green salad as well.

ALSO TRY...

Pommes de terre sarladaises Slice 1½ lb waxy potatoes about 1/16 in thick; don't wash. Heat 3 tbsp goose fat in a heavy frying pan with a lid. When it is hot, add the potatoes and sauté over medium-high heat. Turn for 5–7 minutes to color all over, and season. Cover and reduce the heat to medium-low. Cook for 25 minutes, turning occasionally; it doesn't matter if the slices fall apart. Some bits will become crispy, others soft. Add more fat if they stick and burn. Stir in 2 garlic cloves, chopped, and 2 tbsp chopped fresh parsley. Serve immediately. Serves 4.

Boxty Irish potato pancakes with a buttermilk tang, good with sausages and apple jelly, or smoked fish and beet relish. Peel and grate 1 medium potato and mix with ⅔ cup fresh mashed potatoes, ⅔ cup all-purpose flour, ½ tsp baking soda and enough buttermilk to make a thick batter (about ⅔ cup). Season. Heat a frying pan and melt a pat of unsalted butter—enough to coat the pan. When it is really hot, spoon the batter in to make 3½ in diameter cakes. Cook for 5 minutes on each side, until golden brown. Put on paper towels and keep warm while you make the rest.

Viennese potatoes with pickled cucumber, caraway, and sour cream

Chunks of leftover pork or sausage (especially smoked sausage) are lovely added to this. It's also a good side dish with sausages, pork, mackerel or salmon. If you're eating it in winter, heat the sour cream with the cucumber before serving.

Serves 6

1½ tbsp peanut oil

1 lb cold, cooked waxy potatoes, cut into chunks

2 tsp caraway seeds

1½ tsp hot paprika

1½ tsp sweet paprika

salt and pepper

¼ cup sour cream

1½ tbsp chopped sweet cucumber pickles

1 tbsp chopped dill

1 Heat the oil in a wide frying pan and add the potatoes. Fry over a medium heat until they begin to turn gold. Add the caraway, paprikas and seasoning and cook for another 2 minutes, tossing the potatoes around so they get coated with the spices.

2 Put the potatoes into a serving bowl, spoon the soured cream over and scatter with pickled cucumber and dill.

ALSO TRY…

It sometimes seems mad not to cook extra potatoes just to have the pleasure of making new dishes. Sauté chopped or sliced potatoes in a mixture of unsalted butter and olive oil until golden, adding garlic at the end for a couple of minutes more. Add chopped parsley, thyme, or rosemary, with finely grated lemon zest or even shredded preserved lemon. Don't forget the seasoning.

Batata harra (hot Middle Eastern fried potatoes) Heat 2 tbsp olive oil in a large frying pan. Add 1½ lb cold cooked potatoes, cut into chunks, and fry over a medium-high heat until golden brown. Add seasoning, 2½ tsp ground coriander, and 1½ tsp cayenne and cook for 2 minutes. Toss in 3 tbsp chopped fresh cilantro, squeeze on lemon juice, and serve. For a Spanish spin, use smoked paprika instead of ground coriander and cayenne.

Fried potatoes and wild mushrooms Heat 1 tbsp light olive oil with 2 tbsp unsalted butter in a nonstick frying pan. Cook 4 oz wild mushrooms (or mixed wild and cultivated), sliced if large, until golden. They must have exuded their moisture— and it should have evaporated—or the dish will be soggy. Set aside. Put another tbsp oil in the frying pan, and add 1 lb halved, cooked waxy potatoes; fry until golden. Return the mushrooms to the pan, season, heat through, and add finely chopped fresh parsley. Serve immediately. These are very popular in southwest France, where they sometimes use a bit of walnut oil for the frying.

Red
Lentil

Cut and dried

Beans take time, and we don't have so much of that these days. We're all in too much of a hurry, in thrall to the "dinner in a dash" approach to food that precludes simmering pots of pulses. It's a pity, as nothing quite provides the culinary comfort that beans give; they're good for you, and they cost next to nothing. Simmered long and slow, beans are transformed into a melting mass imbued with the flavors—bacon, lamb, olive oil, duck fat, garlic, onion or herbs—with which you've cooked them.

You do need to think ahead to have your beans ready to cook (stick them in a bowl, cover with water, and leave overnight), though the quick-soak method (bring beans up to a boil, take them off the heat, and leave them to soak for 2 hours) means you can enjoy them on the same day as you get the urge to eat them. You should allow about 2 oz (a tbsp) dried beans per person. Once soaked and cooked, they'll at least double in volume. I always cook more beans than I need for a given dish, as they are great for salads and keep in the refrigerator for several days. (Cover tightly, though, as they are also like sponges for soaking up other flavors.)

Beans may look similar, but they are all distinct and you'll get to know your favorites. I love navy beans. Small, white and not too starchy, they are used for baked beans and cassoulet. Cannellini beans are similar, but a bit bigger with a fluffier texture, and flageolets—which are not the semi-dried version of haricot beans as some people think, but a distinct variety—are pale green with a creamy texture and a delicate flavor. Borlotti beans are large, pink-speckled, and have a hammy, slightly sweet flavor. Black-eyed beans are small and creamy with a black "scar" where they were joined to the pod, and the pinto beans that dominate South American cooking are an orange-pinky color with rust-colored specks and quite a sweet flavor. Kidney beans—the scourge of badly made bean salads—are used in chili con carne, Mexican bean soups, and Caribbean dishes.

Lima beans are large, starchy, and thick-skinned with a potato-like taste, and are good with assertive ingredients and big flavors such as mustard and chorizo. Chickpeas are nutty and firm (in fact they never soften to collapsing) and—though I may well be pilloried for saying this—I can never detect much difference between home-cooked and canned, so rarely cook them from scratch.

There are a few things to watch out for when dealing with dried beans. Make sure that they're not more than six months old—older than that and they take longer to cook; in fact very old ones will never soften at all—and keep checking them during cooking. Age, soaking time, and variety all affect the length of time they need to soften, so it is impossible to give an exact cooking time. The softness to which you cook them depends on what you are going to use them for: salads need a firm bean;

for puréed soups you can cook them further until they are disintegrating; for stews you may want to cook them along with the other stew ingredients, so rescue them when they still retain plenty of bite.

Always throw away the bean-soaking liquid and use fresh water for cooking them. With kidney beans, you need to boil them vigorously in fresh water for 10 minutes to destroy any toxins. Drain and continue to simmer them in fresh water for 45 minutes (no other beans need this treatment).

Lastly, beans need plenty of seasoning. Whether it comes from salt or stock, they require a little help on this front. Not everyone agrees, but I am of the school of thought that thinks that salt added to beans before they are cooked toughens the skins, so I add it only towards the end.

Lentils have an image problem just as much as beans do. We associate them with sandal-wearing hippies and brown vegetarian food. Not one passed my lips until I was 15 years old. Then, as I sat at a simple meal with my French exchange family (all we were eating was bowls of salad, crudités, and baguette, but it stands out as one of the best meals of my life), a big platter of lentils, glossy with olive oil, was set before us. Tossed while still warm in a mustardy vinaigrette, the pulses, with their starchy nuttiness, contrasted beautifully with the sharpness of the dressing. This is still one of my favorite salads, and if I'm cooking lentils I always do a big batch so I have some to eat later in the week. Cooked quite plainly and dressed while still warm, lentils absorb the flavors of any dressing, becoming imbued with oil, lemon, garlic, whatever you put with them. Cooked lentils make a wonderful base for all sorts of other salads. Try them with smoked haddock or sausage; roast pumpkin with goat cheese, celery root and walnuts; or shreds of ham hock and leaves of bitter chicory. Dressings made with nut oils are good, too, and lentils work very well in creamy and spicy vinaigrettes (a creamy curry version is delicious).

Along with beans and potatoes, lentils can truly be described as earthy; in fact they almost taste of soil. They're starchy, prone to collapsing into a purée, and deeply comforting. They don't need to be soaked, and they cook more quickly than other dried beans (they are ready in anything from 20–40 minutes, depending on their age and type). There are quite a few varieties to choose from and they all behave slightly differently. The orangey-red lentils make a great side dish for Middle Eastern or Indian main courses. Cook them in stock or water with onions, garlic, cumin, and maybe a little chile for a dish that provides a low hum of spiciness. Make it hotter and add tomatoes and peppers and you have a great mid-week veggie main course (a staple in my house) to eat with rice and a bowl of raita. Red lentils cook really quickly (in only about 15 minutes) and make a superb soup (have a look in the soup chapter, page 218, for a delicious bowlful).

Then there are the large green or brown lentils. They are whole and unskinned, and therefore retain their shape after cooking. I tend to go for the more expensive versions of these lentils (because even when lentils are "expensive" they're still relatively cheap) and buy those from Puy. These are small and a beautiful green-grey color, the *grand cru* of the lentil world. They have a nuttier flavor and a less starchy texture than regular green lentils. They're great as a side dish with sausages, roasted cod or salmon, or thick slices of ham (banish the idea of potatoes as your starch and think lentils instead). I usually cook them as I do for salads, with sautéed onion, carrot, celery, and perhaps some chunks of bacon in a light chicken stock, though they also take well to being cooked in wine, or having cream or mustard added at the end. Reckon on 20–35 minutes (depending on how old they are) for cooking whole, unskinned lentils.

Split peas, which can be yellow or green (the yellow ones have a sweeter flavor), take just slightly longer to cook than lentils. In 45 minutes you will have a sloppy, starchy purée. They are good in soups (especially when made with a strongly flavored stock, such as ham) and the yellow ones make a lovely Greek mezze–thick with olive oil and flavored with garlic.

If long soaking and cooking seem like too much trouble, there's always canned, though canned beans are more successful than canned lentils (which can tend to be mushy). You can make a great puréed white bean soup with canned beans, and canned flageolets or Great Northerns, tossed with butter, garlic, and parsley are a great pantry standby to serve with lamb. They're more expensive than the dried variety, though, and you will miss out on the comfort of a warm kitchen as they cook. Most important, you don't get the opportunity to flavor them by simmering them along with herbs, spices, and fats. Perhaps the cheapness of beans and lentils has done them no favors. It really is worth cooking your own. Try to free them from their nut-roast image; they can be lip-smackingly good.

Lentil, red pepper, and goat cheese salad

You can cook lentils this way for other salads, too, topping with warm smoked haddock, duck breast, or roasted beets with mackerel. Be sure to dress the lentils while warm, so they stay moist and absorb the vinaigrette.

Serves 6 for lunch

FOR THE SALAD

5 large red bell peppers, halved
  and seeded
olive oil
balsamic vinegar
salt and pepper
½ onion, very finely chopped
1 celery stalk, very finely chopped
1 garlic clove, finely chopped
1¼ cups Puy lentils, rinsed
3 thyme sprigs
1 bay leaf

2½ cups light chicken or vegetable stock,
  or water
good squeeze of lemon juice
2 tbsp chopped flat-leaf parsley
4 oz watercress or arugula
8 oz goat cheese, crumbled

FOR THE VINAIGRETTE

1 tsp sherry vinegar
2 tsp balsamic vinegar
⅓ cup extra-virgin olive oil

1 Preheat the oven to 375°F. Put the peppers in a roasting pan and drizzle with a little olive oil and a slug of balsamic vinegar. Season. Roast for 40 minutes. Cut the flesh into fairly broad strips. Leave these in the pan with their juices.

2 Heat 1 tbsp olive oil and gently sauté the onion, celery, and garlic until soft but not colored. Add the lentils and turn to coat. Chuck in the thyme and bay leaf. Pour on the stock, season, bring to a boil, then reduce the heat and simmer, uncovered, until just tender. This could take 20–35 minutes, depending on the age of the lentils, so watch carefully; they turn to mush very quickly. They should absorb all the stock.

3 Make the vinaigrette by mixing everything together. Pick the bay leaf and thyme from the lentils, add the lemon juice, and stir in 2 tbsp vinaigrette and the parsley. Mix with the peppers and their juices. Check the seasoning.

4 Toss the watercress with 2 tbsp dressing and put all the vegetables in a large, shallow bowl or on a platter. Scatter over the goat cheese. Drizzle with a little more dressing and serve.

ALSO TRY…

Lentil and bacon salad with poached egg Prepare the lentils as above, but sauté 1 small carrot, diced, with the onion. Make the dressing as above but add another 1 tbsp olive oil and ½ tsp Dijon mustard. Toss the lentils with half the dressing and the juice of ½ lemon. Sauté 6 oz bacon, chopped, in its own fat and poach or fry 4 eggs. Toss 4 oz spinach or watercress with 2 tbsp dressing and mix gently with the lentils. Divide between among four plates and throw on the bacon. Top each serving with an egg. Drizzle with more dressing. Serves 4 for lunch.

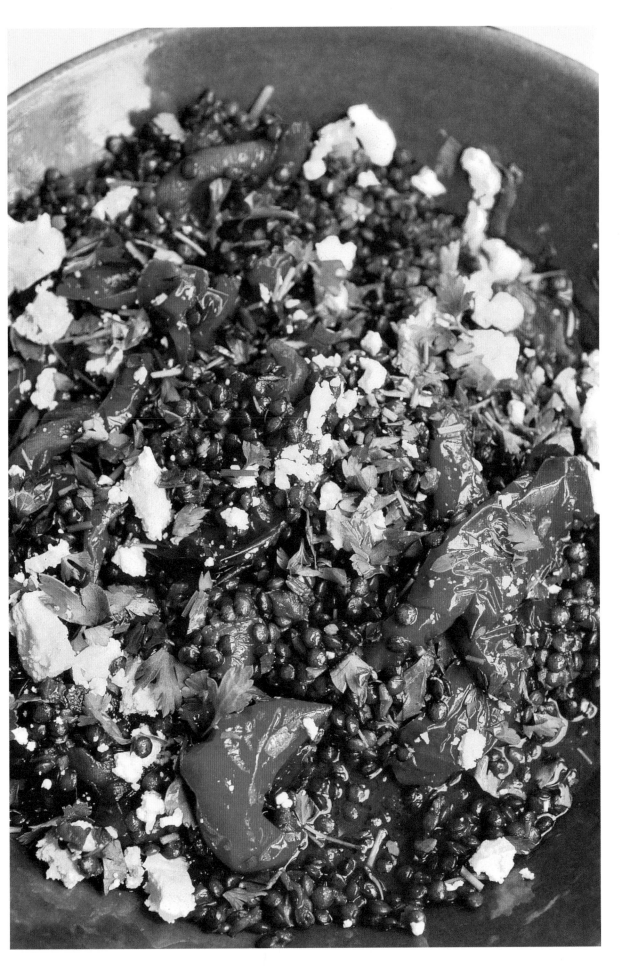

Austrian sweet-and-sour lentils

The French do lentils, the Italians do lentils and—joy of joys—the Austrians do, too, in their own inimitable way. If you have some home-cooked ham (and its stock), this dish is a knockout: you can flake some and stir it into the lentils instead of bacon. Just make sure your stock isn't too salty (sometimes it's unusable, in which case use chicken stock). This makes a great old-fashioned supper with sausages and buttered cabbage, and it's very good with roast pork for Sunday lunch.

Serves 8 as a side dish

FOR THE LENTILS
1 tbsp vegetable oil
6 oz bacon, chopped
1 onion, finely chopped
1 carrot, diced
1 tbsp caraway seeds
2 tsp hot paprika
2 tsp sweet paprika
2¼ cups brown or green lentils
3⅓ cups ham (preferred) or chicken stock
3 thyme sprigs
2 bay leaves

3 tbsp white wine or cider vinegar
good squeeze of lemon juice
salt and pepper
1 tbsp superfine sugar, or to taste
2 tbsp chopped fresh parsley

TO SERVE
sour cream
milk
paprika (optional)
2 tsp caraway seeds (optional)
1 tbsp butter (optional)

1 Heat the oil in a large, heavy saucepan and add the bacon, onion, and carrot. Sauté until the bacon is well-colored and the onion soft and golden. Add the caraway and paprikas and cook over a medium heat for another minute, to release the fragrance. Now stir in the lentils, making sure they get well coated, then add the stock, thyme, and bay leaves. Bring to a boil, reduce the heat, and simmer for 25–35 minutes, until the lentils are tender and the stock has been absorbed (brown lentils lose their shape more quickly than green ones so make sure they aren't overcooking).

2 Add the vinegar, lemon juice, and seasoning (you won't know until now how salty your lentils will be, as it depends on your stock and bacon). Add sugar to taste; the dish should have a good balance of sweet and sour, so go carefully. Stir in the parsley.

3 Serve with sour cream drizzled over the top (dilute with a little milk so it's a bit thinner). Either sprinkle the cream with a little paprika or fry the caraway seeds in the butter and drizzle that over.

LEFTOVERS...

Any extras can easily be made into soup (it's a good idea to plan leftovers so you can make this). Simply add water or stock and purée. If you prefer a chunky soup, add diced carrots, stock, and—later—frozen peas or canned drained and rinsed white beans. Lovely with a swirl of sour cream and a big handful of chopped fresh dill.

Creamy lentils and pumpkin with ginger and cumin

A satisfying vegetarian stew with the flavors of India. Pumpkin or winter squash is brilliant paired with lentils–you get both the sweet and the earthy. This is lovely topped with very thinly sliced onion, fried until dark brown.

Serves 8 as a main course

4 lb pumpkin or butternut squash

olive oil

salt and pepper

2 large onions, sliced into crescent moons

6 garlic cloves, finely chopped

1½ tsp ground cumin

1½ tsp ground coriander

1 tbsp ground ginger

2 fresh red chiles, seeded and shredded

1 cup green or brown lentils

2½ cups chicken or vegetable stock

¼ cup heavy cream

squeeze of lemon juice

¼ cup chopped fresh cilantro

2 tsp garam masala (optional)

2 tbsp toasted flaked almonds

1 Peel the pumpkin, discard the seeds, and cut into large chunks. Heat ¼ cup olive oil in a frying pan or large saucepan and add the pumpkin (you will need to do this in batches to get it all cooked). Season and cook over a high heat until golden on the outside and caramelized in parts (you can do this bit by roasting instead; see page 28 for instructions). Season and set aside.

2 Heat 2 tbsp more olive oil in a large saucepan and cook the onions until softening and golden (rather charred at the tips is good, too). Add the garlic and cook for another couple of minutes, then add the dried spices and chiles. Cook for a couple of minutes to release their flavors, then add the lentils and season. Stir to make sure the lentils get well coated in the cooking juices and spices. Add the stock and bring to a boil. Reduce the heat and cook for about 15 minutes.

3 Add the pumpkin, with any cooking juices, to the lentils and cook until the pumpkin is tender. Stir in the cream. Heat through, add the lemon juice and cilantro, and check the seasoning; this can take quite a lot of salt because of the lentils, but it depends how salty your stock was. Stir in the garam masala, if using, and sprinkle over the almonds. Serve with rice or barley.

Lentils with spring cabbage and peperoncino

I could eat this simple dish by the plateful, with no other accompaniment. Do use a good extra-virgin olive oil; it takes basic food to great heights. And season judiciously.

Serves 4

1¼ cups Puy lentils
½ small Savoy cabbage
olive oil
4 garlic cloves, thinly sliced
1 tsp dried red pepper flakes, or to taste

2 tbsp coarsely chopped fresh flat-leaf parsley
juice of ½ lemon
¼ cup extra-virgin olive oil
2 tsp balsamic vinegar
salt and pepper

1 Cook the lentils in enough water to cover until they are tender but haven't fallen apart, about 20 minutes.

2 Meanwhile, remove the hard core and any tough ribs from the cabbage and cut the leaves into strips. Heat 2 tbsp oil in a large frying pan or wok and stir-fry the greens for a couple of minutes over a medium heat. Add the garlic and red pepper flakes and cook until the garlic is pale gold and the cabbage has wilted, about 4 minutes. Drain the lentils and immediately toss them with the cabbage.

3 Add the parsley, lemon juice, extra-virgin olive oil, balsamic vinegar, and plenty of salt and pepper (lentils take a lot of seasoning). Taste and adjust the seasoning or the amount of oil or lemon as necessary. Serve hot, warm, or at room temperature.

Lentils and broccolini with anchovies and parsley

Serves 4

1 tbsp olive oil
1 small onion, finely chopped
1 fresh red chile, seeded and chopped
2 garlic cloves, thinly sliced
1¼ cups Puy or green lentils
salt and pepper

12 oz broccolini
7 tbsp extra-virgin olive oil
juice of ½ lemon
2 tbsp finely chopped fresh flat-leaf parsley
10 salt-cured anchovies, drained and finely
    chopped

1 Heat the olive oil in a saucepan and sauté the onion until soft; then add the chile and garlic and cook gently for a minute. Add the lentils and stir in the juices; then add water to cover by 2 in. Season. Bring to a boil, reduce the heat, and simmer until tender. Immediately drain and stir in 4 tbsp of the extra-virgin olive oil, with half the lemon juice, parsley, and anchovies. Put into a shallow serving bowl.

2 Boil or steam the broccolini until just tender and put on top of the lentils. Season and drizzle with the remaining extra-virgin olive oil, lemon juice, parsley, and anchovies. Serve warm.

Split pea purée with Greek lemon and oregano chicken

Split peas in the starring role, with herby lemony chicken on the side. Dress with good olive oil (a punchy Greek if you can—they're gutsy and terrific value for money).

Serves 4

FOR THE CHICKEN
8 skin-on chicken thighs
finely grated zest of 1 and juice of 2 lemons
½ cup olive oil
salt and pepper
2 tbsp dried oregano
8 thyme sprigs

FOR THE PURÉE
1 cup split peas
1 small onion, finely chopped

1 fresh chile (red or green), seeded and chopped
2 tsp ground cumin
2 tbsp olive oil
juice of 1 lemon

TO SERVE
½ small red onion, sliced wafer-thin
2 tbsp chopped fresh flat-leaf parsley
extra-virgin olive oil

1 Mix the chicken with the lemon zest and juice, oil, salt and pepper, oregano, and the leaves from half the thyme. Cover and leave for 2 hours (or longer) in the refrigerator. Turn over every so often.

2 Put the peas in a saucepan and cover with 5 cups water. Bring to a boil, skimming off any froth. When the water looks clear, add the onion, chile, and cumin and simmer, uncovered, until the peas collapse into a thick puree, about 30 minutes. Cool, then mash with the oil, lemon juice, salt, and pepper. Taste—it needs good seasoning.

3 Meanwhile, preheat the oven to 400°F. Put the chicken in a roasting pan with the remaining thyme. Cook for 45 minutes, or until the juices run clear when the chicken is pierced. Serve the hot chicken with the pea purée, lukewarm or at room temperature; top with the red onion and parsley and a drizzle of extra-virgin olive oil.

ALSO TRY...

This pea purée is a mezze in Greece, served with other little starters, such as roast peppers, baked beets and tzatziki; it is particularly lovely against sweet things. Try it topped with warm hard-boiled eggs and sliced onions and served with pitta bread.

For a more Indian dish, add 2 tsp ground coriander and a chunk of fresh ginger, peeled and finely chopped, with the cumin. Add chopped fresh cilantro at the end.

Omit the cumin and stir a little heavy cream and a dollop of Dijon mustard into the peas before they collapse; delicious with pork chops.

Add chicken or vegetable stock and make a soup. This is good with really dark, caramelized onions on top, chopped fresh cilantro and a good slug of olive oil.

Lamb, beer, and black bean chili

I came across this recipe in the wilds of Nevada about 20 years ago, when I was snowed in, leafing through my host's stash of ancient *Gourmet* magazines for the most warming dishes.

Serves 6

¼ cup sunflower, peanut, or olive oil

1½ lb boneles lamb shoulder, cubed

1 large onion, coarsely chopped

4 garlic cloves, crushed

2 green chiles, seeded and finely chopped

1½ tsp ground cumin

28 oz can tomatoes in thick juice

2½ cups American or Mexican lager

1 tbsp tomato paste

1 tbsp dark brown sugar

1 tbsp dried oregano

salt and pepper

2 x 14 oz cans black beans, drained and rinsed

juice of ½–1 lime

3 scallions, finely chopped

2 tbsp chopped fresh cilantro

TO SERVE

sour cream or Greek yogurt

avocado slices

grated queso fresco or Monterey Jack cheese

1 Heat the oil in a flameproof Dutch oven and brown the lamb well all over. Remove the lamb and set it aside. Add the onion to the pan and cook until soft and golden, then add the garlic and chiles and cook for 2 minutes. Add the cumin and cook for another minute. Return the lamb to the pot along with the tomatoes, lager, tomato paste, sugar, oregano, and lamb; season well and bring to a boil.

2 Immediately reduce the heat to a very gentle simmer and cook–uncovered–for 1½–2 hours or until the lamb is completely tender. Stir in the beans halfway through.

3 Taste, add the lime juice, scallions and cilantro, stir and taste again. Adjust the seasoning. Serve with sour cream or Greek yogurt, avocado slices, and grated cheese.

ALSO TRY...

Sausage and black bean chili Make as above but, instead of lamb, use sausages–lamb, pork, or venison–and cook for 1 hour.

Turkish black-eyed peas with spicy sausage Heat 2 tbsp olive oil in a flameproof Dutch oven and fry 1 onion, coarsely chopped, and 1 lb spicy lamb sausage, cut into chunks. When these are golden, add 4 garlic cloves, chopped; 1 fresh red chile, seeded and chopped; ½ tsp each ground cinnamon and allspice; and 2 tsp cumin. Cook for 2 minutes, then add a 14 oz can chopped tomatoes in thick juice, a 14 oz can black-eyed peas (drained and rinsed), 1 cup stock or water, and seasoning. Stir in 2 tbsp chopped flat-leaf parsley, 1 tsp dried oregano, and 2 tsp light brown sugar. Bring to a boil, reduce the heat, and simmer for 35 minutes until thick. Check the seasoning (you may want more sugar or chile), stir in more parsley and serve with rice or bulgur. Serves 4.

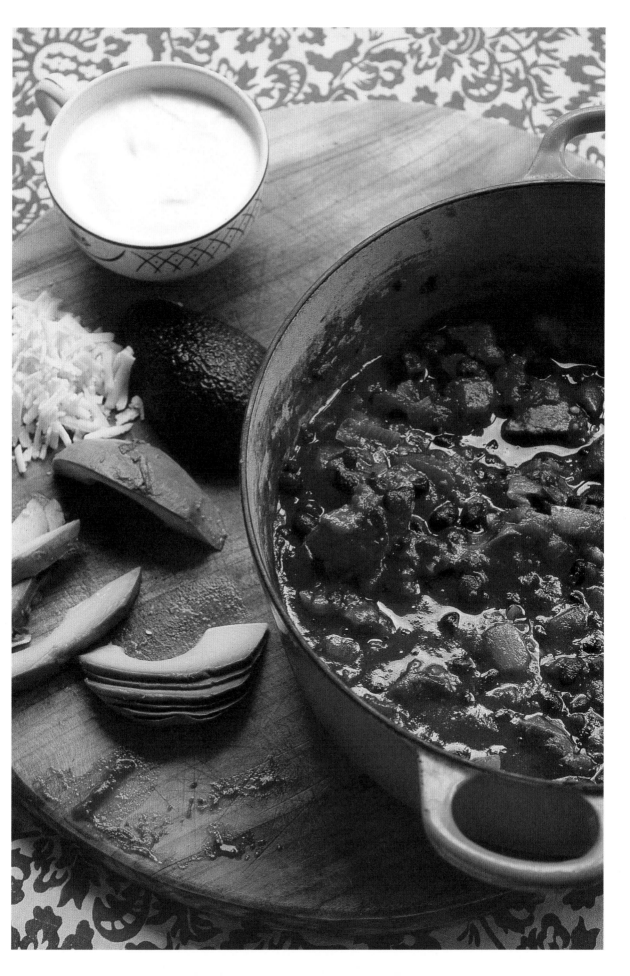

Spanish white beans with blood sausage and chorizo

Serve with rice, or wedges of coarse country bread, and some greens. It's fantastic as a side dish with fish as well (try it with fillets of bream or with farmed cod).

Serves 4

3 tbsp olive oil
1 onion, coarsely chopped
5 oz thick-cut bacon
2 tsp smoked paprika
1⅔ cups white beans, soaked overnight and drained
1 bay leaf
salt and pepper
6 oz Spanish chorizo
6 oz blood sausage or morcilla
¼ cup chopped fresh cilantro or flat-leaf parsley

1 Heat 2 tbsp of the oil and sauté the onion until golden. Add the paprika to the onion and stir over a gentle heat for a minute, then add the beans. Cut the bacon into chunks. In a separate pan, sauté the bacon in its own fat until browned.

2 Add water to come 2 in above the beans and add the bacon and bay leaf. Bring to a boil, then reduce the heat to a gentle simmer. Cook until the beans are almost completely tender, about 2 hours, depending on their age. Keep covered and watch the level of liquid: you want the beans to become stewy and thick, so remove the lid after 1¼ hours or so, but make sure the beans don't become dry. Once they are soft, remove the bay leaf, season, and partly mash some of the beans so they disintegrate.

3 Remove the skin from the chorizo and blood sausage or morcilla and slice. Heat the remaining olive oil and sauté. Add to the beans with the cilantro or parsley. Stir, heat through, and serve.

ALSO TRY…

The cheapness of white beans (and convenience of canned) makes them invaluable. That creamy starchiness is great with strong flavors. Make a salad version of the above, tossing drained cooked beans with chunks of cooked chorizo, strips of roasted red pepper, and lots of fresh cilantro. Or make as above with either chorizo or blood sausage (both would be too much) and serve with roasted cod on top. White beans make a great base for quick salads: toss with dressing, shaved red onions, lots of chopped parsley, and canned tuna, or chopped black olives, tomatoes, and anchovies.

Lima beans with sausages, leeks, and cider Make as above, but instead of chorizo and blood sausage, use 8 good pork sausages (leave whole, brown, and add with the bacon) and omit the smoked paprika. Replace half the water with hard cider, add 6 thyme sprigs, 2 bay leaves, and 2 leeks, cut into chunks and sautéed.

Chickpea, potato, and anchovy salad with preserved lemon and garlic cream

Not a subtle dish but a delicious one. Get a good can of anchovies; it will make a huge difference. I don't presoak the anchovies as I like the saltiness but, if you prefer, soak in milk for 15 minutes, drain, and pat dry. If you use store-bought preserved lemons (which tend to be smaller than homemade), use half instead of a quarter.

Serves 4 as a starter or side dish

FOR THE SALAD

8 oz baby waxy potatoes
1½ cups cooked chickpeas, drained
25 canned anchovy fillets, drained (reserve the oil) and halved
¼ preserved lemon

FOR THE DRESSING

3 garlic cloves
5 tbsp pine nuts
6 tbsp extra-virgin olive oil
juice of ½ lemon
salt and pepper
handful of flat-leaf parsley or cilantro

1 Boil the potatoes until tender and put in a bowl with the chickpeas and anchovy fillets. Moisten with a little anchovy oil. Cut the preserved lemon rind into fine slivers and discard the flesh. Add the rind to the bowl.

2 To make the dressing, put the garlic and pine nuts into a food processor and, with the motor running, pour in the oil. Add the lemon juice, salt, and pepper and check for seasoning. Add the herbs and pulse to blend. Drizzle over the salad and serve.

ALSO TRY...

Chickpea, cauliflower, and roasted pepper salad with feta and smoked paprika
Preheat the oven to 400°F. Brush 2 halved and seeded red bell peppers with oil, put into a roasting pan, and season. Roast for about 30 minutes, or until completely tender, then slice and put into a flat, broad serving bowl. Break a small cauliflower into florets, put into a saucepan, and cover with water. Salt, bring to a boil, and cook until just tender–it must still have bite. Drain well. Add 2 tbsp olive oil to a frying pan and sauté 1 onion, in crescent moon-shaped slices, until soft and pale gold. Add 2 garlic cloves, thinly sliced, and 1½ tsp smoked paprika. Season and cook for another minute. Scrape into a serving bowl and add another 1 tbsp oil to the frying pan (don't clean it). Heat the oil and add the cauliflower. Fry quickly to get color and heat through. Add the cauliflower and a 14 oz can chickpeas, drained and rinsed, to the serving bowl. Pour 2 tsp white wine vinegar into a cup and season. Whisk in ¼ cup extra-virgin olive oil to make a dressing. Pour over the salad, add a generous handful of chopped fresh cilantro and 6oz feta cheese, broken into chunks, and gently mix. Serves 6–8 as a side dish.

Good grains

At university I shared a house with a guy we called Brown Man. His part of the kitchen cupboard was full of foods in shades of taupe, beige, and putty. Chefs and savvy cooks have now fully embraced everything on his shelves; they were weighed down with grains.

Grains are as cheap and healthy as ever, but we now know how to cook them (RIP vegetarian nut roast) and appreciate their range of flavors and textures. Barley is no longer just for granny's Scotch broth, but is one of the coolest ingredients around. If you are keeping a tight hold on your purse strings and want to eat healthily, there's no better food. You have to make a psychological leap, though. When you think "starch", don't reach for the potato peeler; think about barley, bulgur, and farro instead.

There's a grain for every mood. They can be comforting; there's nothing quite like eating cheesy risotto when you are upset. They can startle; I still remember the awe with which I tucked into a dish of *arroz negro*, Spanish rice colored black with squid ink, in a Barcelona restaurant. They can be everyday—one of my favorite meals is the pilaf I make with Sunday roast leftovers—and they can be gorgeous, splattered with pomegranate seeds, nuts, dried fruit, and herbs. Here's the know-how.

FARRO In a modest restaurant in northern Italy, a farro salad won me over. Dressed with olive oil and lemon, tossed with pomegranate seeds and chestnuts, farro was unexpected and delicious. Like barley, farro becomes slightly creamy when stirred in stock, but can also be cooked in water, drained, and used as a salad base or side dish. In texture it is similar to barley, though remains nuttier and firmer.

PEARL BARLEY Barley has become so hip it is now used for risottos (stirred as it cooks) and pilafs. It has more texture and an earthier flavor than risotto or long-grain rice. When it is cooked in stock, so the liquid is absorbed, you are left with a gutsy, savory panful. Chestnuts, leeks, bacon, pumpkin, parsley, and sage are all good in barley pilafs and risottos.

LONG-GRAIN AND BROWN RICE Long-grain rice can be cooked simply in plain water. However, I almost always cook it by the absorption method. Rinse in a sieve until the water runs clear, then sauté chopped onion in butter until pale but soft. Stir in the rice to coat the grains, then add water or stock—I use 1¾ cups liquid for every ¾ cup rice—and bring to the boil, uncovered. In 5 minutes you'll barely be able to see the liquid and the surface of the rice will look "pitted" with holes. Now reduce the heat right down, cover, and cook for 15–20 minutes (but check it). The last bit of liquid will be absorbed and the rice will steam. Don't stir. You should end up with separate, light grains. Fork through very gently before serving. Once you have mastered this, you can make perfect rice flavored in a host of ways—cook spices with the buttery onion, use orange juice or coconut milk to replace some stock, or gently stir in flavored butters or pastes at the end. Brown rice—also long-grained, but with only the husk removed—can be cooked in the same way but takes longer and never softens as much. It has a nutty flavor.

RISOTTO RICE A medium-grained rice; the variety you choose will have a distinct impact on your risotto. Arborio is most common and dependable, but Carnaroli is thought by many to be the king and makes the creamiest risotto. Vialone nano is my favorite (though it's not right for every risotto) as it delivers a more soupy, flowing dish, and seems lighter. It's worth cooking with each, to discover how they differ.

CALASPARRA AND LA BOMBA RICE Spanish calasparra is a short, round-grained rice that gives a moister, stickier consistency than long-grain varieties. It is used for paella and other Spanish rice dishes. La Bomba is more expensive and can absorb up to three times its weight in liquid while retaining a characteristic firmness. You need either Calasparra or La Bomba for Spanish rice dishes—no other rice will do. They're great for lazy cooks as, unlike risotto rice, they mustn't be stirred.

SHORT-GRAIN PUDDING RICE Used to make rice pudding, people either love it or loathe it (creamed rice is one of the great English puddings). Cooked in milk, it can be made on the stove top (the method I find easiest) or baked. Middle Eastern and Indian cooks use it for exotic puddings flavored with flower waters or spices. Substitute risotto rice if you must.

QUINOA A South American grain, this is perhaps the most usable of the "new" grains coming into vogue. Its texture and grain size are somewhere between couscous and bulgur, and it's lovely both hot and cold. Dress it while warm with vinaigrette, then add beans, chopped anchovies, and olives, or slivers of persimmon and chunks of feta, or pomegranate seeds and masses of chopped herbs. There's one caveat: be wary of the package instructions. You are usually exhorted to add too much liquid and end up with gruel. Use 2⅔ cups liquid for every 1¾ cup quinoa to produce grains that are cooked but dry. Toasting the grains in a dry pan beforehand helps, too.

BULGUR Quicker and easier than rice, with more body and flavor than couscous, and wonderfully nutty. Again you need to be careful how much liquid you use. I cook it by the absorption method (see Long-Grain Rice, page 109) and use just under twice the volume of liquid to grain. You can use it in pilafs, sautéing an onion in butter or oil before adding the bulgur. Once it's cooked (it takes 15 minutes), fork it through, then cover and leave for another 5 minutes before serving. Cold bulgur can be made into salad by tossing with other ingredients and dressing, or be reheated by steaming, or frying in butter or oil.

COUSCOUS Not really a grain, but a product of a grain as it's made from pellets of rolled semolina. It's so easy you barely need a recipe. Just pour boiling water or stock over the grains (¾ cup liquid to 1 cup couscous; this will serve four people as a side dish), cover, and leave for 15 minutes. Finish with olive oil or melted butter and seasoning, and whatever other ingredients you want. Reheat in the same way as bulgur.

Classic rice dishes

Pilafs, also known as plovs and pilaus, are found in the Middle East, eastern Mediterranean, India, Pakistan, and some former Soviet states. They are made with long-grain rice cooked by the absorption method (see Long-Grain Rice, page 109). They can be a main course or side dish as they often contain meat or fish, dried fruit, beans, vegetables, herbs, and nuts. Pilafs are great for using up leftovers, so are very useful to have in your repertoire. The other ingredients can be cooked with the rice, or gently forked in afterwards. In Iran, where rice cooking is an art form, they use the absorption method in a very complex way, creating a crust–*tah dig*–in the bottom of the pan with butter and rice (and sometimes also egg, bread, or yogurt too) and layering with different ingredients. Bulgur can also be used for pilafs.

Spanish rice dishes are also made by the absorption method but the other ingredients are usually cooked along with the rice. The rice ends up stickier than long-grain rice but not as creamy as risotto. Leave the rice to cook in its liquid–never stir it–and serve in the cooking vessel.

Risottos aren't just soothing and cheap, they're brilliant for impromptu pantry meals too, using up leftovers and turning humble ingredients into something splendid. If you have risotto rice, stock, and a decent sausage, you can make risotto. It is a very satisfying and sensuous dish as it forms warm waves (as you pour it on to plates, a risotto almost unfolds itself). Don't be fooled by the mystery that surrounds it. Risottos are very easy to make as long as you know the score. Sauté chopped onion in butter or olive oil (or both), add the rice and turn in the fat until glossy. Now add a ladle of stock, which must be simmering, and stir constantly. The stirring helps the risotto develop its creaminess. Add the stock a ladle at a time and add more only when the previous amount has been absorbed. You must never drown the rice in liquid. You then have to judge when your risotto is perfectly cooked, thick, and creamy–the Italians describe the texture as "wavy"–with a *little* bite in the center of each grain. Apart from the stirring, the important thing is the quality of your stock, so gather up those chicken bones and get them into a pot.

Leftover rice is perfect for making stir-fries and can be reheated, either by frying in butter or oil, heating in a microwave, or by adding a little water, covering with a lid, putting over heat, and steaming. But there is one very serious caveat–leftover rice can give you bad food poisoning if you don't handle it properly, so beware. Cool leftover rice quickly then keep it, covered, in the refrigerator and use within 24 hours of it being cooked. The longer cooked rice is left at room temperature, the more likely it is that bacteria, or the toxins they produce, could stop it being safe to eat. When using leftover rice, make sure to heat it through thoroughly, and reheat it only once.

Persian herb chilau

Rice cooked in the Iranian manner with a delicious crust on the bottom. The washing and rinsing of the rice is important, so don't miss out this step. And don't stint on the herbs: it's meant to be a very green, spring-like dish. You can add cooked fava beans to it as well, when they're in season.

Serves 8 as a side dish

FOR THE RICE

2¾ cups basmati rice

3 tbsp butter

⅓ cup olive oil

4 oz mixture of fresh dill and flat-leaf
   parsley or mint, chopped

salt and pepper

TO SERVE (optional)

2 tbsp butter

a squeeze of lemon juice

1 Wash the rice well and rinse it in a sieve until the water runs clear. Cover it with water and leave it to soak for 2 hours. Wash and rinse again. Bring a saucepan of water to a boil, then add the rice. Cook for about 6 minutes, until it's just beginning to soften on the outside. Drain and rinse in lukewarm water.

2 Heat the butter and oil in a saucepan until foaming, then add half the drained rice. Cover with half the herbs, then the remaining rice and, finally, with the rest of the herbs, seasoning as you go along.

3 Reduce the heat to very low and make 3 steam holes in the rice with the handle of a wooden spoon. Wrap the lid of the pan in a cloth towel and put the covered lid on to the saucepan (the cloth towel will stop condensation from falling back into the rice and making it too wet). Leave to cook for another 20 minutes or so. You can check how the rice is cooking (and make sure it isn't burning at the bottom) but try to do this without moving the grains around too much; leaving it alone produces light, fluffy rice with separate grains.

4 Empty the rice into a bowl, making sure you dislodge the lovely crispy bits at the bottom (break these up and add to the rest of the rice). You can serve the rice with extra melted butter on top, though you may feel that the dish is rich enough without it. Persian cooks actually put saffron in the butter before pouring it over. I like a squeeze of lemon as well.

Orange and pistachio pilaf

Beautiful, and not expensive.

Serves 6

2 cups basmati rice	2 garlic cloves, finely chopped
1 orange	1 cup carrots, in matchsticks
3 cups chicken stock	1½ tsp sugar
2½ tbsp butter	3 tbsp unsalted pistachios, chopped
1 onion, finely chopped	3 tbsp chopped fresh cilantro

1 Put the rice in a sieve and rinse until the water runs clear. Cut the zest from half the orange with a very sharp knife in broad strips, slicing away the white pith. Cut the zest into fine julienne. Squeeze the juice from the orange and add to the stock.

2 Heat 1 tbsp of the butter in a heavy saucepan and sauté the onion until pale gold. Add the garlic and cook for 2 minutes. Now add the rice and stir until beginning to toast. Pour in the stock and bring to a boil; the rice will start to look pitted. Reduce the heat to the lowest possible setting and cover for 15 minutes. Do not stir or the rice will become sticky. Check to ensure it isn't burning at the bottom.

3 Melt the remaining butter in a saucepan and sauté the carrots until they lose their raw bite. Remove the carrots and put in the zest. Cook until softening–only 2 minutes– then add the sugar and stir until slightly caramelized. Gently fork this into the rice with the carrots, nuts, and cilantro. Serve immediately.

ALSO TRY...

Egyptian megadara Wash ⅓ cup brown lentils and ¼ cup long-grain rice and soak both for half an hour, then drain. Heat ¼ cup olive oil and sauté 2 onions, thinly sliced, until almost caramelized. Heat a further 2 tbsp olive oil in a heavy saucepan. Stir in the lentils and rice and add 1 tsp ground cumin and ½ tsp ground allspice. Cook for 1 minute, then add 1 cup chicken stock. Cook gently, uncovered, for 25 minutes (don't stir), then cover for 5 minutes so the bottom becomes browned. Stir, breaking the crispy bits from the bottom, and add most of the onions. Mix, check the seasoning, and top with 2 tbsp Greek yogurt. Scatter the remaining onions on top and drizzle with olive oil. Tomato Sauce (see page 119), with 1 or 2 tsp harissa added, makes this a vegetarian main course. Serves 4.

LEFTOVERS...

There are more pilaf recipes in other chapters of this book (see Lamb Pilaf with Figs, Pomegranates, Feta, and Pistachios, page 38 and Salmon and Dill Pilaf, page 150) but if you stick to the method in the main recipe here, you can try salmon, leek, and pea; lamb, date, and eggplant; white fish, dill, and feta; squid, chorizo, and cilantro...The permutations are endless.

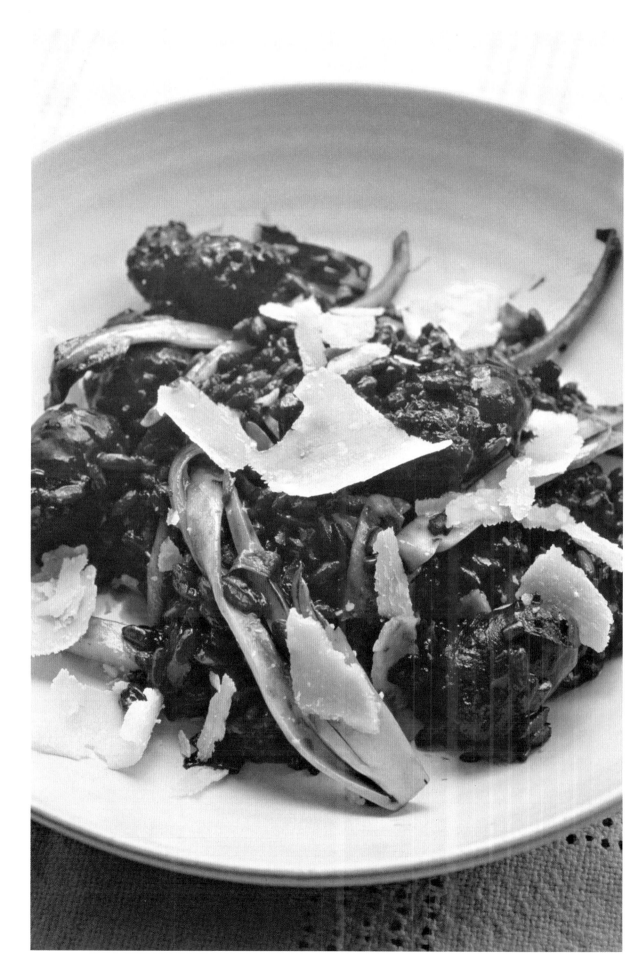

Sausage, radicchio, and red wine risotto

There are nights, I have to admit, when I don't feel much like stirring for the 25 or so minutes it takes to make a risotto....Then I open a bottle of wine, get into the rhythm, and am thoroughly mellow by the time I spoon it into my favorite flat soup plates. Arrive home from work feeling that slow death would be too good for your boss and—within half an hour—you find yourself purring.

Serves 4

6 oz spicy sausage (preferably Italian)
2 tbsp olive oil
1 small onion, finely chopped
2 garlic cloves, finely chopped
1⅓ cups arborio rice
2 cups decent red wine
2 cups chicken stock

1 small head of radicchio (about 6oz),
   halved, trimmed, and sliced
salt and pepper
2 tbsp butter
6 tbsp grated Parmesan cheese, plus more
   to serve

1 Cut the sausage into chunks, about the size of a walnut, then roll them slightly into little balls. Heat the olive oil in a heavy pan, add the sausage and sauté until well browned. Add the onion and cook until just softening. Add the garlic and cook for 1 minute, then add the rice and stir it around to get it coated in the juices.

2 Heat both the wine and the stock separately to the simmering point and keep them simmering. Add the wine a little at a time, stirring continuously and adding more only once the previous lot has been absorbed. Now add the stock a ladleful at a time, stirring continuously. It will take about 25 minutes to add all the liquid. About 10 minutes before the end of cooking time, stir in the radicchio. It will wilt in the heat.

3 Taste for seasoning; both the wine and reduced stock are salty, so see how much salt you need to add. Season with pepper, too. Stir in the butter and the cheese and serve immediately, with extra Parmesan on the side.

ALSO TRY...

Cauliflower, leek, and blue cheese risotto Break ½ head of cauliflower into florets and cook in lightly salted boiling water until just tender. Drain thoroughly. Melt 2 tbsp butter in a saucepan and add 2 leeks, cut into rings and washed really well. Cook over a low heat until soft, about 10 minutes. Add 1⅓ cups risotto rice and cook as above, adding 4 cups hot chicken stock. About 3 minutes before the risotto is ready, carefully stir in the cauliflower (try not to break it up), 6 tbsp grated Parmesan cheese, and 4 oz creamy blue cheese, such as dolcelatte or Cashel blue, broken into small chunks. Serve more Parmesan on the side, if you like, though you shouldn't need it.

Pumpkin, bacon, chestnut, and barley risotto Heat 2 tbsp olive oil in a large frying pan and cook 1¾ lb winter squash or pumpkin (seeded, peeled, and cut into chunks) until slightly caramelized in patches (you don't need to cook it through). You'll probably have to do this in two batches. Lift the pumpkin out with a slotted spoon and set aside. Heat 1 tbsp butter in a saucepan and add 1 small onion, chopped; 2 garlic cloves, chopped; 4 oz bacon, diced, and 1 celery stalk, very finely chopped. Cook over a medium heat until pale gold and the onions have softened. Add 1½ cups pearl barley and proceed as for Sausage, Radicchio, and Red Wine Risotto (see page 117), cooking the barley just like risotto rice. You'll need 4 cups chicken or vegetable stock. Don't forget to season. After about 40 minutes, the barley will soften and become creamy. Stir in the pumpkin halfway through. Towards the end of the cooking time, quickly melt 1 tbsp butter and sauté 1 cup cooked chestnuts (frozen are good) over a medium heat until warmed through. Stir into the risotto with the butter, then stir in 8 leaves of sage, chopped, or 1½ tbsp chopped fresh parsley (both are nice but give different results). Serve with grated Parmesan cheese.

Mussel and fennel risotto Put 4 lb mussels into a sink and clean thoroughly, removing the beards and barnacles. Tap each on the sink and discard any that don't close. Put in a large saucepan over medium heat and add 1 cup dry white wine, a few parsley stems, and 6 black peppercorns. Cover and cook for 4–6 minutes; they should open. Shake the pan a couple of times during the cooking. Strain, reserving the liquor, and remove each mussel from its shell. Discard any that haven't opened. Strain the liquor through a muslin-lined sieve, then heat until gently simmering. Heat 5 tbsp olive oil in a heavy pan and sauté 1 onion, finely chopped; 3 garlic cloves, chopped; and ½ fennel bulb, trimmed and diced, over a medium heat until the onion is soft but not colored. Stir in 1⅔ cups risotto rice. Pour on ¼ cup dry vermouth, then the mussels' cooking liquor a ladleful at a time, as for the method in the main recipe on page 117. If you run out of liquor, use water. When the rice is cooked—after about 20 minutes—stir in the mussels, ¼ cup finely chopped fresh parsley, and a good squeeze of lemon juice, and check for seasoning—mussel stock is salty so you will probably only need pepper. Serve immediately. Fish risottos are not usually served with cheese.

THERE'S LITTLE THAT CAN'T BE MADE INTO A DELICIOUS RISOTTO…

Once you know the basics, you can transform the humblest ingredients into a steaming saucepan of bliss. It's the creaminess of the rice and the goodness of the stock that do all the magic. Try smoked haddock and leek; tomato and mozzarella (let the mozzarella melt into long strings); radicchio and goat cheese; red onion, spicy sausage, and chickpea; saffron and pea; dried wild mushroom; ham and Gruyère or fontina cheese….

Suppli al telefono with tomato sauce

Crisply encased balls of creamy risotto with mozzarella inside that melts into strings as you pull them apart–hence the name, which is Italian for telephone wires.

Serves 4 as a starter

FOR THE TOMATO SAUCE

½ onion, finely chopped

1 celery stalk, diced

2 garlic cloves, chopped

14 oz can diced tomatoes

2 tsp tomato paste

1 tbsp olive oil

1 tsp sugar, or to taste

1 tbsp chopped fresh herbs (parsley, oregano, thyme, or a mixture)

salt and pepper

FOR THE SUPPLI AL TELEFONO

3 large eggs

2¾ cups leftover risotto

⅔ cup grated Parmesan cheese

¾ cup all-purpose flour

⅛ cup fresh white bread crumbs

8 oz fresh mozzarella cheese, drained and diced

2¼ cups oil, for deep-frying

1 Put everything for the sauce into a saucepan with ¾ cup water, bring to a boil, reduce the heat, and simmer for 45 minutes, until soft and thick. Taste for seasoning and purée in a food processor or blender.

2 Lightly beat 1 of the eggs and mix with the risotto and Parmesan. Beat the remaining eggs and put in a wide bowl. Put the flour and bread crumbs on separate plates.

3 Take 2 tbsp risotto and form into a ball. Make a hole in it, place a nugget of mozzarella inside, and reshape the ball. It will be about the size of a tangerine. Make all the other balls in the same way. Roll each in flour– tapping off the excess–then in egg, then bread crumbs.

4 Heat the oil in a heavy saucepan until it's about 320–340°F. (If you don't have an oil thermometer, a cube of bread dropped in should turn golden in 60 seconds.) Deep-fry the balls–three at a time–for 6–8 minutes, turning halfway. Drain on paper towels, and keep the cooked ones warm while you fry the rest. Serve with the sauce.

ALSO TRY...

Risotto cakes with mushroom sauce Mix 1⅔ cups leftover risotto with 1 egg and 3 tbsp grated Parmesan cheese, and season. Pour boiling water over ¼ oz dried wild mushrooms and leave for 15 minutes. Melt 1 tbsp butter and sauté 3 oz fresh mushrooms, chopped, until well colored. Drain the wild mushrooms (reserve the liquor), add to the pan, and cook for 1 minute. Pour on 1½ cups chicken stock and the mushroom liquor and cook until reduced by two-thirds. Add ½ cup heavy cream and simmer until the sauce coats the back of a spoon. Take 3 tbsp risotto at a time, form into a ball, then flatten into a patty. Continue until you have used the mixture up. Dip in all-purpose flour and shake off the excess. Fry in 1½ tbsp olive oil on both sides until golden. Serve with the sauce.

Coconut rice pudding with candied limes

Cheap, easy, and irresistible.

Serves 8

FOR THE CANDIED LIMES

5 limes

2¼ cups granulated sugar

FOR THE RICE PUDDING

1 cup short-grain rice

½ cup superfine sugar

3⅓ cups whole milk

14 oz can coconut milk

¼ cup heavy cream (optional)

1 Fill a large bowl with iced water, then cut the limes into thin, thin slices, discarding any pips. Bring a saucepan of water to a rolling boil. Add the fruit, stir, and cook until softened, about 2 minutes. Drain, plunge into the iced water, then drain again.

2 Bring the granulated sugar and 2¼ cups water to the boil, stirring from time to time to help dissolve the sugar, then reduce heat to medium-low. Add the limes. Simmer gently until translucent and in thick syrup, about 45–60 minutes. Set aside.

3 Put the rice, superfine sugar, and milk in a heavy saucepan and heat gently until simmering. Simmer, stirring occasionally, until the grains are soft and the mixture thick and creamy, about 30 minutes. Take from the heat and stir in the coconut milk. The rice will seem wet, but firms as it cools. Once it is cool, chill. Stir in the cream, if you want to use it. Serve in wide soup plates with the candied limes.

ALSO TRY...

Citrus and spice rice pudding Put ½ cup short-grain rice into a saucepan with 3¾ cups whole milk, ¼ cup superfine sugar, the finely grated zest and juice of 2 lemons, and finely grated zest of 1 orange and juice of ½. Add a pinch of ground cinnamon. Bring to a boil, stirring to dissolve the sugar, then reduce to a simmer. Add ¼ cup mixed dried fruit and candied peel, optional but delicious. Cook until the rice is soft, 20–30 minutes. Add more milk if it's absorbed before the rice is cooked. Cool a little. Stir in ½ cup heavy cream and 3 tbsp Greek yogurt. Refrigerate. Sprinkle with chopped pistachios, toasted pine nuts, or candied citrus zest before serving.

Creamy vanilla rice pudding with simple fruits Make as for Citrus and Spice Rice Pudding above, but add vanilla extract or cook the pudding with a split vanilla pod and its scraped-out seeds. Leave out the zests and juice, dried fruit, and peel. Serve at room temperature with Strawberries in Beaujolais (see page 265), Wine-Poached Apples (see page 272), or fresh cherries.

Rose-and-cardamom-scented rice pudding Make as for Creamy Vanilla Rice Pudding above, but add the ground seeds of 8 cardamom pods instead of vanilla. Once the rice is cooked, add 2 tsp rosewater (don't overdo it) and a squeeze of lemon or lime juice. Serve with chopped pistachios and torn rose petals.

Note: each variation on this page serves 6

Spanish rice with pork and spinach

Layer upon layer of flavor for very little effort.

Serves 6 as a main course

12 oz pork tenderloin

salt and pepper

7 tbsp olive oil

4 oz Spanish chorizo, skin removed,
  in chunks

10 oz unsliced bacon, in meaty chunks

2 large onions, roughly chopped

2 red bell peppers, seeded and sliced

4 garlic cloves, finely chopped

2 tsp smoked paprika

¼ tsp dried red pepper flakes

1½ cups medium-grain rice

4¼ cups hot chicken stock or water

1½ lb spinach

1 lemon

1 Cut the pork in half lengthwise, then slice. Season. Heat 3 tbsp of the oil in a big frying pan and quickly brown the pork on all sides until cooked through. Set aside.

2 Reduce the heat, add a further 3 tbsp of the oil and the chorizo and bacon. Sauté for 2 minutes, then add the onions and peppers and cook over a medium-low heat for 20 minutes until lovely and soft. Add the garlic, paprika, and red pepper flakes and cook for 2 minutes, then add the rice. Stir it well into the juices, add the stock and season. Bring to a boil, then reduce to a simmer. Cook for 15 minutes until there's just a little moisture left. The rice should be almost tender.

3 Meanwhile, wilt the spinach in the remaining oil and season. Distribute over the rice and tuck the pork in, too. Check for seasoning, then reduce the heat to its lowest, cover, and leave for 5 minutes. Squeeze lemon juice over the top and serve immediately.

ALSO TRY…

You must not stir Spanish paella rice, so it's great for the lazy cook. Using the proportions of rice to stock given above, you can create dishes at will: chicken, rabbit, fresh and cured sausage and pork, fish, beans, lentils, and all sorts of vegetables can go in. Just make sure the meat is cooked through.

Spanish rice with chicken and chorizo Make as above with 6–8 bone-in chicken thighs instead of pork (omit the bacon). You need to cook the chicken for longer, so leave it in the pan while you sauté the onions and peppers, then add the rice and stock. Dissolve a good pinch of saffron threads in the stock to flavor the dish and, instead of spinach, add green beans or frozen peas towards the end to cook in the steam created by the covered rice.

Spanish rice with squid, beans, and sausage Make as above, omitting the pork. Cook the rice with canned, drained beans or chickpeas and cooked spicy sausage. Briefly sauté the squid in hot olive oil and fork it through the rice when the dish is just about ready.

Quinoa with lime, chile, cilantro, and rajas

Quinoa should be dry and nutty, not sloppy or wet. I toast it before cooking.

Serves 4

FOR THE QUINOA
1¾ cups quinoa
6 tbsp olive oil
1 small onion, finely chopped, plus
  1 large onion, thinly sliced
2 fresh red chiles, seeded and very thinly
  sliced
4 scallions, chopped
3 garlic cloves, finely chopped
1 tbsp ground cumin
salt and pepper
2⅔ cups chicken or vegetable stock

6 red bell peppers or 12 poblano chiles
finely grated zest and juice of 2 limes
leaves from 1 bunch cilantro,
  coarsely chopped
1 tbsp dried oregano
3 tbsp mild vinegar (such as champagne
  or rice)

TO SERVE
crumbled mild goat or feta cheese
sour cream
lime wedges

1 Heat a frying pan and put in the quinoa. Toast for 2–3 minutes; it should turn a shade darker. Set aside.

2 Put 2 tbsp of the oil into the pan and add the chopped onion. Cook until soft and slightly golden. Add the chiles, scallions, garlic, and cumin and cook for 2 minutes; then add the quinoa and season. Pour in the stock, stir, then bring to a boil. Reduce the heat to the lowest possible and cook, covered, for 18 minutes.

3 Fry the sliced onion in another 2 tbsp of the oil in a frying pan until golden. Roast the peppers (or chiles) over a gas flame, or in your broiler pan. They should be soft with blistered skin, charred in places. Peel off the skin, remove the seeds, and slice the flesh.

4 Reheat the quinoa over a gentle heat and add the remaining oil, the lime juice, and zest. Check for seasoning, then stir in the cilantro. Add the peppers to the fried onion, season, and reheat. Add the oregano and vinegar; it will splutter and reduce.

5 To serve, top the quinoa with the peppers and fried onion. Crumble cheese on top and serve with sour cream and lime wedges.

ALSO TRY...

Fruited quinoa Make as above, but omit the scallions and use ground cinnamon instead of cumin. Toast the grain, then cook with the sautéed onion and spices. Thinly slice 3 plums and half an apple. Soak ⅔ cup dried cranberries and ½ cup dried figs in just-boiled water for 15 minutes and drain. Chop the figs. Melt 2 tbsp butter in a pan, add the fresh fruit and cook until softening. Add 2 tsp soft light brown sugar and caramelize a little, then add the dried fruit. Gently mix with the hot quinoa and 2 tbsp finely chopped fresh flat-leaf parsley or cilantro. Great with roast pork or chicken.

Spring couscous

There are few side dishes you can make with as little effort and have looking this sumptuous. Don't stint on the herbs, this is supposed to be a very green couscous.

Serves 4

1 cup couscous
¾ cup boiling chicken stock or water
salt and pepper
6 tbsp extra-virgin olive oil
zest and juice of ½ lemon

3 tbsp shelled, unsalted pistachio
   nuts, chopped
2 scallions, finely chopped
2 tbsp each fresh flat-leaf parsley, mint,
   and cilantro

1 Sprinkle the couscous into a bowl and add the stock or water, seasoning, and 2 tbsp olive oil. Cover with plastic wrap. Let the couscous plump up for about 15 minutes, then fork it through to separate the grains and aerate it. It will still be hot.

2 Stir in the rest of the ingredients and taste for seasoning.

ALSO TRY...

Autumn couscous Soak the couscous as above. Meanwhile, heat 2 tbsp olive oil and sauté 1 onion, thinly sliced, until golden brown. Add ½ tsp ground cinnamon and ½ tsp pumpkin pie spice and cook for 2 minutes. Now add about ½ cup mixed dried fruit (raisins, golden raisins, cranberries, apples), soaked in boiled water for half an hour, then drained and chopped. Heat through. Add to the couscous along with 3 tbsp chopped fresh parsley or cilantro, the grated zest of ½ orange (plus a good squeeze of juice), and perhaps some chopped toasted nuts (hazelnuts and pecans are lovely). Season and taste. You may want to add want some melted butter or warm olive oil.

LEFTOVERS...

Tunisian red couscous This only works with a leftover dish of fairly plain couscous. Heat 2 tbsp olive oil in a frying pan and sauté 1 onion, finely chopped, until soft and golden. If you want a hot version, add 1 fresh red chile, finely chopped (or ½–1 tsp dried red pepper flakes), then toss in your leftover couscous and stir in 1½ tsp tomato paste mixed with 2 tsp boiling water. Add chopped fresh cilantro or parsley. Squeeze over some lemon and serve.

Couscous, chickpea, and feta salad Combine 2½ cups leftover couscous with 5 tbsp extra-virgin olive oil, the juice of ½ lemon, 6 tbsp chopped fresh parsley, 1 small red onion, sliced wafer thin, 14 oz can of chickpeas (drained and rinsed), and a roasted red bell pepper, sliced. Check for seasoning. Crumble 4 oz feta cheese over and drizzle with more oil. Sprinkle with sumac if you have it. You can add cooked lamb or chicken to this, other vegetables (such as green beans), and shreds of preserved lemon.

Farro with greens, fennel, and chile

If you think healthy food is punishingly dull, try this. It's spicy, nutty, leafy, and glossy with olive oil. Delicious.

Serves 4

4 tbsp olive oil

1 onion, finely chopped

1 celery stalk, diced

¾ cup farro

about 3 cups chicken or vegetable stock
  or water

1 fresh red chile, seeded and chopped,
  (or to taste)

3 garlic cloves, very thinly sliced

2 tsp fennel seeds

1 small Savoy cabbage, weighing about 9oz,
  leaves shredded

3 oz frisée and arugula leaves

salt and pepper

extra-virgin olive oil, to serve

1 Heat half the olive oil in a saucepan and add the onion and celery. Cook over a medium heat until soft but not colored. Stir in the farro and add enough stock or water to come 1½ in above the level of the grain. Bring to a boil, then reduce to a simmer. Cook for about 35 minutes, until the farro is tender but with bite. Try not to stir; you don't want to release any starch. The liquid will be absorbed; if it gets too dry, add more water.

2 Heat the remaining oil in a large frying pan. Add the chile, garlic, and fennel seeds and cook for 2 minutes, or until the garlic is soft. Add the cabbage and a splash of water, cover, and cook for 3 minutes over a medium-low heat, until the cabbage leaves wilt. Now uncover, add the other greens and wilt for 1 minute. Add the cooked farro, season well, increase the heat, and stir. Put into a heated serving dish and drizzle with extra-virgin olive oil.

ALSO TRY…

Farro with pumpkin and feta Cook the farro as above. Preheat the oven to 400°F and roast 1 lb pumpkin or winter squash (seeded, peeled and cut into thin wedges), tossed with 2 tbsp olive oil and seasoning, for about 30 minutes, until tender and slightly caramelized. Gently combine the farro with the pumpkin, 8oz crumbled feta cheese, the juice of ½ lemon, salt and pepper, 3 tbsp extra-virgin olive oil, and 2–3 tbsp chopped fresh flat-leaf parsley, dill, cilantro, or basil.

Lots of farro salads Cook plain farro—you don't need to sauté onion and celery first—in water until tender but still with bite (about 35 minutes), then drain. Add seasoning, lemon juice, and extra-virgin olive oil. Now you have a base for all sorts of lovely nutty salads. Try the ingredients in my barley salads (see page 126); or cherry tomatoes, olives, and basil with chopped anchovies; sautéed zucchini with herbs, crumbled ricotta, and pecorino; apple, hazelnut, watercress, and gorgonzola; smoked meat, blackberries or dried cranberries, and walnuts; roasted cauliflower, red pepper, and feta….

Barley, parsley, and pomegranate salad

Time was when barley turned up only in Scotch broth. Now it has chic, and there are endless ways in which to dress it. Soaked dried sour cherries or cranberries would be good here instead of pomegranates.

Serves 4

¾ cup pearl barley

1½ tsp olive oil

salt and pepper

1 tbsp extra-virgin olive oil

1½ tsp balsamic vinegar

seeds from ½ pomegranate

2 tbsp finely chopped fresh flat-leaf parsley

1 Put the barley in a saucepan and cover with water. Bring to a boil, reduce to a simmer, and cook until just tender, about 30 minutes. It's good if the barley still has a little bite; it tastes nutty that way. It shouldn't cook so much that it becomes "creamy" and starchy.

2 Drain and add the plain olive oil, salt, and pepper. This keeps the barley moist. I don't dress it further until it's cool, otherwise it just soaks up masses of vinaigrette. Once it has cooled, mix with the other ingredients, taste for seasoning, and serve.

ALSO TRY…

Barley, spinach, and mushroom salad Cook the barley as above. Fry 8 oz mushrooms, sliced, in 1 tbsp unsalted butter until well colored and quite dry. Season and toss with the barley along with 3 oz baby spinach, shredded or torn, plus balsamic vinegar, and extra-virgin olive oil as above. Serves 6.

Warm barley, roasted squash, and chile salad The other barley salads here are fine at room temperature, but I prefer squash hot, so cook 1¾ lb winter squash (seeded, peeled and cut into chunks) with 2 tbsp olive oil and seasoning for about 30 minutes in an oven preheated to 400°F. The squash should be completely tender and slightly caramelized. Meanwhile, cook the barley as in the main recipe, but dress it immediately with the 1 tbsp extra-virgin olive oil and 1½ tsp balsamic vinegar. Season and add 2 tbsp chopped fresh cilantro and 2 fresh red chiles, seeded and thinly sliced, and the squash. Serve immediately. Chunks of crumbled feta cheese don't go amiss here, either. Serves 6.

Lots more barley salads… Cook and dress barley (you can eat it hot or cold) and toss with cooked green beans and bacon; soaked dried fruits and hazelnuts; pitted cherries and mint or tarragon; preserved lemon, Spanish chorizo, and mint; smoked fish, watercress, and dill.

Fine fish

We are rather frightened of fish. The rules about cooking meat are simple; after all, we mostly eat only three animals and a few birds. But fish? They're a whole different kettle. Cod, haddock, salmon—we just about know how to deal with these—but venture any further and we're a bit, well, at sea.

Guilt and anxiety now play their part, too. It's impossible to ignore constant warnings about the depletion of fish stocks, and Charles Clover's book, *The End of the Line* (2008), in which he compares trawling to hunters stringing a mile of net between two huge vehicles and dragging it at speed across the plains of Africa, left me feeling morally obliged to get to grips with what and how we should fish.

I know the word "sustainable" can sound uncomfortably worthy, but "sustainable" fish are the only kind we can eat if we are to continue to eat fish at all. We are at a critical point. The UN's Food and Agriculture Organization states that of the 600 fish stocks it monitors, a quarter have been overfished or exhausted, while a further half are being fished at maximum capacity ("Review of the State of World Marine Fisheries Resources", 2002).

More "efficient" fishing has meant landing more fish, but in fact we are taking too much and, too often, indiscriminately. Beam trawling, in which an iron beam with heavy chains is dragged along the seabed, dislodging fish into the net that follows behind, is perhaps the most destructive. It doesn't just catch fish, but all other sea life, which is then dumped back into the ocean...dead.

Campaigning has had a huge impact, so there is hope. Some supermarkets, for example, don't sell any beam-trawled fish and all the major ones have made some effort both to source sustainable fish and consider fishing methods, but you need to shop armed with information on sustainable fish and fishing methods (how fish are caught is almost as important as what is caught). The Monterey Bay Aquarium has an invaluable website (www.montereybayaquarium.org) with information on sustainable fish, fishing techniques, and a pocket guide to what you should buy. You can also look out for the Marine Stewardship Council logo. An international charity, it certifies sustainable fisheries and places its logo on products that have come from its top-rated fisheries. The only drawback is that some varieties are missing from the MSC list because the process of certifying fisheries is voluntary; gurnard, for example, is not mentioned because no gurnard fishery has come forward.

The good news is that the choice of fish we can eat is much larger than you might expect, though supermarkets could go a lot further in the variety they offer. The situation obviously changes from year to year, so you should keep yourself informed by checking the website mentioned above. But at the time of writing, the guide on page 130 is a useful tool. When you scan the list of fish we shouldn't eat (and I've limited the list to the best-known varieties), you'll probably think that doesn't leave much. Not so. There is a wealth of fish and seafood out there we can eat with a clear conscience. It's a good choice, especially if you can get excited about varieties you've never tried. Remember that monkfish was once derided as poor man's scampi.

Avoid

Albacore tuna (that is not troll/pole caught)

Atlantic flounders, halibut, sole

Atlantic or Pacific cod

Bluefin tuna

Chilean seabass

Mahi mahi

Monkfish

Red snapper

Salmon (farmed, including Atlantic)

Shark

Skate

Tilapia (Asian farmed)

Yellowfin tuna

Eat

Albacore tuna (troll/pole caught)

Arctic char (farmed)

Catfish (US farmed)

Clams (farmed)

Cod (Pacific and Alaskan longline)

Crab (Dungeness and stone)

Haddock

Mussels (farmed)

Oysters (farmed)

Rainbow trout (farmed)

Salmon (wild Alaskan)

Sea Bass (farmed)

Scallops (farmed)

Skipjack tuna (troll/pole caught)

Striped bass (farmed)

Tilapia (US farmed)

Fish farming

Managing wild stocks is not enough. There will have to be fish farming, too; otherwise fish will become a treat only for the very rich. But fish farming has created as many problems as it has solved.

Farmed fish are often stocked at a high density, so they don't swim enough to develop flesh that will taste good. Worse than that, high stocking increases the risk of disease and parasites, which can be transmitted to wild stocks, and the strong chemicals used to treat sea-lice have a detrimental effect on the ecosystem surrounding fish farms. Farmed fish can also escape and mate with wild fish, creating hybrids that can't cope with the open sea.

But perhaps the worst thing is that farmed fish are fed on a diet of fish meal made from wild fish. Not only does this fish have to be vacuumed up but also, if we are processing it, it's not there for other wild fish to eat. The World Wildlife Fund estimates that it takes about 3 tonnes of wild fish to produce 1 tonne of salmon. You don't need me to tell you that that's a crazy use of resources.

But it is not all gloom. Like all kinds of farming, there is good fish farming and bad fish farming. We just need to buy the good stuff. For one thing, some types of fish take much better to being farmed. Shellfish, for example, present few problems. Mussels, scallops, and oysters don't even require much "farming," as they will eat whatever is in the water. All the fish farmer has to do is capture them while they are young and put them in a good site.

There are conscientious farmers of salmon and now cod, who practise good husbandry and are as concerned about ecology as they are about making a profit. They will in almost all cases use sustainable feed; this comes from the fish-processing industry, where the off-cuts and bones they don't need are made into fish meal.

If buying farmed fish, I always buy organic (apart from ecological considerations, it definitely tastes better) and even then I want to know where it is from—not just the area but the farm—and a good fishmonger (including one in a caring supermarket) should be able to tell you this. I buy farmed salmon, cod, seabass, trout, bream, and shellfish. Farmed salmon is a naturally beige color, but this was thought to be off-putting for consumers, so many farms add dye to their fish meal. Instead of the natural pale pinky-orange of wild salmon, farmed stuff can be a startling orange color. Also look at the texture. Farmed salmon gets less exercise than wild salmon, but it should still get some. Specimens that look over-fatty, or whose white stripes of fat look very broad, will taste fatty, too.

The way forward

Shop armed with knowledge and always ask questions about where and how a fish was caught or farmed. Fish will rarely be a cheap option, though many varieties, such as mackerel, squid, and gurnard, offer great value. They don't lend themselves to leftovers either, because the flesh spoils quickly (although there are lots of recipes in this chapter on what to do with leftover salmon, because that is something you can end up with in the summer months).

Fish has to be regarded as a treat, especially when we are talking about prized varieties such as wild seabass and salmon. I hate to think that there may be a time when it is impossible to sit at a seaside café, the smell of iodine in the air, squeezing lemon over a plate of succulent fish flesh, or to enjoy fish and chips on a beach at twilight. If we are responsible in our shopping and imaginative in our cooking, we should be able to eat fish both now, and for a long time to come.

Spanish baked sea bass

The Spanish have lots of sea bass recipes, none of them too complicated. It has a great flavor and I often buy it. If you don't like smoked paprika, leave it out. Or sauté bacon pieces and sprinkle over before serving.

Serves 4

FOR THE SEA BASS

4 x 10 oz sea bass, gutted,
   trimmed, and scaled
7 tbsp olive oil
juice of 1 lemon
salt and pepper
5 tsp smoked paprika

4 garlic cloves, crushed
¾ cup fresh white bread crumbs
small handful of fresh flat-leaf parsley,
   finely chopped

TO SERVE
extra-virgin olive oil
wedges of lemon

1 Preheat the oven to 375°F. Brush the fish inside and out with olive oil, squeeze on some lemon juice and season well. Lay the fish–in a single layer but close together–in an ovenproof dish. Mix the smoked paprika, garlic, and bread crumbs together and season. Sprinkle this all over the fish, then drizzle on the remaining olive oil and lemon juice.

2 Bake for 20 minutes. Throw on the parsley when the fish has cooked for 15 minutes. The bass is cooked when the flesh near the bone is white and opaque. Drizzle with extra-virgin olive oil and serve with lemon wedges.

ALSO TRY...

Bake the sea bass drizzled with olive oil, seasoned, and served with any of these sauces:

Anchovy and rosemary sauce In a mortar crush 2 tbsp rosemary leaves with 12 salt-cured anchovies (rinsed, soaked in milk for 15 minutes, then drained) to a paste. Slowly pestle in the juice of 1 lemon and about ½ cup olive oil. Taste to see if you want more lemon or oil. Stir in some black pepper. (You can also use a mini blender.)

Sherry vinegar and parsley sauce Put ⅓ cup each of sherry vinegar and chicken stock and 3 tbsp unsalted butter in a small pan and bring to a boil. Boil for about 2 minutes, until quite syrupy. Stir in 1 tbsp finely chopped fresh flat-leaf parsley, 1 shallot, very finely chopped; and ½ tsp Dijon mustard. Taste and season. Spoon this warm sauce over the fish.

Fennel, anchovy, caper, and mint salsa Trim 1 large fennel bulb, quarter, remove the core and dice the flesh. Heat 2 tbsp olive oil in a frying pan and cook the fennel and 2 garlic cloves, chopped, over a medium heat, just until the fennel stops tasting raw but isn't yet soft. Pour into a bowl and add a 1.75 oz can anchovies, drained and chopped; 1½ tbsp finely chopped fresh mint leaves; 2 tbsp capers, rinsed; 2 tsp balsamic vinegar, pepper, and 6 tbsp extra-virgin olive oil. Stir.

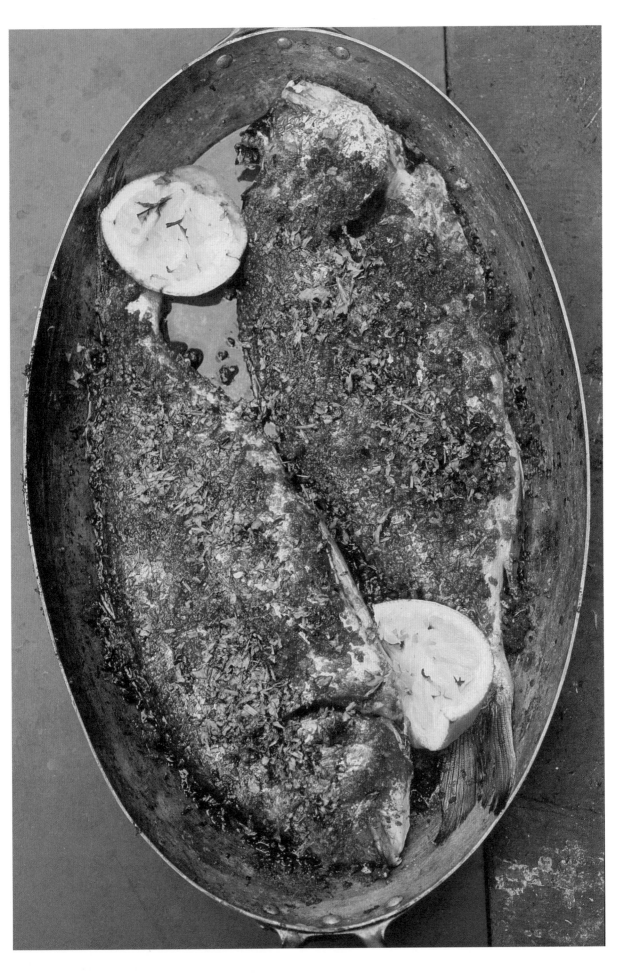

Fish pie with leek mash potatoes

Everyone needs a recipe for fish pie, and it doesn't have to be expensive. You can use cheap fish–such as pollock–and replace the shrimps with more white fish (even hard-boiled eggs). Mustard and lemon help the flavor and I have my secret ingredient (don't be snobbish–try it!), but it isn't mandatory....

Serves 6

2 lb skinless white fish fillets, in large chunks	1 tbsp Dijon mustard
1 cup whole milk	1½ tbsp Miracle Whip (optional)
½ cup butter	½ cup heavy cream
6 tbsp all-purpose flour	3 tbsp finely chopped fresh dill or parsley
salt and pepper	8 oz cooked, peeled shrimp
juice of ½ small lemon	1 lb leeks
	1¾ lb baking potatoes, in chunks

1 Put the fish into a sauté pan and pour on the milk. Bring to simmering point and poach for about 3 minutes. Remove the fish with a slotted spoon and set both it and the milk aside.

2 Melt ¼ cup of the butter in a saucepan and add the flour. Stir, then remove from the heat and gradually add the milk a little at a time, beating well after each addition to keep the mixture smooth. Return to the heat and bring to a boil, stirring. It should be very thick. Season, add the lemon juice, mustard, and Miracle Whip, if using. Reduce the heat and cook for 2 minutes. Add the cream and herbs and simmer for another minute. Taste; this needs to be well-flavored.

3 Put the fish and shrimp into a 2½ qt casserole dish. If there is any liquid under the fish, stir it into the sauce, or it will make watery patches in the pie. Pour the sauce over the fish and carefully mix. Taste and adjust the seasoning. Leave to cool, then refrigerate to make it easier to spread the mash on top. Preheat the oven to 400°F.

4 Melt the remaining butter in a heavy saucepan and add the leeks. Turn to coat, season, add 2 tbsp water, cover, and sweat over a low heat for about 15 minutes until really soft and sloppy. Add a splash of water every so often to ensure they don't burn.

5 Cook the potatoes in boiling, lightly salted water until tender, then drain. Return the potatoes to the saucepan, cover with a clean cloth towel and a lid. Place over a very low heat for a couple of minutes to dry out a bit–this produces a better mash.

6 Mash the potatoes until smooth, add the leeks and their juices, and season well. Spread the mash over the fish. Bake for 30 minutes, until golden and bubbling.

Gurnard on crushed potatoes with olives, parsley, and lemon

Gurnard (sea robin) fillets are small and sweet-tasting. It is the chef's favorite to serve in place of cod or haddock, though its flakes are much smaller than those of cod, and I think it has a better flavor than haddock. It is still quite plentiful. If olives seem too strongly flavored you can make a more subtle dish by crushing the potatoes with watercress (remove the coarse stems). The leaves wilt slightly in the heat.

Serves 4

FOR THE POTATOES
1¾ lb new potatoes
salt and pepper
1¼ cups pitted black olives in olive oil
½ cup extra-virgin olive oil, plus more to drizzle
juice of ½ lemon and finely grated zest of 1
2 tbsp coarsely chopped fresh flat-leaf parsley

FOR THE GURNARD
8 gurnard fillets (or substitute red or gray mullet), each weighing about 4 oz
¼ cup olive oil
1 tbsp unsalted butter
good squeeze of lemon juice

1 Boil the potatoes in salted water until tender. Drain the olives and chop coarsely. Drain the cooked potatoes and leave them in the pan in which they were cooked with a lid on, just to keep warm while you cook the fish.

2 Dry the gurnard fillets and season them all over. Heat the olive oil and butter in a nonstick frying pan and cook the fillets, flesh side down first, until pale gold and cooked through, about 2½ minutes each side. Squeeze over some lemon juice.

3 Crush the potatoes with a fork or potato masher—you just want to break them up, not mash them—and add all the other ingredients. Season and fork everything through. Serve on warm plates, with two fillets laid over the top of each portion of potatoes. Pour the pan juices from the fish over the fillets. Drizzle with a little more extra-virgin olive oil.

Sushi any way you like it

Purists should look away now because I see no reason why you can't simply offer the elements and let your friends assemble their own sushi DIY-style. You can try to get a grip on making your sushi look beautiful with strips of nori or whatever (it's quite fun), but the main thing is you get to eat gorgeous (and cheap and healthy) food. Serve with green tea or beer.

Serves 4

FOR THE SUSHI
1¼ cups sushi rice
¼ cup mirin
8 oz really fresh mackerel fillets
8 oz really fresh wild Alaskan or
    organically farmed salmon fillet
6 nori sheets

TO SERVE
1 small cucumber, cut into batons
pickled ginger
wasabi paste
Japanese soy sauce
chopped scallions

1 Wash the rice really well in a sieve. Put into a saucepan and pour over 3 cups water. Bring to a boil, then reduce the heat and simmer for about 25 minutes. The water should have been absorbed. Remove from the heat, cover, and leave to stand for 10 minutes.

2 Pour the rice onto a tray and spread it out so that it can cool down. Sprinkle on the mirin. The rice has to get completely cool before you can serve it.

3 Cut the mackerel and salmon into strips about the length of your little finger.

4 Serve the rice in a bowl and the fish on a platter with the nori, and all the accompaniments in little bowls. Let everyone help themselves.

Moroccan fish cakes, minted cucumber salad, and hot sauce

Fish cakes are good when you need to stretch fish. This recipe turns inexpensive white fish into something exotic, not unlike Thai fish cakes in texture, but with different spices. The sauce does have one expensive ingredient–saffron–but you use only a pinch and can leave it out. The sauce is worth making for plain grilled or roast fish, too.

Serves 6

FOR THE HOT SAUCE

2 tbsp olive oil
2 red bell peppers, seeded and sliced
1 carrot, chopped
2 shallots, chopped
1 fresh red chile, seeded and sliced
¼ tsp saffron threads
¼ cup sugar
¼ cup white wine vinegar

FOR THE FISH CAKES

1½ lb white fish, skinned and filleted
  (pollock, cod, haddock, sea bass,
  whatever is available)
1 tbsp ground cumin
½ tsp dried red pepper flakes

3 garlic cloves, chopped
½ preserved lemon, chopped
1 egg, lightly beaten
small handful of chopped fresh cilantro, or
  a mixture of cilantro and parsley
salt and pepper
all-purpose flour, to dust
neutral-tasting vegetable oil, for frying

FOR THE CUCUMBER SALAD

1 large cucumber
4 tsp white wine vinegar
4 tsp superfine sugar
2 tbsp olive oil
handful of chopped fresh mint leaves

1 To make the hot sauce, heat the olive oil in a frying pan and cook the peppers, carrot, shallots, and chile until completely soft (after they get a good turn in the oil, reduce the heat, add a splash of water, cover, and leave to sweat). Add the rest of the ingredients and ½ cup water, cook on a low heat for 10–15 minutes, then leave to cool. Purée in a blender until you have a nice smooth mixture; set aside.

2 To make the fish cakes, put all the ingredients except the flour and oil in a food processor and pulse to blend very briefly; you just want everything to blend together, not to turn the fish into a paste. Put flour on your hands and make the mixture into little cakes. You should get 24 out of this mixture, or 4 for each serving.

3 Just before you cook the fish cakes, prepare the cucumber. Peel the cucumber, halve it lengthwise and scoop out the seeds with a teaspoon. Discard the seeds. Thinly slice the cucumber and mix with the vinegar, sugar, oil, and mint. Season.

4 Put about 1½ in of oil in a sauté pan and heat. Cook the cakes for about 6 minutes, turning them over halfway through. (Test one by looking inside to see whether the fish in the middle has cooked.) Set on paper towels to soak up excess oil and sprinkle with sea salt. Serve with the sauce (either reheated or at room temperature) and the cucumber salad.

Mackerel with spiced rhubarb relish

Mackerel with rhubarb has been regarded for years as a winning combination, but I didn't know why until I made this. The relish is wonderful with all oily fish, and also with pork.

Serves 6

FOR THE RELISH

1 cup cider vinegar

1½ cups sugar

2 star anise

1 globe preserved ginger in syrup, shredded (available online and in Asian markets)

1 small fresh red chile, seeded and shredded

1 red onion, very thinly sliced

12 oz rhubarb, cut into short, even lengths

FOR THE MACKEREL

salt and pepper

12 mackerel fillets

1 tsp unsalted butter

good squeeze of lemon juice

1 Put the vinegar and sugar in a pan and bring to a boil, stirring to help the sugar dissolve. Add the spices and simmer for 10 minutes. Add the onion and cook, simmering, for 10 minutes. The onion will soften and the mixture become thicker. Now add the rhubarb and simmer gently for 4 minutes, or until just tender. Don't overcook; you want the rhubarb pink and the pieces intact. Leave to cool. The mixture will thicken as it cools.

2 Season the mackerel on both sides and melt the butter in a nonstick frying pan. Fry the fillets, skin side down, until golden, then carefully turn and cook the other side for about 3 minutes. Squeeze over some lemon juice.

3 Serve the mackerel with the relish alongside.

ALSO TRY...

Salad of mackerel, anchovies, and leeks with a soft-boiled egg Put 1 tbsp white wine vinegar, ½ tsp Dijon mustard, salt, and pepper in a cup; then whisk in ½ cup extra-virgin olive oil. Add a pinch of sugar and taste for seasoning. Cook 8 oz waxy potatoes until tender. Drain and leave in the pan, covered, to keep warm. Plunge 8 oz baby leeks into a large pan of boiling salted water and simmer for 5 minutes. Drain really well and season. Slice the potatoes into rounds slightly thicker than a quarter. Carefully toss with the leeks, 12 salt-cured anchovies (drained), 1 tbsp finely chopped fresh parsley and about two-thirds of the dressing. Cook 4 eggs in boiling water for 4½ minutes, then plunge into cold water and leave until cool enough to shell. Score 4 large mackerel fillets (each 6 oz) 4 times across their width. Season, lightly flour, and shake off the excess. Heat 2 tbsp oil in a nonstick frying pan and fry the fish over medium heat for 2–3 minutes each side. Divide the salad among four plates and set a mackerel fillet on top. Carefully shell the eggs. Break an egg over the top of each serving so the yolk spills onto the mackerel and drizzle with the remaining dressing. Serve immediately. Serves 4.

Beet, celery root, and sweet smoked mackerel salad

Smoked mackerel is good for you and a little goes a long way, so it's a wise option if you are watching the pennies. I have suggested sweet smoked mackerel (you do sometimes see it), but if you can't get that, regular smoked mackerel will do.

Serves 6

FOR THE DRESSING
2½ tsp white wine vinegar
½ tsp Dijon mustard
good pinch of superfine sugar
salt and pepper
¼ cup olive oil
2 tbsp finely chopped dill

FOR THE SALAD
1 lb celery root
juice of ½ lemon
3 cups cooked beets in wedges
12 oz sweet smoked mackerel
2 oz watercress

1 To make the dressing, just mix everything together. Taste; it should be quite sweet, so make any adjustments necessary. Refrigerate until needed.

2 Peel the celery root and cut the flesh into thick matchsticks. Put these immediately into a bowl of water mixed with lemon juice to prevent discoloration. Halve or quarter the beets, depending on size.

3 Break the fish into very large flakes, discarding the skin. Drain the celery root and pat it dry. Toss it with the fish, watercress and most of the dressing. Add the beets (at the last minute, or they will stain the other ingredients) and drizzle on the remaining dressing. Serve immediately.

ALSO TRY...

Smoked mackerel with lentils, Jerusalem artichokes, and mustard dressing
Make the same dressing as above but leave out the dill and use only a tiny pinch of sugar. Rinse 1½ cups green lentils (regular or Puy), then cover with cold water, bring to a boil, and cook until tender, 20–30 minutes. Meanwhile, gently sauté ½ onion and 1 celery stalk, both finely chopped, in 1½ tsp oil until soft but not colored. Add the lentils, stir, and add most of the dressing, and 1½ tbsp finely chopped fresh flat-leaf parsley then season to taste. Cook 12 oz Jerusalem artichokes in boiling, salted water, to which you've added a good squeeze of lemon (to stop discoloration). Once they are tender, drain and slip off the skins. Slice into rounds, about ¼ in thick. Gently combine with the lentils. Put a mound of lentils and Jerusalem artichokes on each of six plates and top with a smoked mackerel fillet. Drizzle with the remaining dressing, add a good grind of black pepper, and serve.

Roasted mackerel on potatoes, lemon, garlic, and thyme

Serve this in the dish in which it's been cooked.

Serves 4

2 lb small waxy potatoes, halved

2 onions, cut into wedges

1 head of garlic, cloves separated

2 lemons, plus more wedges, to serve

8 thyme sprigs

salt and pepper

olive oil

4 whole mackerel, gutted

1 Preheat the oven to 400°F. Put the potatoes and onions into a very broad, shallow ovenproof pan or roasting pan with the garlic. Cut 1 of the lemons into wedges and toss it in, then squeeze over the juice of the other. Add the thyme, season, and pour on ½ cup olive oil. Turn with your hands to coat.

2 Roast for 30 minutes, then lay the mackerel on top. Drizzle with oil, season, and cook for another 20 minutes. Check to see if they are cooked; if the fish are very big, they could take another 5 minutes.

ALSO TRY...

Roasted mackerel with cumin and chermoula Make chermoula (see page 160). Mix 1½ tsp ground cumin with 2 tsp cayenne, salt, and pepper and ¼ cup olive oil. Rub this over 4 whole gutted mackerel, inside and outside. Put into a roasting pan or ovenproof dish and cook as above. Spoon the chermoula over and serve with couscous or Barley, Parsley, and Pomegranate Salad (see page 126).

Indian-spiced mackerel with mango, coconut, and chile salad Put 1 cup dried coconut into a bowl and cover with boiling water. Leave for 30 minutes. Put the coconut, 1 tsp mustard seeds, 2 tsp superfine sugar, salt, and 1½ tsp dry sherry into a blender and blend to a coarse paste. Layer up 2 ripe mangoes, sliced, with spoonfuls of the coconut paste, squeezing on lime juice and sprinkling with 2 fresh red chiles, seeded and shredded. Add a generous handful of mint leaves, torn (don't add the mint until ready to serve). Put 2 tsp coriander seeds, 2 tsp cumin seeds, 3 cloves, and a ¾ in cinnamon stick into a small frying pan and toss for 2 minutes; the coriander will begin to "pop." Leave to cool, then grind with 4 garlic cloves, ¾ in fresh ginger, peeled and finely grated, 2 tsp cayenne pepper, 2 tbsp sunflower oil, and seasoning. You should have a lumpy paste. Take 4 whole gutted mackerel and make small slashes in the flesh on both sides, ¾ in apart. Rub the spice paste all over, outside and inside. Put the fish on oiled foil on a broiler rack and broil for 5 minutes each side. Check they are cooked. (Roast them if you prefer, following the temperature and timings in the main recipe above.) Serve immediately with the salad.

Baked mackerel with Sicilian flavors

Mackerel, since they have an assertive taste, are good at standing up to other strong ingredients such as the classic sweet-savory flavors so prevalent in Sicilian cooking. This is a simplified version of a Sicilian recipe that traditionally uses sardines. Coarsely chopped almonds and raisins will do just as well as pine nuts and currants.

Serves 4

1 large fennel bulb
about 6 tbsp olive oil
3 garlic cloves, finely chopped
1¾ cup fresh white bread crumbs
½ cup currants
6 tbsp pine nuts
1 tsp dried red pepper flakes
small handful of flat-leaf parsley,
   finely chopped

small handful of mint leaves, torn
salt and pepper
1¾ lb mackerel fillets
juice of ½ lemon

TO SERVE
extra-virgin olive oil
lemon wedges

1 Preheat the oven to 400°F. Remove any tough or discolored outer layers from the fennel. Quarter lengthwise, cut the little hard core out of each piece, discard, and finely chop the rest. Heat 2 tbsp of the olive oil in a frying pan and gently sauté the fennel until just beginning to soften. Add the garlic and cook for another minute, then remove from the heat and add the bread crumbs, currants, pine nuts, red pepper flakes, herbs, salt and pepper.

2 Layer up the mackerel in an ovenproof dish with the bread crumb mixture, seasoning and drizzling on lemon juice and the remaining oil as you go. You should finish with a layer of bread crumbs. Put into the oven and bake for 10 minutes.

3 Drizzle with extra-virgin olive oil and serve with lemon wedges.

Baked salmon with Scandinavian cucumber

Baked salmon is the quintessential summer dish. It is a beautiful sight–grand and celebratory–but there are two problems. First, it can be overcooked, so be careful with your timings. Second, as with Thanksgiving turkey, there are always leftovers, so I've given a raft of things to do with them on the following pages. (I often enjoy those dishes more than the original.) I have suggested butter here as the fat to use, but this is only if you are serving the dish warm. To serve cold, use olive oil instead (butter will congeal).

Serves 6–8

FOR THE SALMON
5 lb organically farmed salmon,
    cleaned and gutted
⅓ cup butter, melted
salt and pepper
good fistful of fresh parsley, chervil, and
    tarragon, coarsely chopped
⅔ cup dry white wine or vermouth
juice of ½ lemon

FOR THE CUCUMBER
1 large cucumber
2 tbsp flaked sea salt
2 tbsp rice wine vinegar
3 tbsp superfine sugar
2 tbsp chopped dill

1 Cut the ends from the cucumber and slice the rest into almost transparent slices. Layer in a colander with the salt, place a plate on top, and set over a bowl. Leave for 2 hours. Rinse the cucumber and pat dry. Mix with the remaining ingredients and keep covered, in the refrigerator.

2 Preheat the oven to 425°F. Wash the salmon inside and out and pat dry. (Wash bloody bits well; they make the salmon bitter.) If you've taken it straight from the refrigerator, leave for about 30 minutes so the chill goes off it. Melt the butter.

3 Put a large sheet of foil–big enough to enclose the salmon with room to spare–on a baking sheet or in a large roasting pan. Brush with some butter. Season the fish inside and out and put it on the buttered foil. Put the herbs inside, then drizzle the butter over and inside. Pour on the wine and lemon juice. Tent the salmon with the foil (it needs room to steam). Scrunch the edges together to make it airtight.

4 Bake for 45 minutes. It should be ready, but to check rub the skin with the tip of a blunt knife: if it slips off easily, the salmon is done.

5 Remove the salmon from the parcel, being careful not to lose the juices. If you're serving the fish hot, drain the juices into a pan and reheat them slightly, then pour into a warmed sauce boat. Serve the salmon whole on a platter, or remove the skin and lift pieces onto individual plates. Serve the cucumber alongside.

6 To serve it cold, leave the salmon to cool in the foil package and remove the skin before serving.

Salmon, mango, and wild rice salad with ginger and chile

It's worth having cooked salmon around just to make this. You might not think it sounds like the perfect combination, but mango is a surprisingly good partner for salmon as long as there are Thai flavorings (chile and ginger) in the mix. This also works with leftover chicken and pork.

Serves 6

FOR THE SALAD

⅔ cup wild rice

1 cup brown rice

3 cups chicken stock or water

8 oz green beans, trimmed and halved

salt and pepper

2 small mangoes

14 oz cooked salmon

⅔ cup unsalted pistachios, chopped

leaves from a small bunch of cilantro, coarsely chopped

squeeze of lemon juice

FOR THE DRESSING

1½ tbsp cider vinegar

¼ tsp Dijon mustard

1 garlic clove, crushed

1 tsp honey, or to taste

1 globe preserved ginger, finely chopped, plus syrup from the jar (available online or from Asian markets)

2 fresh red chiles, seeded and shredded

salt and pepper

3 tbsp peanut oil

¼ cup olive oil

1 Put the wild and brown rice into a saucepan with the stock or water. Bring to a boil, cover, and cook for about 30 minutes. Wild rice never gets completely soft, but retains a nutty bite. It should absorb the stock as it cooks, but keep an eye on it to make sure the rice doesn't become dry and add a little water if you need to.

2 Cook the beans in boiling salted water until *al dente*. Drain and rinse under cold water to set the green color. Peel the mangoes and cut off the "cheeks"—the fleshy parts on either side of the stone. Slice these to about the thickness of a quarter. (Use the rest of the mango flesh for something else.)

3 Make the dressing by whisking all the ingredients together and stir it into the warm rice with the green beans. Break the salmon into chunks and add it to the rice along with the mango, pistachios, cilantro, salt and pepper, and a squeeze of lemon juice (the dish can take quite a lot of salt, though it depends on whether you've used stock or water for cooking the rice). Taste everything for seasoning and adjust if you need to.

Salmon and dill pilaf

Pilafs are great vehicles for leftovers (read more about them in the chapters on grains (page 114) and roasts (page 38)). You can stir cooked buttery leeks or chopped wilted spinach into this as well and, if you have it, pour a slug of dry vermouth into the rice before adding the stock.

Serves 6

1⅔ cup long-grain rice	salt and pepper
1 onion, finely chopped	1 lb cooked salmon
2 tbsp butter	¼ cup fresh dill or parsley, finely chopped
3½ cups fish or chicken stock	lemon juice, to taste

1 Rinse the rice in a sieve until the water runs clear. Sauté the onion in the butter until soft but not colored. Stir in the rice to coat the grains. When it is really glossy, add the stock, season, and bring to a boil with the lid off. In 4–7 minutes you will barely be able to see the liquid and the surface will seem "pitted" with holes. Now reduce the heat, cover, and leave to cook (about another 15–20 minutes, but keep checking). The last little bit of liquid will be absorbed during this time and the rice will steam. Don't stir or it will spoil the texture.

2 When the rice has about 4 minutes of cooking time left, gently put the salmon on top and replace the lid. The salmon will warm through in the steam.

3 Gently fork the rice and salmon together with your chosen herb. Add a good squeeze of lemon juice and taste for seasoning. You should end up with separate, light grains and warm salmon.

ALSO TRY...

Making this with smoked haddock or smoked cod.

Simple kedgeree Proceed as above but use 3 tbsp butter to sauté the chopped onion and fry some spices (½ tsp ground cinnamon, ground seeds from 5 cardamom pods, ½ tsp ground turmeric, and 1 tsp curry powder) for 2 minutes along with the onion once it has softened. Use cooked salmon or cooked undyed smoked haddock (or a mixture). Add quartered hard-boiled eggs, fried onion slices (cut thinly and fry until golden brown in peanut or sunflower oil) and chopped cilantro (omit the dill or parsley). Stir in 1–2 tbsp cream if you have it just before serving and make sure the dish is well seasoned.

Salmon hash

There are lots of variations on the hash theme, all using leftovers, and, in my opinion, quite often you end up with something better than the original dish. They are all basically fry-ups, and this is rather more healthy than most. You don't need to use any smoked salmon—you can use all fresh cooked salmon—but it is lovely, and I always think those little packs of inexpensive smoked salmon trimmings are crying out to be used.

Serves 4

2 tbsp unsalted butter

1½ tsp oil

1 onion, finely chopped

2½ cups cooked potatoes, in chunks

12 oz cooked salmon and smoked
    salmon trimmings (in a 2:1 ratio)

10 oz spinach leaves, coarse stems
    discarded and shredded

salt and pepper

squeeze of lemon juice

small bunch fresh flat-leaf parsley or dill,
    finely chopped

1 Heat the butter and oil in a large frying pan and add the onion and potatoes. Fry over a medium heat until the onion is soft and both potatoes and onion are golden. The potatoes will be brown in places.

2 Flake the cooked salmon into large chunks, discarding the skin (and look out for the bones, too) and stir this in along with the smoked salmon and spinach. Stir everything around gently and allow the spinach to wilt a little and the salmon to heat through.

3 Season to taste, add the lemon juice and your chosen herb. If you want to smarten this dish up, serve with creamy mustard sauce (see page 155).

ALSO TRY...

Making the above with undyed smoked haddock or a mixture of haddock (or pollock) and smoked haddock.

Salmon on lentils with herb relish

Salmon fillets–like chops–are one of the things we turn to most often for an easy meal. Farmed organic fillets are reasonably inexpensive, healthy, and there's never any waste. This recipe is also lovely made with gurnard (cook as on page 135).

Serves 4

FOR THE LENTILS

2 tbsp olive oil
½ small onion, finely chopped
1 celery stalk, diced
1 small carrot, diced
¾ cup Puy lentils
2 thyme sprigs
1 cup chicken stock or water
salt and pepper
squeeze of lemon juice
extra-virgin olive oil

FOR THE HERB RELISH

¾ cup fresh herb leaves (flat-leaf parsley,
    basil, mint, and chives)
1½ tbsp capers, rinsed
2 garlic cloves, very finely chopped
juice of 1 lemon
½ cup extra-virgin olive oil

FOR THE SALMON

1 tbsp unsalted butter
1 tbsp peanut oil
4 x 6 oz salmon fillets

1 To make the lentils, heat the oil in a saucepan and gently cook the onion, celery, and carrot until softening. Stir in the lentils, thyme, and stock. Season with pepper. Bring to a boil, reduce to a simmer, and cook for 15–20 minutes. Watch carefully; the lentils can collapse very quickly.

2 Meanwhile, chop the herbs very finely and mix with the other relish ingredients.

3 Heat the butter and oil for the salmon in a large frying pan. Season the fish on both sides and cook over a medium heat, flesh down, for 1½–2 minutes, until golden. Turn and cook for 1½–2 minutes. Reduce the heat, cover, and cook until done but still moist.

4 When the lentils are cooked, add the lemon juice and a good slug of extra-virgin olive oil and taste for seasoning. Put some lentils on each plate and top with salmon and a good spoonful of relish.

ALSO TRY…

Crispy-skinned salmon with Vietnamese caramel sauce Heat 1½ tsp peanut oil and sauté 1 in fresh ginger, peeled and finely chopped, and 2 garlic cloves, chopped, until soft. Add 3 tbsp light soy sauce and ½ cup light brown sugar. Stir to melt and cook over a high heat until you smell caramel. Immediately add 1½ tbsp fish sauce and 2 tbsp water. It will splutter, so take care. Add 2 tsp tamarind paste and the juice of ½ lime and stir. Taste; it should be syrupy and intense. You may want another splash of water. Season 4 salmon fillets and heat 2 tbsp peanut oil until hot. Put the salmon in skin side down, and cook for 3 minutes until crispy. Turn and cook for 2–3 minutes, until golden. Check for doneness on the flesh side with a fine, sharp knife. Serve with the warm sauce, boiled rice, and stir-fried greens.

Fillet of salmon with sweet-sour beets and dill crème fraîche

Scandinavia is the perfect place to look for salmon recipes as so much of it is eaten there. Beet is an excellent partner and, after years in the wilderness, seems to be making a comeback and rightly so, as it's both inexpensive and gorgeous.

Serves 6

FOR THE DILL CRÈME FRAÎCHE
1 cup crème fraîche
2 tbsp whole-grain mustard
1½ tbsp chopped fresh dill

FOR THE BEETS
10 cooked beets (2 in diameter)
¼ cup unsalted butter
1½ tsp peanut oil
2 red onions, very thinly sliced

2 tbsp sugar
1½ tbsp red wine vinegar
salt and pepper

FOR THE SALMON
2½ tbsp unsalted butter
1 tbsp oil (sunflower, peanut or olive)
6 x 6 oz salmon fillets
good squeeze of lemon juice

1 To make the dill crème fraîche, simply mix the crème fraîche, mustard, and dill together. Refrigerate until you need it.

2 Pat dry the beets with paper towels. Cut each globe into quarters or, if they are small, halves. Set aside.

3 Heat the butter and oil in a frying pan and cook the onions over a medium heat until completely soft. Add the beets and increase the heat. Cook for 2 minutes, then add the sugar and stir until the mixture is beginning to caramelize. Add the vinegar and let it bubble. Season and taste for sweet-sour balance; you may want more sugar or vinegar. Set aside; you can reheat the beets before serving or serve at room temperature.

4 Heat the butter and oil in a large frying pan. Season the salmon on both sides and cook over medium heat, flesh side down, for 1½–2 minutes or until golden. Turn over and cook for 1½–2 minutes. Reduce the heat, cover, and cook until done but still moist. (How long this takes depends on the fillets' thickness.) Squeeze on some lemon juice.

5 Serve the salmon with beets and dill crème fraîche. Boiled new potatoes are the obvious accompaniment, but I also love it with a warm barley salad (see page 126).

ALSO TRY...

Salmon with mushrooms, melted butter and fresh horseradish Cook the salmon as above. Meanwhile, melt ¼ cup butter and briskly cook 8 oz mushrooms (mixed wild and cultivated), sliced, until well colored. Season and add a squeeze of lemon juice and 1½ tsp finely chopped fresh parsley. Melt ¼ cup butter. Put a salmon fillet on each of four plates, spoon the mushrooms around, drizzle with butter, sprinkle with 5 tbsp fresh horseradish, grated, and serve.

Smoked haddock stovie with fried eggs and mustard sauce

A combination of fish cakes and bubble and squeak and just the kind of dish I always want for Saturday night supper: British, substantial, soothing. Perfect for tucking into in front of the television. You only need a fork.

Serves 4

FOR THE SAUCE
1¼ cups heavy cream
1½ tbsp whole-grain mustard
generous squeeze of lemon juice
salt and pepper

FOR THE STOVIES AND EGGS
2 large baking potatoes
8 oz undyed smoked haddock
1 cup milk

2 large leeks, cut into chunks, and washed really well
1 tbsp grated horseradish (or horseradish cream)
2 tbsp finely chopped fresh flat-leaf parsley
peanut or sunflower oil, for frying
2 tbsp butter
4 eggs

1 Make the sauce first so you just have to reheat it before serving. Heat the cream until boiling, then boil for about 4 minutes to reduce. Add the mustard, lemon juice, and salt and pepper. The sauce will thicken because of the lemon. Taste for seasoning.

2 Preheat the oven to 400°F. Bake the potatoes for about 50 minutes, or until just tender (not falling apart; they'll be cooked further).

3 Put the haddock into a saucepan or sauté pan and cover with the milk. Bring to a boil, then immediately reduce the heat to very low. Cover and poach for 4–5 minutes. Once the fish is cool enough to handle, remove from the pan, break into large flakes, discarding the skin and any little bones. (You could use the poaching milk to make a parsley sauce, see page 196).

4 Cook the leeks in boiling salted water for 5–6 minutes, until tender. Drain really well, then transfer to a bowl. Remove and discard the skin from the potato, then coarsely chop the flesh and add to the leeks with the haddock, horseradish, and parsley. Season really well and mix everything together.

5 Heat 1 tbsp oil and all the butter in a large nonstick frying pan. Add the mixture and flatten into a large pancake. Cook for about 6 minutes over a medium heat, then turn it over by inverting it onto a plate, and then sliding it back into the pan. Cook for another 4–5 minutes, until the bottom is golden and has a good crust. While the stovie is in the last stages of cooking, fry the eggs in more oil.

6 Reheat the sauce. Cut the stovie into 4 wedges and serve each topped with a fried egg and a generous drizzle of sauce.

Smoked haddock brandade with spinach and poached egg

This is a British version of the French classic made with salt cod. It makes a little bit of smoked fish go a long way. If you aren't a great egg poacher, serve with a soft-boiled egg instead. Take a look at Salad of Mackerel, Anchovies, and Leeks with a Soft-boiled Egg (see page 140) for how to do that.

Serves 4

FOR THE BRANDADE
1 baking potato, about 8 oz
8 oz undyed smoked haddock
1½ cups milk
2 garlic cloves, coarsely chopped
1 large bay leaf
¼ cup heavy cream
2 tbsp extra-virgin olive oil
juice of ½ lemon
¼ cup grated Parmesan cheese
4 large eggs

salt and pepper
8 oz young spinach leaves

FOR THE VINAIGRETTE
½ tsp Dijon mustard
pinch of superfine sugar
1 tbsp white wine vinegar
3½ tbsp extra-virgin olive oil

TO SERVE
extra-virgin olive oil
couple of pinches of cayenne pepper

1 Bake or boil the potato (in its skin) until tender. Meanwhile, make the vinaigrette by mixing the mustard, sugar and vinegar with salt and pepper in a cup and whisking in the olive oil. When the potato is ready, halve it, and scoop the flesh into a large bowl. Mash with a fork and season.

2 Put the haddock in a pan and cover with the milk. Add the garlic and bay leaf. Bring to a boil, then immediately reduce the heat and poach–covered–for about 4 minutes, or until just firm. Strain off the milk (discard the flavorings) and reserve. Break the fish into fine flakes, discarding the skin and checking for bones as you go.

3 Mash the fish with the potato until well blended, then beat in about 5 tbsp of the reserved milk, the cream, and extra-virgin oil using a wooden spoon. Add the lemon juice and Parmesan. Check the seasoning. Keep the brandade mixture warm while you poach the 4 eggs.

4 Dress the spinach with the vinaigrette and divide among four plates. Top with the brandade and a poached egg. Sprinkle with a little extra-virgin olive oil and cayenne and serve.

Genoese squid with potatoes

If you're a squid enthusiast you are in luck, as it's cheap and plentiful. The smell of it frying reminds me so much of the sea and sand that cooking it always makes me feel as though I'm on vacation. Portugal, Spain, Greece…it reeks of hot sun and blue skies, which makes it very cheering to eat. Squid must be cooked with care, though, to avoid a plateful of rubber. The rule of thumb is to cook it quickly at a very high heat, or slowly over a gentle one. Both approaches produce flesh that is quite melting. Your fishmonger can clean and prepare squid for you.

Serves 4

2¼ lb squid, cleaned

1¼ lb waxy potatoes

5 tbsp olive oil

4 garlic cloves, chopped

1½ cups dry white wine

leaves from 2 oregano or marjoram sprigs

2½ tbsp chopped fresh flat-leaf parsley

14 oz can tomatoes in thick juice

salt and pepper

extra-virgin olive oil, to serve

1 Wash the squid and check whether there's any gunge inside the bodies. If there is, pull it out and discard. Cut the bodies into 1 in thick rings. Cut the knobbly bit off the bottom of each tentacle and slice the wings into 2 or 3, depending on size. Cut the tentacles in half if they're large. Rinse in a sieve and dry well with kitchen paper.

2 If the potatoes have thin skins you don't need to peel them; just wash well and cut into 1½ in thick slices.

3 Heat the olive oil in a saucepan or sauté pan. When it's really hot, add the squid and garlic. Turn these over in the hot oil, frying briskly for about a minute. Add the wine, oregano, 1½ tbsp of the parsley, and the tomatoes. Season, cover, reduce the heat, and simmer for 30 minutes.

4 Add the potatoes, season again and cover. Cook over low heat for about 30 minutes, until the potatoes are tender. Taste for seasoning, sprinkle with the remaining parsley, and serve. A little extra-virgin olive oil drizzled over just finishes it off.

ALSO TRY…

Braised squid with fennel Make as above but, before you fry the squid, heat half the olive oil and fry 1 small onion, finely chopped, for a few minutes. Add 1 large fennel bulb, trimmed, cored and finely sliced lengthwise, and sauté until the fennel is golden and the onion soft. Add 3 cloves garlic, finely chopped, and cook for another couple of minutes. Put the remaining oil in another pan and sauté the squid very fast over high heat. Add the squid to the onion and fennel, then add the wine and tomatoes as above. Add 2 tbsp chopped parsley. Cook as above, adding only 1 lb potatoes. Stir in another 2 tbsp chopped parsley before serving. You could also add a small handful of black olives in the last 5 minutes.

Squid, chorizo, and bean stew with chile and cilantro

This started off one night as a stir-fry, and sheer hunger (that's never going to be enough, I thought as I looked at the pan) caused it to grow. It features the irresistible Iberian combination of pork and seafood.

Serves 6

8 oz Spanish chorizo

2 lb squid, cleaned

olive oil

1 large onion, in crescent moon-shaped slices

1 lb waxy potatoes, cubed

2 fresh red chiles, seeded and chopped

4 garlic cloves, crushed

8 large plum tomatoes, cut into wedges

salt and pepper

1½ cups cooked cannellini or other white beans, rinsed

2¼ cups light chicken, fish or vegetable stock

juice of ½ lemon

generous bunch of fresh cilantro, coarsely chopped

1 Pull the skin from the chorizo and cut into chunks. Wash and prepare the squid as for Genoese Squid, opposite.

2 Heat 2 tbsp olive oil in a large saucepan and sauté the onion and potatoes until the latter are golden and the onion is soft. Add the chile and garlic and sauté for another minute. Add the tomatoes, season, and sauté for 3 minutes.

3 Heat 2 tbsp olive oil in another frying pan and sauté the chorizo until colored. Add to the stew with the beans, then the stock. Bring to a boil, reduce the heat, and simmer for 5 minutes. Remove from the heat.

4 Meanwhile, heat 2 tbsp olive oil in a frying pan and sauté the squid in batches, over a high heat, for 1 minute. Season, squeeze over a little lemon juice, and add to the stew.

5 Stir the stew, heat it through, add the remaining lemon juice, check the seasoning, and stir in the cilantro. Serve in flat soup plates with good coarse country bread.

ALSO TRY...

Hot stir-fried squid It's amazing that something this delicious—and with multi-dimensional flavors—is this quick to make. Heat 1 tbsp peanut oil in a wok and add 2 garlic cloves, finely sliced; ½ in fresh ginger, peeled and finely chopped; 2 lemon grass stalks (optional), chopped; and 1 red chile, seeded and shredded. Cook for 1 minute. Add 2 lb cleaned squid, prepared as on page 158. It's very important that it is dry or it won't fry properly. Cook over a very high heat for 1 minute. Reduce the heat, add 4 scallions, diagonally sliced, 1–2 tsp superfine sugar, and 1 tbsp dry sherry. Cook for another minute, then serve on warmed plates with rice and stir-fried greens. Serves 4.

Griddled squid with chickpeas, peppers, and chermoula

Despite relatively inexpensive ingredients–squid and chickpeas–this dish has a certain magnificence. The sight of griddled squid, in all its tentacled loveliness, and the green of chermoula (a Moroccan herb and spice blend) against the red of roast peppers laid out on a big platter is very impressive. And then there's the aroma…. Be sure to provide plenty of lime wedges on the side.

Serves 8

FOR THE SQUID

5 red bell peppers, halved and seeded
olive oil
salt and pepper
2 x 14 oz cans chickpeas, drained
  and rinsed
2¼ lb squid, cleaned
½ lime

FOR THE CHERMOULA

juice of ½ lime
1 fresh red chile, seeded and thinly sliced
½ cup extra-virgin olive oil
½ tsp ground cumin
½ tsp hot smoked paprika
⅓ cup fresh chopped cilantro
2½ tbsp chopped fresh flat-leaf parsley

1 Preheat the oven to 350°F. Brush the peppers with olive oil, season, and put into a roasting pan. Cook for about 35 minutes, depending on size. They should be completely tender and slightly blistered. I don't skin them as I like the slightly charred skin. Slice in broad strips once cool enough to handle.

2 To make the chermoula, just mix everything together. Mix the peppers and the chickpeas with the chermoula in a broad, shallow bowl.

3 Cut the little wings from the squid and put them aside with the tentacles. Cut the bodies down one side so they open out. If your squid are very big, halve the main body lengthwise. Clean the inside (there's always a little bit of gunk). Score the flesh on the inside and dry well on paper towels. Put in a bowl with enough oil just to moisten the outside and heat a griddle pan until very, very hot.

4 Season the squid and cook it on both sides on the griddle pan in batches. It needs only about 20 seconds on each side. The squid will turn opaque and should have lovely griddle marks and a really good golden color. I like to squeeze lime over it as soon as it is ready. Toss the cooked squid with the other ingredients in the bowl. Taste everything for seasoning. You can serve this either now while the squid is hot, or at room temperature.

Thai mussels with coconut, chile, and lime

Serving mussels to friends creates a kind of holiday feeling. It's the fact that you eat them with your hands, actively digging out the food, and you get messy. Before long the table is littered with shells (what beautiful debris—the bluish wash inside looks as if it were applied by the most careful watercolorist), squeezed lemon wedges, and crumpled napkins. Another bottle of wine is opened and people decide to stay "just a bit longer." Food that has this profound an effect is definitely worth cooking. Mussels are also good for you, cheap, and sustainable. What more could you want? This dish is utterly addictive.

Serves 4

FOR THE MUSSELS
4½ lb mussels
1½ tbsp groundnut oil
1 onion, finely chopped
2 garlic cloves, finely chopped
¾ in square fresh ginger, peeled
  and finely chopped
2 fresh red chiles, seeded and shredded
2 x 14 oz cans coconut milk

juice of 1 lime
1½ tsp soft light brown sugar
2 kaffir lime leaves, cut into strips (or
  grated zest of 1 lime)

TO SERVE
2 kaffir lime leaves, cut into strips (or
  grated zest of 1 lime)
¼ cup coarsely chopped cilantro
½ fresh red chile, seeded and shredded

1 Wash the mussels really well, scrubbing off barnacles and removing any "beards." Tap each on the side of the sink. If it doesn't close, chuck it away. Rinse the mussels well.

2 Heat the oil in a large saucepan. Add the onion, garlic, ginger and chiles. Cook over a medium heat until the onion is soft and very pale gold. Add the coconut milk, lime juice, sugar, and lime leaves. Bring to just under a boil, then add the mussels.

3 Cover and cook for 4 minutes, or until the mussels have opened, shaking the pan a couple of times. Throw away any that haven't opened (and remind your diners to do the same).

4 To serve, stir, then throw the lime leaves, cilantro, and chile on top.

ALSO TRY...

Spanish mussels with cider and chorizo Prepare 2½ lb mussels as above. Heat 3 tbsp olive oil in a large pan and sauté 8 oz Spanish chorizo (skinned and cut into chunks) and 2 onions, finely chopped, until slightly colored and the onions have softened. Add 2 garlic cloves, finely chopped, and cook for 2 minutes to soften. Throw in the mussels, 2¼ cups dry hard cider and pepper, and cover. Bring to a boil, reduce the heat to medium, and leave the mussels to steam open, about 4 minutes. Throw away any that haven't opened (or tell your diners to do so), stir in 3 tbsp finely chopped fresh parsley, and serve immediately in soup plates.

Rediscovered cuts

When I was growing up–and certainly when my parents were–we cooked cuts of meat that children (and most adults) now would barely recognize. Those cuts–beef shank, pork cheeks, brisket–have lots of connective tissue, which dissolves during slow cooking. They require time and care to cook to tenderness, but your reward is meat that practically falls apart as you stick your fork in it. They provide the sweetest, most melt-in-the-mouth kind of eating.

It seems crazy that many of these bargain cuts are now routinely used in inferior, commercially made pies, sausages, and pet food. These days we're all for grilling, searing, and flash-frying; many people don't know how to cook any other way. We want food instantly, and this requires leaner, more expensive meat. Trying old-fashioned cuts means slower cooking, making a bit more effort, and acquiring some new knowledge.

I have always been careful with the food budget. Fillet or sirloin of beef, for example, is rarely on the menu in my house, and I have routinely cooked less expensive cuts, but over the last few years I've cooked them even more. A workshop I attended on old-fashioned cuts not only convinced me that I would eat more enjoyably if I explored them, but also showed me that it's the only sane way to eat, as you use the whole beast. What kind of society takes the leanest meat from an animal and–because the rest of the carcass is too much trouble to cook or, on the part of the retailer, make money from–turns it into substandard sausages and pet food?

Since I have gone back to the cuts of my childhood I have saved money–but it has also changed the feel of my house. Beef shank has simmered away on the stove, we've had pot after pot of sticky oxtail, and neck of lamb has once again been on my shopping list. The kitchen smells very like my mother's and my grandmother's. There is proper cooking going on, and I have had to use more imagination.

I am not saying you shouldn't buy expensive cuts–in fact there's a whole chapter on them at the beginning of this book–but cooking them sometimes means turning to cheaper cuts at other times. It's a balance. And it does make for more satisfying eating.

You may well feel daunted by my exhortations to try old-fashioned cuts. It's scary to ask a butcher for something with which you're unfamiliar. But persist. Get to know your butcher and ask him questions. There is real pleasure in turning cheaper cuts into great food. You get a kick out of knowing you haven't simply cooked "the best" of what's available, but that you have made the best of what's available. You know that saying, "You can't make a silk purse out of a sow's ear"? It ain't true.

Buying unusual cuts

The majority of large supermarkets don't buy whole animals (only the parts we most use), so for more unusual cuts you need to find a good butcher.

In the past, your mum or granny cultivated a butcher, visited regularly, and relied on him to supply good meat, track down special orders, and issue sound advice. For cooking old-fashioned cuts, a relationship with a good butcher is vital. At first you may find he doesn't have what you are looking for (of course, he stocks what he can sell), but I bet he'll be pleased you are interested and will be glad to source cuts for you.

The alternative is to buy directly from good meat producers and farm stores. Many sell online. And there's something very rewarding about connecting with the people who produce the food you eat.

Beef cuts

SHANK The smell of a rich pot of beef shank simmering on the stove takes me back to when I was nine years old. Shank comes from the top of the leg and is great value. It can be cooked on the bone in a soup or stew; cut in cross sections and cooked like osso bucco with wine, onions, and tomatoes; or cut off the bone and braised. My mum would simmer it for a few hours with onions, carrots, and celery and use the stock as the basis for a soup or stew, leaving the meat to cool before removing it from the bone.

BRISKET Quite fatty as it comes from the belly, but full of flavor and very good for salting, so you can use it for the salt beef in this chapter. Brisket is highly prized for slow-cooked genuine barbecue (not grilling).

RUMP The rear end of the cow is divided into the rump on top and the round on the lower portion. It is often cut into steaks (top round) or roasts. Because it is lean, some people roast it wrapped in fat. It takes reasonably well to slow pot-roasting.

ROUND The round may be ground or cut into steaks, roasts, or chunks for braising and stewing. My granny braised steaks with carrots and onions.

CHUCK The chuck is full of connective tissue and therefore is quite flavorful but requires long, slow cooking. When it comes to both the round and the chuck, a "steak" just means that it is cut into a thinner piece than a "roast." Chuck is often sold ground and makes excellent burgers.

FLANK The flank is lean and muscular with long fibers. It may be cut into roasts or steaks, which may be called flank steak, London broil, or skirt steak. It is lean but very tasty when cooked long and slow. It can also be beaten and marinated to break down the fibers and tenderize, then cooked more quickly.

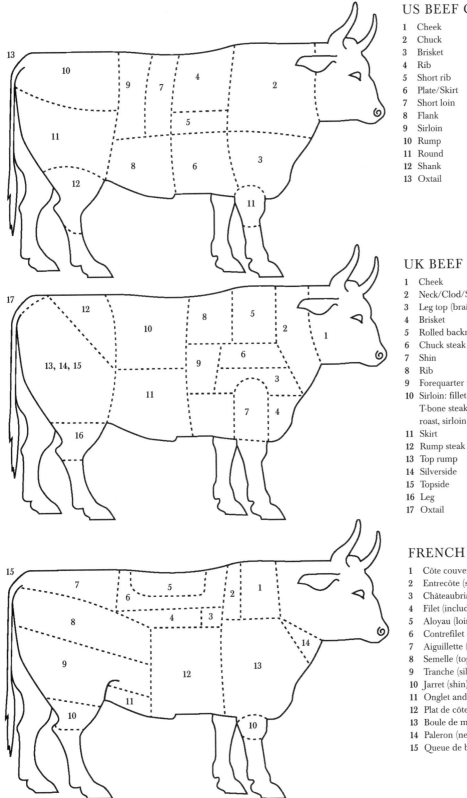

US BEEF CUTS

1 Cheek
2 Chuck
3 Brisket
4 Rib
5 Short rib
6 Plate/Skirt
7 Short loin
8 Flank
9 Sirloin
10 Rump
11 Round
12 Shank
13 Oxtail

UK BEEF CUTS

1 Cheek
2 Neck/Clod/Stewing steak
3 Leg top (braising steak)
4 Brisket
5 Rolled backrib
6 Chuck steak
7 Shin
8 Rib
9 Forequarter flank, short ribs
10 Sirloin: fillet and fillet steak,
   T-bone steak, wing rib, sirloin
   roast, sirloin steak
11 Skirt
12 Rump steak
13 Top rump
14 Silverside
15 Topside
16 Leg
17 Oxtail

FRENCH BEEF CUTS

1 Côte couvert (rolled rib)
2 Entrecôte (steak)
3 Châteaubriand (thick end)
4 Filet (includes Châteaubriand)
5 Aloyau (loin)
6 Contrefilet or faux filet (sirloin)
7 Aiguillette (rump)
8 Semelle (topside)
9 Tranche (silverside)
10 Jarret (shin)
11 Onglet and hampe (skirt)
12 Plat de côte (plate)
13 Boule de macreuse (shoulder)
14 Paleron (neck)
15 Queue de boeuf (oxtail)

OXTAIL No cut of beef makes your mouth as sticky with melting meat as oxtail.? There's no mistaking the cut—it looks like a tail—and it is usually cut into short lengths to make it easier to deal with. It needs to be cooked gently and slowly (at least 3 hours), but you're rewarded with the tenderest meat that is beautifully rich.

BEEF CHEEKS Cheeks of beef are dark in color, and require even longer gentle cooking than pigs' cheeks. Braise them with beer, shallots, and carrots, with pickled walnuts, or with Chinese flavorings. Other beef stews will seem pale in comparison. Substitute braising beef if you can't find beef cheeks, and cook until tender.

Pork cuts

SHOULDER A whole pork shoulder is massive—too big for most gatherings as it feeds about 20—but you can buy part of one. It makes a most delicious meal (I actually prefer it to belly) as it becomes so soft you can almost spoon it. Despite its being cheap there is something very feast-like and celebratory about a shoulder. It can take strong flavors such as mustard and spices. Roast it either on or off the bone. Cut into cubes, blade shoulder is what is usually sold for braising.

BELLY The sound says it all. "Belly" is soft and yielding, fatty and succulent. But pork belly has come into vogue only recently, the result of chefs turning to more old-fashioned cuts. Formerly, in Britain at least, it was the kind of cut you bought only if you were going to make your own pâté or terrines. Commercially, it was mostly used for bacon, pancetta and salt pork. Now it is almost a cliché of gastropub menus and at last, thankfully, it has made its way into our home kitchens. The bit at the head end, called the thick end, is the best bit for roasting and produces the crispiest crackling, but there is much more to it than roasting, something the Chinese know well. You barely need teeth to eat pork belly when it has been cut into chunks and braised slowly, it simply dissolves in your mouth. In composite dishes with beans, like French cassoulet, chunks of pork belly don't just provide the meat element but flavor the cooking liquid and the beans, too, and exude fat that creates an unctuous texture. And soft but crispy chunks are even good in salads.

LEG Sold either on the bone or boned and rolled, leg of pork can be roasted, though it's a lean cut so needs a good layer of fat on it if it isn't to dry out. (I certainly prefer shoulder or belly.) It's best suited to slow roasting, but whack up the heat at the end for good crackling. The leg can also be cubed and used for braised dishes.

HOCK I usually cook this only in its cured form, when it is called ham hock. It looks a bit like a small lamb's shank and is unappealing in appearance when cooked—it is covered in gelatinous skin and fat—but the flesh is soft and moist with a rich, hammy flavor. You just have to take the meat off the bone and discard the fat. It's a great plateful to have with parsley or mustard sauce, piccalilli, or beets and horseradish. It's also a good cut to use for making terrines, the best, most chunky ham sandwiches,

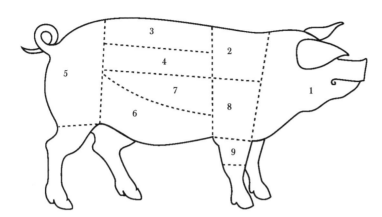

US PORK CUTS

1 Cheek
2 Shoulder
3 Loin
4 Tenderloin
5 Leg
6 Belly
7 Sparerib
8 Picnic shoulder
9 Hock

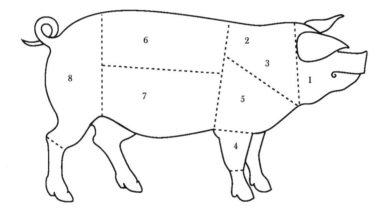

UK PORK CUTS

1 Cheek
2 Spare rib
3 Shoulder
4 Hock
5 Hand and Hock
6 Loin: rack of pork, loin chop,
  tenderloin (pork fillet), escalope,
  chump chop
7 Belly, rack of spare ribs
8 Leg

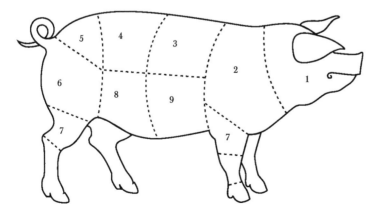

FRENCH PORK CUTS

1 Cheek
2 Echine (shoulder)
3 Carré (spare rib)
4 Filet (loin)
5 Pointe (tenderloin)
6 Jambon (leg)
7 Jambonneau (hock)
8 Poitrine (belly)
9 Plat de côte (forequarter flank)

and for tossing into warm salads (with bitter greens or lentils and a punchy mustardy vinaigrette), and provides great stock for soup (it makes particularly good lentil and bean soups). If you are using it for stock, make sure it isn't too salty; sometimes it can be unusable, or needs watering down.

SPARERIBS Great to get your teeth round; I always forget just how satisfying spareribs are. I have tended to keep them for barbecue weather or Halloween, but don't leave them just for special times of the year—pork ribs are uniquely suited to both cold and warm weather eating and are terrific value for money. The cut is made up of the trimmed ribs from inside the belly and they usually come as a rack of five or six. Marinate spareribs in Asian flavors (a sweet-and-sour glaze) and bake in the oven, protecting your roasting pan with foil. They're always a huge hit with children.

CHEEKS Pig cheeks: that's exactly what they are and they come in the most beautiful little medallions about the size of the fleshy bit of your palm. Braise them with Chinese spices (they're great with star anise, orange, and ginger) or with wild mushrooms and onions. They can be hard to track down.

Lamb cuts

SHANK The vogue for "peasant food" has driven up the price of lamb shanks, which used to be relatively cheap. A smallish shank serves one person and, braised, they make a warming, succulent dish. Because they are sweet, shanks take well to strong flavors such as Asian ingredients (see Vietnamese Lamb Shanks, page 180).

SHOULDER Many people prefer this fantastic cut to a leg of lamb. It has sweet, melting flesh and is particularly good with sharp, salty ingredients (anchovies and mustard, or Middle Eastern preserved lemons, are all wonderful). I usually cook it boned and stuffed, when you can either roll and tie it—the fat is then within the roast and lubricates the meat as it cooks—or cook it *en ballon*, where the meat is pulled up round the stuffing to make a ball-shaped parcel (so you can use more stuffing).

NECK Neck was the only meat I cooked at college. I used it to make navarin of lamb, braising it slowly with tomatoes, carrot, and rutabaga before adding peas or beans, and for Irish stew. The only laborious thing is removing the meat from the bones after cooking before returning it to the pot.

GROUND LAMB Ground lamb doesn't have to be lean; the fat gives flavor and keeps dishes, such as kofta (meatballs) moist and tender. There's a wealth of great Middle Eastern dishes (some in this chapter) to be made with ground lamb.

BREAST Some cooks think this an underrated cut, but I find it so fatty that I rarely cook it. It can be stuffed and slowly pot roasted, but I prefer to roast it flat, cut it up, and use it in slow-cooked bean dishes, such as Cassoulet (see page 172).

US LAMB CUTS

1 Neck
2 Shoulder
3 Rib
4 Saddle
5 Loin
6 Leg
7 Hind shank
8 Breast
9 Fore shank

UK LAMB CUTS

1 Scrag end
2 Neck fillet/Middle neck
3 Shoulder
4 Rack of lamb (best end of neck)
5 Loin, loin chop
4 & 5 Saddle
6 Breast
7 Chump, chump chop
8 Leg
9 Shank

FRENCH LAMB CUTS

1 Collet (scrag end)
2 Epaule (shoulder)
3 Carré (rack and best end of neck)
4 Careé de côtes premières (cutlets)
5 Filet (loin)
6 Selle (saddle)
7 Gigot (leg)
8 Gigot d'agneau (shank)
9 Poitrine (breast)

Cassoulet

I often make this particularly inexpensive version of cassoulet without duck confit, but always include breast of lamb. It is a cheap cut I find difficult to use—it's so fatty—except in dishes where that fat melts to flavor and season other cheap ingredients (such as beans). Then it's perfect.

Serves 10

2 lb (5 cups) dried haricot or navy beans

8 oz bacon, in one piece

1 onion, studded with 6 cloves

1 bouquet garni

8 garlic cloves, crushed

1¾ lb boned breast of lamb

12 oz pork shoulder

8 oz good-quality sausages,

10 large tomatoes, very coarsely chopped

leaves from 8 thyme sprigs

2½ tbsp fresh flat-leaf parsley, coarsely chopped

salt and pepper

1 tbsp tomato paste

about ½ cup fresh white bread crumbs (you may need more)

1 Soak the beans overnight in cold water. Drain, rinse well and put in a pan with fresh water to cover completely. Cut the rind off the bacon and add, together with the onion with its cloves, bouquet garni, and half the garlic. Bring to a boil, skim, then reduce the heat and simmer for 1¾ hours, or until the beans are tender (it partly depends on how old they are).

2 Preheat the oven to 375°F. Put the lamb, pork, bacon, and sausages into a roasting pan and cook in the oven for 30 minutes. Pour out and reserve the fat. Cut the pork, bacon, and lamb into chunks about 1–1½ in square and slice the sausages into thick rounds.

3 When the beans are tender, drain off and reserve the liquid. Discard the bacon rind, onion, and bouquet garni. Reduce the oven temperature to 350°F. Layer the meat, sausages, tomatoes, remaining garlic, and the herbs in a large casserole, starting and finishing with a layer of beans. Season really well as you go. Measure 2½ cups of the bean liquor and mix it with the reserved meat fat and the tomato paste. Pour this over the dish. Sprinkle some bread crumbs on top (reserve some for later). Cover and put in the oven for 1½ hours. After 45 minutes, uncover and stir, put more bread crumbs on top, and return to the oven.

4 You now have to work on the cassoulet's thickness while it finishes cooking. If it isn't thick enough, add more bread crumbs to the surface, let them go golden, then stir them in. If, on the other hand, it is a bit dry, add more bean liquor. It is hard to be prescriptive about quantities as it depends how much liquid your beans absorb. When the cooking time is up there should be a layer of golden crumbs on top. Watch the seasoning: this dish needs a lot because of the quantity of beans. Be prepared to add more herbs if you think it necessary.

Spanish lamb with beans and chorizo

Dead easy, as long as you remember to soak your beans the day before. It's best served with plain boiled rice or rice pilaf and greens on the side (kale is good).

Serves 6

1½ cups dried navy or lima beans
  (or other white beans)
1 piece of bacon rind, if available
  (ask your butcher)
2 onions
3 bay leaves
3 tbsp olive oil
1½ lbs braising lamb, in
  large chunks

8 oz Spanish chorizo, in chunks
4 garlic cloves, finely chopped
1½ tsp ground cumin
1½ tsp smoked paprika
28 oz can tomatoes in thick juice
a few thyme or rosemary sprigs
pinch of sugar
salt and pepper
3 tbsp coarsely chopped fresh flat-leaf
  parsley

1 Cover the beans with cold water and soak overnight. Drain and rinse. Put into a saucepan with the bacon rind, 1 of the onions, quartered, and 2 of the bay leaves. Cover with cold water and bring to a boil. Skim the surface and reduce the heat to low. Cover and cook until the beans are almost tender. It could take 45 minutes, it could take 1½ hours, depending on their age.

2 Heat the olive oil in a large saucepan or flameproof Dutch oven and brown the lamb on all sides, in batches so that it doesn't sweat but browns properly. Set the meat aside. Add the chorizo to the pan and briskly color that, too. Set aside.

3 Coarsely chop the remaining onion and fry it in the pan in which you browned the lamb. When it's soft and golden, add the garlic and spices and cook for a couple of minutes, then add the tomatoes. Return the lamb and chorizo with the remaining bay leaf, the herbs, sugar, and seasoning. Add the beans and their cooking water (discard the onion and bacon rind). Stir everything and bring to a boil, then reduce the heat and cook, uncovered, for 1½ hours. Check the seasoning. The beans should be soft and some should have collapsed (to thicken the stew). Stir in the parsley and serve.

Lamb with olives and preserved lemons

Not authentically Moroccan, because Moroccan cooks wouldn't brown the meat, but I think it produces a better flavor. A company called Belazu makes preserved lemons but the lemons are very small (a Moroccan variety), so if you're using homemade preserved lemons you'll need just one of them.

Serves 6

6 tbsp olive oil	good pinch of saffron threads
2 tbsp butter	salt and pepper
3½ lb lamb shoulder, in 2 in chunks	3½ cups lamb or chicken stock or water
2 large onions, finely chopped	1 large or 2 small preserved lemons
4 garlic cloves, finely chopped	1¼ cups green olives in brine, rinsed
1 tbsp ground ginger	2 tbsp each coarsely chopped fresh flat-leaf
2 tsp cayenne	parsley and cilantro
¾ tbsp ground cumin	

1 Heat the olive oil and the butter in a heavy pan and brown the lamb on all sides. Add the onions, stir them round in the juices, and cook for a minute, then add the garlic, spices, and seasoning (easy on the salt as the preserved lemons make the dish salty later on) and cook for another minute.

2 Add the stock or water, bring to a boil, then reduce to a simmer. Put the lid on the pan and reduce the heat to very low. Cook for 1 hour, stirring from time to time.

3 Discard the preserved lemon flesh and cut the rind into shreds. Take the lid off the pan and add the olives and most of the lemon. Cook for another 15 minutes, during which time the juices will reduce. Check the lamb: it should be tender. Stir in most of the herbs, sprinkle with the remaining lemon and herbs and serve.

ALSO TRY...

Tajine of lamb with apricots, saffron, and honey Heat olive oil and butter and brown the lamb as above. Add the onions as above, then add 4 garlic cloves, finely chopped; 1 tbsp ground ginger; 2 tsp ground cinnamon; and seasoning and cook for another minute. Throw in 1¾ cups dried apricots and 6 tbsp dried sour berries (cranberries or sour cherries). Add 3½ cups lamb or chicken stock or water and a good pinch of saffron, if you have it. Cook as above for 1 hour, then remove the lid and cook for 15 minutes. The lamb should be tender. Stir in 2 tbsp honey, a good squeeze of lemon juice, and 2 tsp orange flower water, if you have it. Add 2 tbsp coarsely chopped fresh flat-leaf parsley, mint, or cilantro and check for seasoning and flavor; you may want more honey. Sprinkle with 2 tbsp chopped pistachios or almonds before serving.

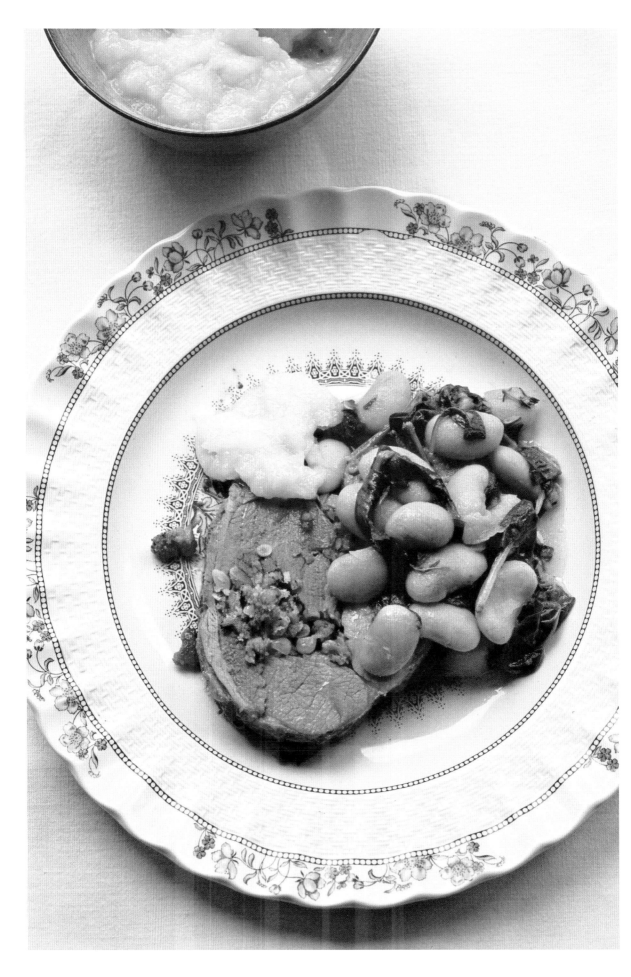

Roast lamb shoulder with lima beans, spinach, and apple aioli

Lamb shoulder is one of the cheapest roasting cuts you can buy, so it's brilliant for a crowd, and it has a sweeter flavor than leg. This is earthy country food with a Catalan twist. Apple and garlic aioli works brilliantly and is made without egg yolks. It's good with rabbit, pork, and chicken as well.

Serves 6

4 lb boneless lamb shoulder

FOR THE STUFFING
½ onion, finely chopped
4 oz pancetta or bacon, chopped
1 tbsp olive oil
3 tbsp pine nuts or almonds, toasted
2¼ cups fresh white bread crumbs
1 small egg, beaten
leaves from 4 thyme sprigs
3 tbsp chopped fresh flat-leaf parsley
salt and pepper

FOR THE AIOLI
2 Granny Smith apples, peeled, cored, and
  cut into chunks

2 garlic cloves
½ tsp rock salt
⅓ cup fruity extra-virgin olive oil
1 tsp white wine vinegar
1½ tbsp honey

FOR THE BEANS
10 oz spinach, washed
¼ cup olive oil
leaves from 1 thyme sprig
4¾ cups cooked lima beans, drained
good squeeze of lemon juice

1 Preheat the oven to 425°F. For the stuffing, sauté the onion and pancetta or bacon in the oil until golden. Put in a bowl with all the other stuffing ingredients and mix. Open the lamb out and trim any excess fat. Season well inside, then stuff. Roll up and tie up using thin kitchen string. Season the outside, put in a roasting pan and cook for 20 minutes. Reduce the heat to 325°F and cook for another 50 minutes (reckoning on 15 minutes per pound).

2 To make the aioli, put the apples in a small saucepan and cover with water. Cook until very tender. Drain. Chop the garlic cloves and crush with the rock salt in a mortar, then add the apple and crush to a purée. When it is quite smooth, slowly add the extra-virgin olive oil, a drop at a time, beating as you go (as if making mayonnaise), until you have a thick sauce. Add the vinegar and honey and refrigerate until needed.

3 When the lamb is cooked, cover with foil, insulate with cloth towels, and allow to rest for 25 minutes or so.

4 Wilt the spinach in the water that clings to it after washing. It should take 4 minutes. Drain, squeeze out the water, and chop. Heat the oil in a wide pan. Add the spinach, salt, pepper, and thyme. Cook for a minute, stirring, then add the beans, being careful not to break them up. Cook until hot, then add the lemon juice and more seasoning (beans need quite a lot). Serve with the lamb and aioli.

ALSO TRY...

Stuffed Samos lamb This Greek dish is to die for; you'll relish the gasps as you take it to the table. It's very simple to put together, and the ingredients won't break the bank, but it looks like the centerpiece of a wonderful feast. Preheat the oven to 425°F. Saute ½ red onion, finely chopped, in 2 tbsp olive oil. Add 1 small fennel bulb, trimmed and chopped (reserve any little feathery fronds). Once the onion is soft, add 3 garlic cloves, finely chopped, and cook for 2 minutes, then add 1 cup basmati rice, which you've rinsed until the water runs clear. Pour on enough water just to cover. Season. Bring to a boil and boil hard until the water has disappeared and the surface looks "pitted", then reduce the heat, cover, and cook gently for about 12 minutes. The rice should still be a bit *al dente*. Fork it gently and mix with the finely grated zest of 1 lemon and 3 tbsp each finely chopped fresh dill and parsley (this is a very herby stuffing). Check for seasoning. Prepare and stuff the lamb as on page 177, using a 5 lb boneless shoulder. Season the outside, squeeze over the juice of ½ lemon, and drizzle with olive oil. Roast for 20 minutes, then reduce the heat to 325°F and cook for another 1¼ hours. Rest and insulate the lamb as on page 177 and serve on a heated platter. Serves 8.

Lamb shawarma Mix together 1 lb lamb shoulder, thinly sliced, with 1 onion, finely sliced; 2 cloves garlic, coarsely chopped; the juice of 1 lemon; ¼ cup olive oil; 1 tsp each ground cinnamon and ground allspice; the leaves from 3 thyme sprigs; and salt and pepper. Cover and put in the fridge to marinate for 3 hours, turning occasionally. If you have a griddle pan, warm it until it is very hot. Lift the meat from the marinade and griddle briefly (it needs only a couple of minutes on each side, it is so tender), adding more seasoning. Lift the onion out of the marinade and fry on the same griddle–but on a lower heat–until golden brown. Spoon on the marinade and let it bubble away to almost nothing. If you don't have a griddle pan, you can use a frying pan instead (you just won't get the marks). Serve hot with warm pita bread and Greek yogurt (you can add chopped cucumber and mint) or tahini dressing (see page 82). The contrast of temperatures is fantastic.

Lamb, blood sausage, and mustard hot pot

I've tinkered with the original hot pot recipe, but if you prefer to be traditional
leave out the blood sausage and mustard.

Serves 4

3 tbsp peanut or sunflower oil
   or dripping
2 large onions, thinly sliced
12 oz blood sausage, sliced
8 lamb chops (shoulder chops)
2 lb potatoes, very thinly sliced

2 tbsp wholegrain mustard
salt and pepper
5 tbsp finely chopped fresh parsley
leaves from 6 thyme sprigs
3¾ cups lamb or beef stock,
   or stock and water
1 tbsp butter

1 Heat half the oil in a frying pan and cook the onions until soft and turning golden.
Set aside. Add the remaining oil to the pan and fry the blood sausage for a minute each
side. Set aside. Briefly cook the chops over high heat to get a good color. Set them
aside, too. Preheat the oven to 350°F.

2 Starting with the potatoes, layer them with the onions and meat in a Dutch oven in
which everything fits snugly. Dot the mustard over the blood sausage, season well, and
sprinkle with herbs as you go. You should have two layers of chops and end with a
layer of potatoes.

3 Arrange the top layer of potatoes in neat overlapping slices. Heat the stock and pour
it on, then melt the butter and brush the top. Cover and bake for 1½ hours, then
uncover and continue to cook and bake for a further 30 minutes.

ALSO TRY...

My Irish stew People have remarked that my Irish stew is not "traditional", but
I grew up with this and I am Irish! It's a great way to use a cheap cut. Put 3¼ lb neck
or shoulder of lamb into a large saucepan with a handful of parsley stems, 1 onion,
halved, 1 large carrot, halved, and 6 black peppercorns. Cover with water, bring to
a boil, and skim. Reduce to a simmer, cover, and cook until tender. It should take
1–1½ hours. Strain and reserve the stock. Cut another 3 large carrots into rounds
and 4 large, peeled, baking potatoes into chunks. Coarsely chop 2 large onions. Put
the vegetables into a clean saucepan, and add the stock, 3 thyme sprigs, and seasoning.
Bring to a boil, reduce the heat, and cook, uncovered, until the vegetables are tender
and the potatoes partly fallen apart (they thicken the stew). Remove the lamb from the
bones and cut into large chunks. Add the meat to the stew. Heat through and check the
seasoning. Sprinkle with finely chopped fresh parsley before serving. Serves 4–6.

Braised lamb shanks with gremolata

Lamb shanks aren't as cheap as they were, but are still good value and great reheated, so can be eaten over a couple of meals. You'll have to take whatever size shanks the butcher has, which makes cooking times difficult to specify. Just cook them gently until the meat is parting from the bone. The timings here are for the weight of shanks given; if yours are smaller, check to see when they're ready.

Serves 8

FOR THE SHANKS
8 lamb shanks, about 12 oz each
salt and pepper
5 tbsp olive oil
2 onions, chopped
8 carrots, chopped
4 celery stalks, chopped
3 x 14 oz cans tomatoes in thick juice
3 cups dry white wine

several rosemary sprigs
2 bay leaves
3 strips orange zest

FOR THE GREMOLATA
finely grated zest of 1 unwaxed orange
4 garlic cloves, very finely chopped
about ¼ cup finely chopped fresh
  flat-leaf parsley

1 Preheat the oven to 300°F. Remove the fat covering the lamb with a sharp knife. Season the meat. Heat the oil in a large flameproof Dutch oven and brown the lamb, in two batches, on all sides. Set aside. Add the vegetables to the Dutch oven and cook until the onions are soft but not colored. Add the tomatoes, wine, and flavorings and bring to a boil. Return the shanks and put in the oven with the lid on for 3–3½ hours, or until the meat is falling from the bone.

2 Remove the lamb and reduce the liquid by boiling until quite thick. Meanwhile, make the gremolata by mixing the ingredients together. Sprinkle over the shanks and serve.

ALSO TRY...

Vietnamese lamb shanks with sweet potatoes Gorgeously fragrant and quite "brothy", so serve in broad, flat soup plates. Preheat the oven to 325°F. Heat 2 tbsp peanut oil in a heavy Dutch oven, season 4 lamb shanks (about 12 oz each) and brown well. Remove from the casserole. Briskly fry 2 onions, in crescent moon-shaped slices, until golden, then add 1 in fresh ginger, peeled and finely chopped; 2 fresh red chiles, seeded and thinly sliced, and 3 garlic cloves, thinly sliced. Reduce the heat and cook for a minute. Stir in 1 tbsp dark brown sugar, 3 star anise, 2 bruised lemon grass stalks, 4¾ cups lamb stock, 1½ tbsp tomato paste and seasoning. Add 4 sweet potatoes, peeled and cut into chunks, and return the lamb. Bring to a boil, reduce the heat and cook in the oven with the lid on for 2½ hours, or until the meat is almost falling off the bones. Stir in 2 tbsp fish sauce, the juice of 2 limes, and another tsp of brown sugar. Taste for seasoning, sprinkle with torn basil and mint and serve with boiled rice. Serves 4.

Turkish lamb kofta with cherries and yogurt

Ground meat, though much maligned, can be made into dishes that aren't just good, but have magic. Kofta are little meatballs eaten in the Middle East, India, Pakistan, all over the eastern Mediterranean, in Russia, and many other parts of the former Soviet Union. They are so easy to make; just spiced, pummelled ground meat formed into little balls and fried. This, dark red with cherries and splattered with yogurt, is a lovely-looking dish. It's obviously best made when cherries are slightly less expensive (though they're never cheap). Increase the quantity of dried cherries to replace some of the fresh if you want, or make with a mixture of fresh and dried apricots instead.

Serves 6

2¼ lb ground lamb
1 tbsp ground cinnamon
2 tsp ground cumin
1 tsp ground cloves
1 tsp cayenne pepper
salt and pepper
3 tbsp olive oil
1 tbsp butter
1 onion, finely chopped
12 oz fresh cherries, pitted

¾ cup sour dried cherries, soaked
   in just-boiled water for 15 minutes
   and drained
1–2 tbsp light brown sugar
juice of ½ lemon
½ cup lamb or chicken stock

TO SERVE
Greek yogurt
a little milk or buttermilk
chopped fresh mint, parsley, or cilantro

1 Put the lamb in a bowl and add all the spices except 1 tsp of the cinnamon. Season. Pummel the meat until really soft and everything is well blended. If you don't mind raw lamb (it won't do you any harm), eat a tiny bit to check the seasoning and spicing (otherwise fry a little chunk, then taste; the seasoning and spicing are paramount). With wet hands, form into walnut-sized balls.

2 Heat the oil in a large sauté pan and fry the kofta in batches, making sure they are well browned. Scoop them out onto paper towels as you cook them.

3 Pour the oil out of the pan, return it to the heat, and add the butter. Heat until foaming, then add the onion and sauté until soft and golden. Add about half of the fresh cherries and all the dried ones with the remaining cinnamon and cook for a minute until softening, then add the sugar and lemon juice.

4 Return the kofta and add the stock. Bring to a boil, then reduce to a simmer and cook for 20 minutes, uncovered, until cooked through and the mixture is thick. Press some of the cherries so they disintegrate. If your mixture isn't thick enough, remove the meatballs and boil the liquid to reduce, then return the kofta. Put the remaining fresh cherries in towards the end of cooking to soften slightly and heat through. Serve drizzled with Greek yogurt (diluted with a little with milk or buttermilk) and sprinkled with fresh chopped parsley, mint, or cilantro.

ALSO TRY...

Tajine of kofta and dates with preserved lemons Heat 2 tbsp olive oil in a frying pan and gently sauté 1 small onion, grated (squeeze out excess liquid first), until soft. Add 3 garlic cloves, crushed, 1 tsp each ground ginger, pumpkin pie spice, and cayenne, and 1 tbsp ground cumin. Cook for another minute. Mix into 2 lb ground lamb (use your hands) and season really well. Using wet hands, form into golf-ball-sized rounds. Heat another 2 tbsp oil in a flameproof Dutch oven and brown the kofta on all sides in batches. Remove with a slotted spoon as you go and set aside. Add 1 onion cut into slim wedges, and fry in the remaining oil until golden. Add 1 tbsp each ground cumin and ground ginger and cook for another minute. Return the kofta to the Dutch oven and add 8 pitted dates and 4 cups lamb or chicken stock. Stir in a good pinch of saffron threads and 1 tbsp honey. Season. Bring to a boil then immediately reduce to a simmer and cook for 15–20 minutes. The kofta should be cooked but tender and the cooking liquid should have reduced. Remove and discard the flesh from 1 preserved lemon. Cut the rind into slivers and add to the Dutch oven with ¼ cup torn fresh mint leaves. Taste for seasoning. Serve with Arab flatbread, couscous, or rice. Serves 6.

Kofta don't always have to be served in a stew or sauce. Use different spices to flavor them (see page 183) or put them onto skewers, broil and serve them with the following accompaniments:

Tahini sauce (see page 82)

Greek yogurt, mixed with chopped garlic and mint

Orange and Pistachio Pilaf (see page 114)

Split Pea Purée (see page 103)

Tarator (see page 58)

You can also brown kofta, then add them to Kaye Korma Curry (see page 74), Turkish Potatoes with Tomatoes and Black Olives (see page 85), or Creamy Lentils and Pumpkin with Ginger and Cumin (see page 101). They need to cook in these dishes for 15–20 minutes.

Pork rillettes with sweet-and-sour plums

Rillettes are very cheap to make and a good thing to stash in the refrigerator if you have a crowd of friends coming. With some dressed lentils, a few cornichons and decent bread you have a perfect lunch. They also make wonderful picnic food.

Serves 8–10, makes about 2¼ lb

FOR THE RILLETTES
- 1 lb boneless pork shoulder
- 1 lb pork belly (bones and rind removed)
- 10 oz rendered pork fat or lard
- 4 thyme sprigs
- 3 bay leaves
- 4 cloves
- ¼ tsp ground pumpkin pie spice
- very generous grating of nutmeg
- salt and pepper

FOR THE PLUMS
- ⅓ cup red wine vinegar
- ⅓ cup sherry vinegar
- ½ cup sugar
- 2 in cinnamon stick
- 12 oz fresh ripe plums

1 Cut the pork shoulder into strips ¾ in across, slicing along the grain. Cut the pork belly into slices ½ in thick. Put the fat and ½ cup water into a broad, heavy pan and set over a very low heat. Add the meat. Tie the thyme, bay leaves, and cloves in a square of muslin and put this in, too.

2 Cook over a very low heat so the liquid is shivering, not bubbling, for about 4 hours, on top of the stove where you can keep an eye on it. The meat shouldn't brown; just poach. Make sure it doesn't stick and turn it occasionally. It's ready when you can pull it gently apart.

3 Leave to cool, remove the spices and herbs and shred the meat with two forks into soft strands. Add the pumpkin pie spice and nutmeg and season well with salt and pepper. Put into a couple of bowls and cover with waxed paper that you've greased with more pork fat or lard.

4 The rillettes taste better after a couple of days in the refrigerator, but I find them too much of a temptation. If you pack the rillettes into jars with no air pockets and cover with a good ¼ in pork fat, they should last for about 4 months.

5 To make the plums, put the vinegars into a saucepan and add the sugar and cinnamon. Dissolve the sugar over a low heat, stirring from time to time, then bring to a boil. Reduce the heat immediately and simmer for 7 minutes, until slightly syrupy. Halve and stone the plums, add them, and simmer for 4 minutes, depending on ripeness; they should be just tender. Leave to cool. The fruit will develop a good flavor in the syrup and the liquid will thicken as it cools.

6 Serve the rillettes with the plums, lightly dressed salad, and good baguette or sourdough bread. Rillettes are also wonderful in the summer with pickled cherries.

Succulent pork belly with soy and star anise

A pot of Asian deliciousness that is irresistibly more-ish. It also takes very little effort. Mushrooms make a good addition if you want to extend the dish with vegetables. You can obviously tailor this to suit your palate; not everyone is a big fan of star anise, for example, but stick to Asian flavors.

Serves 6–8

3⅓ lb pork belly, bones removed, rind left on

½ cup dark soy sauce

⅓ cup Chinese rice wine or dry sherry

1½ tbsp rice vinegar

2½ tbsp light brown sugar

2 in square of fresh ginger, peeled and thinly sliced

3 star anise

3 garlic cloves, thinly sliced

1 fresh red chile, seeded and thinly sliced

12 scallions, sliced on the diagonal

1 Cut the pork belly into chunks (or ask your butcher to do it for you) about 2 in square. Put these in a saucepan and add enough water to cover. Bring to a boil, reduce the heat so that the water is simmering and cook the pork for 5 minutes. Skim the surface of any scum that rises.

2 Strain the pork (discard the cooking water), rinse the pan, and return the pork. Add about 4¼ cups water (or light chicken stock if you have it), plus all the other ingredients (using only half the scallions). Bring this up to a boil, then immediately reduce to a gentle simmer, cover tightly with a lid, and leave to cook very gently for about 2 hours, or until the pork is completely tender. Make sure it doesn't boil dry and add more water if needed.

3 Scoop the pork out of the cooking liquor with a slotted spoon and set aside. Reduce the cooking liquor by boiling it until you have a good, intensified flavor (but don't take it so far that it is unpalatably salty). Return the pork to the liquid and heat through. Serve in bowls over noodles, or with boiled rice, with the rest of the scallions sprinkled over the top. Some kind of stir-fried greens–cabbage or bok choy–are good served on the side, too.

Crispy pork belly with potatoes, eggs, and gribiche dressing

It may seem unusual to put chunks of pork belly in a salad, but this French dish works beautifully. Cooked this way chunks of pork belly can also be used for salads made with lentils dressed in a good mustardy vinaigrette, or in Asian-style salads with noodles, bean sprouts, mushrooms, and strongly flavored greens tossed in a spicy dressing.

Serves 6

FOR THE SALAD
6 thick slices of pork belly
1 lb small waxy potatoes
6 eggs
6 oz salad greens (watercress or
   spinach are both good)

FOR THE DRESSING
smidgen of Dijon mustard
salt and pepper

1½ tsp white wine vinegar
¼ cup extra-virgin olive oil
1 small shallot, very finely chopped
2 large gherkins, finely chopped
1 tbsp capers, rinsed and chopped
leaves from 2 tarragon sprigs, chopped
2 tbsp chopped fresh flat-leaf parsley

1 Preheat the oven to 350°F. Pierce the skin side of the pork belly pieces with a fork and plunge them into boiling water (this helps them crisp up more). Remove, place the pieces on a rack set over a roasting pan and cook in the oven for 1 hour. The pork should be tender and crisp. Cut into bite-sized chunks.

2 Half an hour before you are ready to eat, make the dressing and boil the potatoes. To make the dressing, put the mustard, salt, pepper, and vinegar into a small bowl and whisk in the olive oil. Add all the other dressing ingredients and check for seasoning. Cook the potatoes in boiling salted water until just tender. Drain and carefully halve the potatoes lengthwises. Toss them straight away in a little of the dressing and keep them warm.

3 Cook the eggs in boiling water for 5–6 minutes. They should be just between boiled and hard-boiled. Take their shells off once they are cool enough to handle, and halve lengthways.

4 Gently toss the greens, warm potatoes, and pork with most of the dressing. Divide among six plates. Add the warm halved eggs and drizzle more dressing over the top. Serve immediately.

Thyme-roasted belly of pork with baked apples

Pork belly has everything going for it. It can be roasted with a crispy crackling or braised to produce tender, melting mouthfuls. And it's cheap.

Serves 8

4 lb thick end of pork belly, rind
   scored (ask your butcher for the last 6 ribs)
leaves from 1 small bunch of thyme
fine flaked sea salt
freshly ground black pepper
8 smallish apples, preferably with
   russet skin

1 cup dry hard cider, white wine,
   or apple juice
¼ cup light brown sugar
juice of ½ lemon

1 Preheat the oven to 425°F. Lay the meat, skin side up, in a roasting pan. Rub the thyme leaves and salt and pepper into the skin. Be generous with the salt as this gives crisp crackling. Roast for 30 minutes.

2 Run a knife horizonally around the middle of each apple and put in a baking dish. Heat the cider and sugar gently until the sugar dissolves. Bring just to a boil, add the lemon juice, and pour over the apples. Reduce the oven temperature to 350°F. Put the apples in the oven and roast them alongside the pork for another hour (but do check before then: they should be tender yet not collapsing).

3 Test the pork: the juices should run clear when the meat is pierced. If the crackling isn't crispy enough, increase the oven temperature to 425°F and check again after 5 minutes. Serve each person some meat and crackling, a baked apple and its juices.

ALSO TRY...

Spiced pork belly with fennel, chile, and lentils Crush together 1½ tbsp fennel seeds, 1½ tsp dried red pepper flakes, 2½ tsp thyme leaves, and 2½ tsp flaked sea salt. Mix in 3 tbsp olive oil and rub over 3¼ lb pork belly (rind scored). Refrigerate, covered, for an hour. Preheat the oven to 425°F. Roast the pork, skin side up, for 30 minutes. Reduce the heat to 350°F and pour in 1½ cups white wine or hard cider. Cook for 1½ hours, pouring in another 1½ cups liquid (wine, hard cider or water) after 1 hour. Heat 2 tbsp olive oil and gently sauté 1 small onion, chopped; 1 carrot, diced; and 1 celery stalk, diced; for 10 minutes. Add 1½ cups green lentils, 2 cups chicken stock or water, and 1 bay leaf and bring to a boil. Reduce to a simmer, season, and cook, covered, for 25 minutes. Take the pork from the oven and insulate to rest. Skim the fat from the juices. Stir 1 tbsp red wine vinegar, 2 tbsp extra-virgin olive oil, and 2 tbsp chopped fresh parsley into the lentils. Serve the pork with the lentils and cooking juices. Serves 6.

Slow-roasted shoulder of pork with stuffed squash

Sunday lunch can seem dauntingly expensive if you're trying to feed a crowd. But slow-cooked pork shoulder is one of the most satisfying roasts (so tender) and, relatively, very cheap. It also looks magnificent. You can vary the stuffing by using dried fruit instead of mushrooms, or add grated Parmesan or wilted spinach.

Serves 8

FOR THE PORK
sea salt and pepper
6 lb boneless pork shoulder roast,
    rind scored
¼ cup olive oil
4 cups dry hard cider or white wine

FOR THE SQUASH
2 small winter squash or pumpkins
¼ cup butter

1 onion, finely chopped
3 oz pancetta, chopped
8 oz mushrooms, quartered
1 cup brown basmati, wild, and Camargue
    red rice (or just brown and wild)
2¼ cups chicken stock or water

1 Preheat the oven to 400°F. Season the inside of the pork. Roll up and tie at intervals with kitchen string. Rub with oil and season well. Put in a roasting pan and roast in the oven for 25 minutes. Reduce the heat to 325°F and pour in half the alcohol. Cook for another 25 minutes per pound–about 2½ hours in total–basting and adding more cider or wine as you go.

2 Meanwhile, halve the winter squash and scoop out the fibers and seeds. Score a lattice on the flesh. Put in a roasting pan and smear with 1 tbsp of the butter. Season and roast for 20 minutes. Remove from the oven.

3 Melt another 1 tbsp of the butter in a saucepan and sauté the onion until quite soft. Add the pancetta, mushrooms, and remaining butter and sauté until colored. Stir in the rice to coat, season, and add the stock or water. Cover, bring to a boil, reduce the heat to low and cook for 15 minutes.

4 When the pork is cooked (the juices should run clear, with no trace of pink, when you pierce the meat), take it from the oven and put on a heated platter. Cover with foil, insulate well, and rest for 30 minutes. Increase the oven temperature to 375°F.

5 Spoon the rice stuffing into the winter squash cavities, mixing it with the butter that has collected there. Return to the oven for 30 minutes. The flesh should become completely tender and the tops golden.

6 Meanwhile, pour the cooking juices from the pork into a pitcher and remove the fat. Deglaze the roasting pan with more hard cider, white wine, or water (only about ½ cup), add the pork juices, and bubble away until you have a thin, tasty gravy. Serve the pork with the gravy and squash.

ALSO TRY...

Porc au four A brilliant celebration or big Sunday lunch dish. The pork is practically melting. Serve with roasted potatoes or lentils, watercress salad, and baked red onions (see page 32). Put 7 garlic cloves, chopped, ¾ tbsp sea salt flakes, a generous grinding of black pepper, and the leaves from 5 thyme sprigs into a mortar and pound to a rough paste. Add 3 tbsp Dijon mustard and 5 tbsp olive oil. Make small incisions all over the flesh of a 5 lb bone-in pork shoulder roast. Paint the mustard mixture all over the flesh (not the rind), pushing it into the slits. Cover loosely and refrigerate for a few hours, or ideally overnight. Bring to room temperature and preheat the oven to 425°F. Season the rind with sea salt. Roast the pork for 30 minutes, then reduce the heat to 325°F and roast for 25 minutes per pound–just over 2 hours. Cover with foil about two-thirds of the way through. Once the pork is cooked, remove from the oven, cover, and insulate for 30 minutes to rest. Make a light gravy, (see page 190). Serves 10.

Lechon asado Cuban roast pork. The last time I made this, I couldn't get people to sit down to eat it; they stood at the kitchen counter and pulled it from the bones. Serve with rice and–preferably–black beans, or an avocado, spinach, and orange salad. The marinade (*mojo*) is also great with roasted chicken or lamb. Dry-fry 1½ tbsp cumin seeds and 1½ tsp black peppercorns until fragrant, then grind with 6 fat garlic cloves, sea salt flakes, and 1 tbsp dried oregano until you have a paste. Stir in the juice of 1 orange and 2 limes plus 2 tbsp rum and 2 tbsp olive oil. Pierce a 4 lb bone-in pork shoulder roast all over with a sharp knife. Put into a large bowl and pour the marinade over. Cover loosely and refrigerate for 12–24 hours, turning regularly. Preheat the oven to 425°F. Lift the pork from the marinade and put into a roasting pan. Roast for 30 minutes, then reduce the heat to 325°F and roast for 1 hour 40 minutes, or until cooked through, regularly basting with pan juices and the marinade. Transfer to a carving board, cover loosely with foil, insulate and rest for 30 minutes. Pour the juices into a saucepan and skim the fat. Bring to a boil. Carve the pork and serve with the juices. Serves 6–8.

Pigs' cheeks with mustard lentils

The first time I ate pigs' cheeks was in Paris (braised, with wild mushrooms) and I just couldn't wait to get my hands on them. There's nothing squeamish about them—we are not talking piggy tails or ears, they are little medallions about the size of the fleshy bit of your palm and cook into the most tender chunks of meat. You'll have to make a special order with your butcher though.

Serves 4

FOR THE PIGS' CHEEKS

8 pigs' cheek
salt and pepper
all-purpose flour, to dust
1 tbsp sunflower or peanut oil
½ cup dry hard cider
1 cup chicken stock

FOR THE LENTILS

1 tsp butter
1 small onion, finely chopped

1 celery stalk, diced
1 carrot, diced
1 cup Puy lentils
1 thyme sprig
2 cups chicken stock
½ cup heavy cream
8 tsp Dijon mustard
chopped fresh flat-leaf parsley, to serve

1 Trim the cheeks and remove any excess fat. Drop them in seasoned flour—shaking off the excess—and heat the oil in a Dutch oven. Brown the cheeks on both sides, then add the cider and let that bubble away. Pour on the stock and bring to a boil.

2 Immediately reduce the heat to very low, cover, and simmer gently for 2 hours. Make sure the cheeks don't boil dry: add a little more water but don't drown them— you just need enough to keep the cooking ticking over. The cheeks will eventually be soft and falling apart.

3 You need to start cooking the lentils about half an hour before the pork is ready. Melt the butter and gently cook the onion, celery, and carrot until just softening but not colored. Add the lentils and stir them in the fat and cooking juices, then add the thyme and stock. Season with pepper. Bring the stock to a boil, then reduce to a simmer and leave to cook. The lentils should take 20 minutes but keep an eye on them: they should be tender but not collapsing and can go soft very quickly. The stock should all be absorbed (for this reason, there isn't too much liquid here, but make sure that the lentils don't boil dry).

4 When the lentils are cooked, add the cream and mustard, stir, and heat through. The cream will reduce as it heats. You don't want a "soupy" mixture. Adjust the seasoning. Lift the cheeks out of their cooking liquid and boil to reduce until quite syrupy. Return the cheeks to heat through. Serve with their cooking juices and the lentils, sprinkling everything with parsley.

Mexican tinga poblana

At least one up on regular chile, this uses pork shoulder and is adapted from a recipe by Mexican expert Rick Bayless. If you can't find Mexican chorizo, use another spicy sausage but add 2 tsp smoked paprika with the cumin. Chipotle chiles are smoked as well as dried.

Serves 6–8

FOR THE TINGA POBLANA
4 dried chipotle chiles
3 lb plum tomatoes, halved
olive oil
salt and pepper
1½ tsp sugar
8 oz Mexican chorizo or other spicy sausage
3 lb pork shoulder, cut into 1½ in cubes
2 onions, coarsely chopped
3 garlic cloves, crushed
1 tsp ground cumin

3 thyme sprigs
1 tsp dried oregano
about 1 cup chicken stock or water
brown sugar, to taste (optional)

TO SERVE
2 ripe avocados
juice of 1 lime
1 cup soured cream
6 oz mild soft goat cheese or feta cheese, crumbled
about 2 tbsp coarsely chopped fresh cilantro

1 Preheat the oven to 375°F. Cover the chipotles with just-boiled water and leave to soak. Put the tomatoes, cut side up, in a roasting pan where they fit in a single layer. Drizzle with oil, season, and sprinkle with sugar. Roast for 50 minutes, until soft, slightly scorched, and shrunken.

2 Remove the sausage from its casing and break into pieces. Heat 1 tbsp olive oil in a large frying pan and sauté the sausage pieces until well colored. Put into a flameproof Dutch oven, retaining the fat in the pan. Brown the pork well in this fat to a really good color (cook the pork in batches so the temperature stays high and you are frying, not steaming, the meat).

3 Remove the meat and put it in the Dutch oven, leaving behind any fat. Add a little more oil to the frying pan if needed and fry the onions to a good deep gold. Add the garlic and cumin and cook for 2 minutes more, then add to the Dutch oven with the thyme, oregano, seasoning, and enough stock or water to cover. Simmer, partially covered, over a low heat until just tender (about 50 minutes).

4 Fifteen minutes before the cooking time is up, add the tomatoes and juices into the Ducth oven. Remove the chiles from their liquid, take off the stems, and seed. Coarsely chop the flesh and add this, with the soaking liquid, to the casserole. Gently cook for 15 minutes. Check the seasoning; you may want to add a little brown sugar.

5 To serve, slice the avocados and squeeze lime juice all over them. Season. Put the meat into a large broad bowl (or leave it in the casserole) and spoon over the sour cream, add the avocado slices, then sprinkle with the cheese and cilantro. Serve with boiled rice.

Silesian heaven

Braised pork, Eastern European style. I sometimes add leeks as well (cut a couple into chunks and sauté along with the onions). Be careful to get the sweet-savory balance right: taste and alter with a little more cider vinegar or brown sugar.

Serves 4

8 oz dried fruit (apples, pears, sour
  cherries, prunes)
1 cup cold tea
1 tbsp sunflower oil
1 tbsp butter
2¼ lb boneless pork shoulder, cut into
  large cubes
1 large onion, cut into crescent
  moon-shaped slices
1 celery stalk, diced

1 tbsp pumpkin pie spice
3 tbsp all-purpose flour
salt and pepper
about ½ cup dry hard cider (optional)
1 tbsp dark brown sugar
1 tbsp cider vinegar
3 thyme sprigs
1 bay leaf
chopped fresh parsley, to serve

1 Soak the dried fruit overnight in just enough cold tea to cover. Heat the oil and butter in a large flameproof Dutch oven and brown the pork on all sides. It's best to do this in batches so it browns properly instead of sweating. Remove the pork and, in the same pan, sauté the onion and celery until soft and lightly colored. Add the pumpkin pie spice and cook for another minute. Return the pork and stir in the flour and seasoning. Cook for another minute.

2 Drain the fruit. Measure the fruit soaking liquid and make it up to 1½ cups with the hard cider, if using, or water. Add to the pork with the fruits, sugar, vinegar, thyme, and bay leaf. Season. Bring to a boil, then reduce the heat to very low. Stir well and cover. Cook gently for 1½ hours, uncovering after 1 hour so that some of the liquid can evaporate, but keep an eye on it as you don't want the mixture to become too dry. Replace the lid or add more liquid as necessary. The meat should be completely tender and melting.

3 Adjust the seasoning and sprinkle with chopped parsley. I love this with brown rice or bulgur, with Greek yogurt on the side.

Ham hock with parsley sauce and cabbage

One of my mum's dishes, this shows how worthwhile it is to try less-common cuts. It's a wonderful supper and provides great leftovers for lots of dishes.

Serves 6

FOR THE HAM

2¾ lb ham hocks
8 peppercorns
1 large carrot, cut into chunks
1 onion, quartered
2 celery stalks, chopped
1 bay leaf
handful of parsley stems, bruised

FOR THE PARSLEY SAUCE

3 cups whole milk
½ onion, sliced
small bunch of fresh flat-leaf parsley, stalks separated and leaves finely chopped

8 peppercorns
1 bay leaf
3 tbsp butter
3 tbsp all-purpose flour
salt and pepper
6 tbsp heavy cream
really generous squeeze of lemon juice
dollop of Dijon mustard (optional)

FOR THE CABBAGE

1½ lb Savoy cabbage
2¼ tbsp butter

1 Soak the hocks for 24 hours, changing the water twice.

2 Put the hocks in a large pan and cover with water. Add the other ingredients and bring to a boil. Skim and cook gently until the meat is falling off the bone. It usually takes 2–3 hours. (You can also cook this in advance and gently reheat in the stock.)

3 To make the sauce, heat the milk with the onion, parsley stems, peppercorns, and bay leaf. Bring to a boil, remove from the heat, and infuse for 15 minutes. Strain.

4 Melt the butter in a heavy saucepan and add the flour. Stir over low heat for a minute. Slowly add the infused milk, stirring to incorporate before you add more. Return to the heat. Bring to a boil, stirring, then simmer for 4 minutes. Season, add the cream, finely chopped parsley leaves, and lemon juice. Taste; you may want mustard, more lemon juice, or extra seasoning. Cover to keep warm.

5 Core and shred the cabbage. Melt the butter in a heavy saucepan, add the cabbage, season, and add 2 tbsp water. Reduce the heat to low, cover, and cook for 4 minutes, shaking. Stir, so the butter coats the cabbage. Cover, but don't let it sit for too long.

6 Remove and discard the fat from the hocks and break the meat into large pieces. Serve the ham with the parsley sauce, and the cabbage. It's also great served with boiled potatoes.

LEFTOVERS…

Break the ham into large flakes and toss with watercress, warm waxy potatoes and mustardy dressing. Make a hash (see page 151) or a stovie (see page 155) with ham instead of fish. Or add to bubble and squeak (see page 89).

Ham hock and wholegrain mustard terrine

This, served at The Potting Shed pub (attached to the Rectory Hotel in Malmesbury in Wiltshire, England), is one of the best terrines I have ever eaten and really moist. If you've never made one before it can seem a bit daunting…but just look how simple this is!

Serves 6

1 carrot

½ onion

1 celery stalk

1 large ham hock, soaked in water
   for 24 hours (see page 196)

3–4 thyme sprigs

1 bay leaf

1 garlic clove

1 star anise (optional)

1 tbsp wholegrain mustard

3 tbsp finely chopped fresh flat-leaf parsley

salt and pepper

1 Coarsely chop all the vegetables and put them in a large pan with the ham hock, thyme, bay, garlic, and star anise. Cover with water. Bring to a boil then turn the heat down low and simmer until the meat begins to fall off the bone (2–3 hours). Check the hock during this time to make sure the water is still covering it; top up as required.

2 Once it is cooked, remove the hock and leave to cool. Shred the meat with your fingers, picking through it and discarding any fat or sinew. Add the mustard and parsley.

3 Reduce the ham cooking liquor by boiling until only 1 cup remains. Add it to the meat and season to taste. Press the mixture into a terrine or small loaf tin lined with clingfilm and chill. Or, if you don't have a terrine dish, the mixture can be put into ramekins and served as "potted ham". It's best to leave it for a couple of days before eating. Serve with pickles, chutney or Piccalilli (see page 209) and good toast.

Asian pork balls with chile dipping sauce

Another spin on the meatball theme, these aren't remotely authentic but are what I make when I want to serve a selection of Asian-inspired main courses or starters. They're as good tossed with noodles and hoisin sauce as eaten with the chile sauce below and a bowl of plain rice. This recipe makes more chile sauce than you need, but I can never see the point of making enough for just 6 people. It keeps in the refrigerator for months.

Serves 6

FOR THE CHILE SAUCE

6 large fresh red chiles, 3 seeded and
   coarsely chopped
2 in fresh ginger, peeled and
   coarsely chopped
grated zest of 3 and juice of 2 limes
12 garlic cloves
1 large bunch of cilantro, leaves only
1½ cups superfine sugar
¼ cup Thai fish sauce
½ cup white wine vinegar

FOR THE PORK BALLS

2¼ lb minced pork
8 oz bacon, very finely chopped
4 garlic cloves, crushed
¾ in fresh ginger, peeled and grated
1 fresh red chile, seeded and chopped
grated zest of 1 and juice of ½ lime
3 scallions, finely chopped
3 tbsp cilantro, finely chopped
salt and pepper
peanut oil, for frying

1 First make the chile sauce. Put the chiles, ginger, lime zest and juice, garlic, and cilantro leaves into a food processor and purée into a coarse paste. Put the sugar into a heavy pan with 6 tbsp water and place on medium heat until the sugar dissolves. Increase the heat slowly and gradually boil until the syrup becomes a caramel colour. Stir in the paste, fish sauce, and vinegar and simmer for 2 minutes. Leave to cool.

2 Mix everything for the pork balls (not the oil) together in a large bowl, combining all the ingredients with your hands to make sure they get well mixed. Season well. Pull off chunks and form into balls about the size of a walnut. It is better to chill these before cooking them, otherwise they tend to fall apart, so lay them on a baking sheet, cover with plastic wrap, and refrigerate for an hour or so.

3 Heat about ½ in oil in a frying pan and cook the pork balls in batches, coloring them all over. It takes about 4 minutes, but do check you are frying them long enough for the pork in the middle to be cooked.

4 Serve with the chile sauce (or indeed a store-bought dipping sauce, such as Thai sweet chili or plum) and eat with plain boiled rice and stir-fried vegetables.

Beef and carrots in stout with parsley and horseradish dumplings

The stout mellows in the oven to a lovely deep, chocolatey flavor. You don't need potatoes, making this dish very cook-friendly. Buttered cabbage is delicious with it.

Serves 4–6

FOR THE BEEF
3 tbsp peanut or sunflower oil
2¼ lb braising beef, in large chunks
12 oz carrots, sliced
12 oz leeks, sliced
1¾ oz pearl barley
1 x 12 oz bottle stout
salt and pepper

FOR THE DUMPLINGS
½ onion, very finely chopped
1 tbsp butter
¼ cup finely chopped fresh parsley
1¾ cups fresh bread crumbs
1 large egg
3 generous tbsp creamed horseradish

1 Preheat the oven to 325°F. Heat 2 tbsp of the oil in a heavy flameproof Dutch oven and brown the meat in batches. Remove and set aside. Add the remaining oil to the pan and fry the vegetables until lightly colored, then pour in the barley.

2 Add the stout and stir to deglaze the pan. Pour in 2¾ cups water, return the meat, and season. Bring to the boil, reduce the heat, cover and put in the oven for 2 hours. Check to make sure the casserole hasn't become dry; add more water if needed.

3 Make the dumplings: sauté the onion in the butter, put into a bowl, and add the remaining ingredients. Bring the mixture together and form into 12 little golf ball-sized dumplings. The mixture will be rather loose, but persevere. Dot the dumplings on top of the beef. Cook, covered, for 20 minutes, then uncover and cook for another 10 minutes.

ALSO TRY...

Braised beef with anchovies and olives Preheat the oven to 350°F. Heat 3 tbsp olive oil in a heavy flameproof Dutch oven and brown 4½ lb braising beef, in chunks, in batches. Set aside. Add 1 tbsp more oil and fry 1 large onion, coarsely chopped; 8 garlic cloves, chopped; and 2 fennel bulbs, trimmed and diced, until dark gold. Add 12 salt-cured anchovies, drained, cook until they disintegrate, then add 1 tsp ground cinnamon. Cook for another minute. Add a bottle of red wine and stir to deglaze the pan. Return the meat and add 1 tbsp tomato paste, 2 broad strips of orange zest and the juice of 1 orange, 2 rosemary sprigs, and pepper. Bring to a boil, reduce the heat, and cover. Cook in the oven for 2 hours. Uncover, mix in 1 cup small wrinkly black olives and cook for 20–30 minutes. Chop together a small handful of fresh flat-leaf parsley, 2 garlic cloves, and the finely grated zest of 1 unwaxed lemon to make a gremolata. Stir some into the beef and sprinkle the rest on top. Serves 6.

Granny Miller's beef, potato, and parsley stew

Along with Irish stew, this was a core dish of my childhood. Funnily enough, I used to think everybody cooked it…but in fact it's a dish that only my grandmother made. It would be hard to think of a cheaper meal: you take a cheap cut of beef and add potato, celery, leek, and parsley. It's a great lunch dish on a cold Saturday.

Serves 6

2¼ lb beef shank

2 lb baking potatoes, halved or quartered, depending on size

2 celery stalks (and any celery leaves you have), coarsely chopped

2 leeks, diced

salt and pepper

⅔ cup fresh parsley, coarsely chopped

1 Put the beef into a big saucepan (big enough to hold all the vegetables later) and add enough cold water to cover. Bring to a boil, then reduce the heat, and simmer steadily for 1½ hours, or until the beef is falling off the bone. Skim from time to time. Lift the meat from its cooking liquid and leave to cool.

2 Add the potatoes to the beef stock and cook for about 30 minutes, until they start to break up (you should have a mixture of potato chunks and a soupy potato purée). Now add the celery and leeks and season really well. (There is so much potato in this it needs it.) Simmer for a further 15 minutes.

3 When the beef is cool enough to handle, remove it from the bones, discarding any fatty bits and sinew. I find using my hands is the easiest way. The meat should be in bite-sized chunks, but it doesn't have to be exact. Stir the beef into the stew with the parsley and heat it through. Check the seasoning and serve the stew in flat soup plates.

Marinated skirt steak with horseradish butter

A very interesting cut, so called for its wide, open-grained fibers that look "pleated". Ask the butcher for "outside" skirt. Properly trimmed, skirt makes a terrific steak. It benefits greatly from marinating, and this marinade is based on a recipe by the great American chef Thomas Keller. Serve medium-rare.

Serves 6

FOR THE STEAKS
½ **head of garlic**
6 thyme sprigs
2 rosemary sprigs
1 tbsp black peppercorns
⅔ **cup olive oil**

6 x 6 oz thin-cut skirt steaks
salt and pepper

FOR THE BUTTER
½ **cup butter, softened**
freshly grated horseradish

1 Bash the unpeeled garlic cloves with a rolling pin. Put the herbs, pepper, and garlic in a pan with the oil and bring to a simmer. Leave to cool. Remove excess fat and any silverskin from the meat. Put in a dish, pour the marinade over, cover, and refrigerate overnight.

2 Mash the butter with the horseradish and season. Refrigerate until firm, then work into a sausage shape and roll in parchment paper. Chill until completely firm.

3 Bring the steaks to room temperature. Lift them from the marinade and pat dry with paper towels, then lightly rub with oil. Heat a griddle or nonstick frying pan and, when it is very hot, sear the steaks on both sides for a couple of minutes, then reduce the heat and cook until done to your liking. Slice across the grain.

4 Serve the steaks with melting rounds of horseradish butter and watercress salad. Roasted regular or sweet potato wedges are great alongside.

ALSO TRY…

With soy sauce and wasabi Prepare and cook the steaks as above. Serve with bowls of soy sauce and wasabi, boiled rice, and cucumber batons.

With chimichurri Put a generous bunch of flat-leaf parsley (leaves only), 3 garlic cloves, chopped, 2 tbsp red wine vinegar, juice of ½ lime, 1 tsp each ground cumin and smoked paprika, 2 tbsp oregano leaves, and ½ cup extra-virgin olive oil into a blender and blend. Season to taste. Serve with the steaks, cooked as above.

Sandwich with horseradish cream Mix 1 heaped tbsp grated fresh horseradish with 1 cup crème fraîche, 1½ tsp Dijon mustard, and seasoning. Thinly slice 1 onion and cook over a medium heat in 2 tbsp oil. Increase the heat and cook the onion until almost crisp. Prepare and cook the steaks as above and make into baguette or sourdough sandwiches with the onion and horseradish.

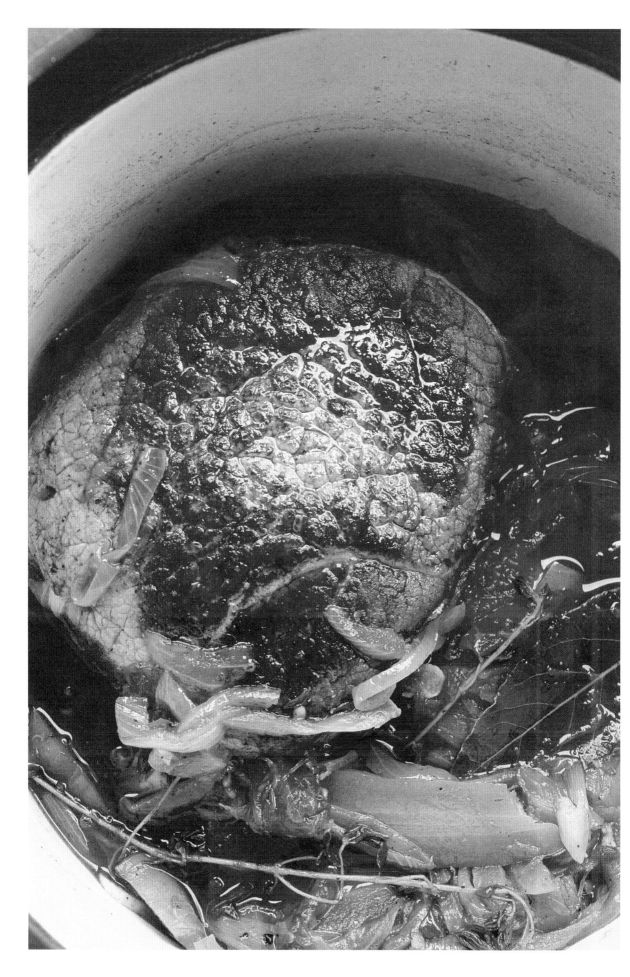

Clothilde's beef with wine, bay, and thyme

I had never eaten a pot roast until I went on an exchange to France where my opposite number, Clothilde (only 15 and a very accomplished cook) made this. A slow-cooked pot roast turns into lovely savory slices with copious amounts of juice and completely soft vegetables. Everything tastes so much of itself; it's a pure dish. My French family didn't eat this with potatoes, but with bread or a delicious gratin of macaroni. The macaroni was either moistened with juice from the pot roast or with cream, then topped with Parmesan or Gruyère cheese and baked or grilled. It makes an excellent side dish for braised beef.

Serves 4

salt and pepper

2¼ lb beef bottom round

1 tbsp peanut oil

2 onions, halved and cut into crescents

3 garlic cloves, chopped

⅔ cup dry white or red wine

4 carrots, halved lengthwise

2 plum tomatoes, quartered

3 thyme sprigs

3 bay leaves

⅔ cup chicken or beef stock

1 Preheat the oven to 275°F. Season the beef and heat the oil in a frying pan. Brown the roast well all over. Remove and put into a Dutch oven. Add the onions to the frying pan (use the same oil and don't wash out the pan) and cook until golden. Add the garlic for another couple of minutes, then add the wine and bring to a boil, scraping the pan to make sure all the flavor goes into the liquid. Put this into the Dutch oven with the beef and add the other vegetables and the herbs.

2 Heat the stock in the frying pan and pour that over, too. Season well, cover, and put into the oven for 2½ hours. The meat and vegetables should be tender. Serve from the Dutch oven, cutting the meat into thick slices.

LEFTOVERS...

Remove the meat and vegetables from the cooking juices and chop them. Reduce the cooking juices, then toss the meat, veg, and reduced juices with pasta and grated Parmesan. Chopped finely, the meat can also provide the base for a cottage pie.

ALSO TRY...

Rare roast rump Preheat the oven to 425°F. Rub a 3 lb rump roast (at room temperature) with olive oil and sprinkle with seasoning. Put in a roasting pan and roast for 30 minutes. Reduce the heat to 300°F and cook for another 25 minutes. This will give lovely rare beef; don't be tempted to cook it for longer. Take the beef from the oven, insulate, and leave to rest. Serve hot, with the usual accompaniments, or leave to cool, then refrigerate. It makes great sandwiches. Serves 8.

Oxtail with prunes and orange

Sweet, sticky, unctuous, there is no mistaking a pot of braised oxtail. I don't know why people don't cook it more, since it is the tenderest and most wonderfully flavored cut. A dish for the depths of winter.

Serves 4–6

2 oxtails, cut into 1 in lengths
salt and pepper
all-purpose flour
2½ tbsp oil
1 large onion, coarsely chopped
2 celery stalks, finely chopped
2 garlic cloves, finely chopped
1½ cups red wine
2¼ cups chicken or beef stock

juice of 1 orange and 2 broad strips of zest
½ cinnamon stick
8 juniper berries, crushed
1 bouquet garni
16 shallots or baby onions
pat of unsalted butter
2 tsp superfine sugar
16 moist prunes
2 tbsp finely chopped fresh flat-leaf parsley

1 Preheat the oven to 300°F. Wash and dry the oxtail pieces. Cut off any excess fat and toss the pieces in seasoned flour. Heat most of the oil in a heavy flameproof Dutch oven and color the oxtail all over: you need a good brown color. Remove the oxtail from the pan, add another drizzle of oil, and sauté the onion and celery until soft and golden. Add the garlic and cook for another couple of minutes, then pour on the wine and scrape up all the bits of juice that have stuck to the bottom of the pan.

2 Return the meat and add the stock, orange juice and zest, cinnamon, juniper, and bouquet garni. Season. Bring to a boil, then immediately reduce to a simmer, cover, and put in the oven for about 3 hours, or until the meat is falling off the bone. Check every so often to make sure the liquid is still just about covering the meat.

3 I like to add the baby onions and prunes 1½ hours before the end of the cooking time, otherwise they completely fall apart. To prepare the onions, fry them in the butter until golden all over, then add the sugar to caramelize the outside a little. Add these to the stew with the prunes.

4 Lift the bouquet garni and cinnamon out before serving. If you happen to see it and it hasn't disintegrated, take the zest out, too. If the juices seem a little runny, lift out the meat, small onions, and prunes and reduce the juices by boiling. Return the meat, onions, and prunes and heat through. Serve the oxtail with the parsley scattered over the top. Mashed potato seems an obvious accompaniment and is glorious but rich. I prefer to serve this stew with farro or even bulgur.

Indian beef with peas

Based on a recipe called Kheema Matar in Madhur Jaffrey's *Indian Cookery* from 1982, I've been cooking it ever since. Her family ate it lukewarm on picnics with parathas, but I serve it hot.

Serves 6

2 tbsp oil	¼ tsp cayenne
1½ lb ground beef	1¼ cups beef or chicken stock
2 onions, finely chopped	or water
6 garlic cloves, finely chopped	1 tbsp tomato paste
1 in fresh ginger, peeled and	pinch of dark brown sugar (optional)
very finely chopped	salt and pepper
2 green chiles, seeded and finely	1½ cups fresh or frozen peas
chopped	6 tbsp chopped fresh cilantro
1 tsp ground coriander	juice of 1 lime
2 tsp ground cumin	1 tsp garam masala

1 Heat the oil in a Dutch oven or sauté pan. Cook the beef over a high heat to a good brown color (in batches if your pan isn't big enough for all of it at once). A good color gives a dark, deep-tasting dish, rather than a pile of gray mush. Remove to a bowl.

2 Add the onions to the pan, reduce the heat and cook until soft and pale gold. Add the garlic, ginger, chiles, coriander, cumin, and cayenne and cook for another couple of minutes. Return the beef, add two-thirds of the stock or water, the tomato paste, sugar (if using), and seasoning and bring to a boil. Reduce the heat and cook, covered, for 30 minutes.

3 Add the peas and remaining stock or water and cook for 10 minutes more. You should have a thick mixture. If not, turn up the heat to boil off some liquid. Stir in the chopped cilantro, lime juice, and garam masala and taste. Serve with rice or warm Indian bread. Try chutney and chopped cucumber with yogurt and mint on the side.

ALSO TRY...

Picadillo Sauté 1½ lb ground beef as above. Set aside. Add 1 onion, 1 red bell pepper, and 1 green bell pepper (all chopped) to the pan and cook until soft and the onion is golden. Add 4 garlic cloves, chopped; 2 fresh red chiles, seeded and chopped; and 1½ tsp ground cumin. Cook for another minute, then add a handful of fat raisins, a 14 oz can of tomatoes in thick juice, 1 tbsp tomato paste, 1 tsp dark brown sugar, and 1 cup stock or water. Cook, uncovered, for 40 minutes, stirring occasionally. The result should be thick, like chile con carne. Add the juice of a lime, with 1 cup green olives, pitted and chopped, and seasoning. Stir in a handful of chopped fresh cilantro and sprinkle with toasted almonds. Serve with rice or warm tortillas, avocado slices, sour cream, and grated cheddar or Monterey Jack cheese.

Spiced meatballs in tomato sauce

The word "meatball" doesn't generally inspire, yet there are wonderful versions from all over the world (quite a few appear in this book). It was a plateful of chile-hot meatballs in Tuscany which alerted me to their potential. I made this shortly after and have tweaked the spicing over time. Add the chile according to taste, but don't stint on the cinnamon—it gives a lovely sweet warmth.

Serves 6

FOR THE SAUCE	FOR THE MEATBALLS
28 oz can tomatoes in thick juice	3 tbsp olive oil
1 onion, finely chopped	1 onion, finely chopped
2 garlic cloves, crushed	4 garlic cloves, crushed
leaves from 4 oregano sprigs	1 fresh red chile, seeded and chopped
1½ tsp tomato paste	2 lb ground beef
3 tbsp olive oil	1 tbsp ground cinnamon
1 tbsp light brown sugar	1 tsp freshly grated nutmeg
salt and pepper	2 tsp pumpkin pie spice
	3 tbsp finely chopped fresh parsley

1 First make the sauce. Put all the ingredients into a saucepan (no need to brown anything) and bring to a boil. Reduce to a simmer and leave to cook for 30 minutes; the sauce will thicken and the tomatoes collapse. Stir from time to time, adding a little water if needed. Taste and adjust the seasoning.

2 For the meatballs, put 1 tbsp of the oil in a pan and cook the onion until soft and pale gold. Add the garlic and chile and cook for another minute and a half. Put this into a bowl with the beef, spices, and parsley. Season really well. Pull off a little chunk and fry in some oil. Eat. This helps you decide whether you need more seasoning or spices. Form the beef into meatballs using wet hands.

3 Heat the remaining oil in a frying pan and brown the meatballs in batches. You don't need to cook them through; just color the outside. Once they are done, add to the tomato sauce and stir gently. Cook for 10–15 minutes.

4 Serve with pasta (penne or spaghetti are both good; you'll need 4 oz per person). Stir it with the sauce and meatballs in a large heated shallow bowl and serve.

ALSO TRY...

Baked meatballs with penne Preheat the oven to 350°F. Increase the tomato sauce quantities in the main recipe by half. Make the sauce and meatballs as above, then cook 12 oz penne and drain. Season the pasta and add a pat of butter. Layer in a deep gratin dish with the meatballs and sauce and 1 lb packets mozzarella cheese, sliced (reserve some). Lay the reserved slices on top and sprinkle on 1½ cups grated Parmesan. Bake for 20 minutes or until golden and bubbling.

Corned beef

I love corned beef but it seemed a lot of bother to make until I tried it. It was simple. You'll get a feast from an inexpensive cut with plenty left for sandwiches.

Serves 10, with leftovers

FOR THE BRINE
1 lb light brown sugar
3⅓ lb coarse sea salt
2 tsp black peppercorns
2 tsp juniper berries
4 cloves
4 bay leaves
2 thyme sprigs
3 tbsp saltpeter (optional)

FOR THE BEEF
6½ lb beef brisket
1 bouquet garni
1 large carrot, coarsely chopped
1 onion, coarsely chopped
1 celery stem, coarsely chopped
1 leek, cut into chunks
½ head of garlic

1 Put all the brine ingredients, with 5 quarts water, into a very large saucepan and bring to a boil, stirring. Bubble for 2 minutes. Cool completely. Put the beef in a large, crock and cover with brine. (Weigh it down if necessary.) Leave in a cool place for 7 days.

2 Take the beef from the brine and soak in fresh water for 24 hours, changing the water a couple of times. Put in a pan with the other ingredients and cover with water. Poach gently for 2½–3 hours until tender. Serve with Piccalilli (see below), and boiled potatoes.

Piccalilli

The British love this relish with their corned beef.

Makes 3 x 12 oz jars

2¼ lb vegetables, including summer squash,
   cucumber, green beans, baby onions,
   cauliflower, and carrot
3 tbsp fine salt
¼ cup cornstarch
1½ tsp English mustard powder

1 tbsp ground turmeric
1½ tsp yellow mustard seeds
1½ tsp ground ginger
1 tsp crushed coriander seeds
2½ cups cider vinegar
1 cup light brown sugar

1 Halve the summer squash and cucumber, scoop out the seeds, and cube. Trim and halve the beans. Halve the onions, break the cauliflower into florets, and cube the carrots. Layer in a large bowl, sprinkling with salt. Cover and leave for 24 hours. Rinse and drain.

2 Mix the cornstarch and spices with a little vinegar to make a paste. Put the rest of the vinegar in a saucepan with the sugar and bring to the boil, stirring to dissolve the sugar. Pour some of the liquid (about ¼ cup) over the paste, stir, and back add to the pan.

3 Bring gently to a boil so the sauce can thicken. Boil for 4 minutes. Add the vegetables, stir, and simmer for 2 minutes. Ladle into warm sterilized jars, seal, and store in the refrigerator. Leave for 4 weeks before eating.

Soup, beautiful soup

Soup is just about the most sensible dish you can make. For a start it is based on stock that you can use cooked, leftover bones to produce. Food writers are forever exhorting us to use only what is spanking fresh, but I often make soup from carrots that are getting soft, or wilted salad (vinaigrette and all, see page 216). And leftover braises are a perfect base for a warming bowlful. But soup is not dull. A pot of soup is something you hug to yourself like a secret. Hurrying home on a cold day, you can feel miserable until you remember that there is soup in the house. The prospect is as cheering as being greeted by someone you love.

In our house, soup is often made on a Sunday night and eaten over the next three days. The carcass from the Sunday-lunch chicken is thrown into a pot with onion, carrot, celery, parsley, and peppercorns; then covered with water and simmered for a few hours. (Never add salt, skim the surface when it needs it, and don't boil as it makes the stock murky.) The stock you use is paramount–your soup will only be as good as your stock–and judicious seasoning is also important, but a cooking course opened my eyes to another important element. We made a creamy vegetable soup (just leeks, potatoes, and carrots) the prospect of which didn't particularly wow me, but it was one of the loveliest I have ever tasted. Why? The slow, careful sweating of the vegetables to bring out their sweetness. Of course the butter you use adds greatly to the flavor but–in case your health alarm bells are ringing–you don't need much. Just melt enough to get the vegetables to exude their juices, cover the pan, and regularly add splashes of water to keep everything moist and stop the vegetables from sticking. In soups that are Mediterranean in tone, olive oil does the same job.

A bit of thought given to garnishes opens up new worlds, too. There is nothing wrong with a humble bowl of spiced lentil soup, but top it with yogurt and spicy fried onions and you have a wonderful interplay of hot and cold, a trip for your tastebuds. Flavored creams–such as chile for a pea and cilantro soup, for example– can take your bowl to new heights, and more gutsy embellishments, like chunks of ricotta salata or shavings of cheese, transform a plain dish into a special one.

With careful sweating of the vegetables, good stock and judicious seasoning (with soup you have to taste, taste, taste, and a good squeeze of lemon juice will often heighten and bring the flavors together more than another scattering of salt), you can make a dish that hasn't broken the bank and somehow becomes more than the sum of its parts. Soup is a perfect example of sane and feel-good cooking.

Chilled roasted tomato soup with anchovy and Parmesan toasts

Long, slow cooking brings out the flavor of tomatoes. You can also serve this hot.

Serves 8

FOR THE SOUP
5½ lb plum tomatoes, halved
½ cup olive oil
salt and pepper
1½ tbsp sugar, plus more if needed
1 large onion, finely chopped
2 garlic cloves, finely chopped

FOR THE TOASTS
16 slices baguette, about ⅓ in thick
3 tbsp butter, melted
5 tbsp grated Parmesan cheese
8 canned anchovies, halved

1 Preheat the oven to 350°F. Put the tomatoes in a roasting pan (or pans) where they can lie in a single layer. Add 6 tbsp of the oil, season, and turn to coat. Sprinkle with the sugar. Roast until soft and slightly caramelized (about 40 minutes).

2 Heat the remaining oil in a heavy pan and sauté the onion until soft but not colored. Add the garlic and sauté without browning. Add the tomatoes, their juices, and about 3¾ cups water. Bring to a boil and simmer for 10 minutes.

3 Purée in a food processor (not a blender, which crushes the seeds and makes the soup bitter), then push through a sieve. Adjust the seasoning–you may need more sugar–and add water until you have the consistency you want (it thickens considerably once cool). Refrigerate until serving.

4 To make the toasts, preheat the oven to 350°F. Brush both sides of the bread with butter and set on a baking sheet. Sprinkle with cheese and top each with a halved anchovy. Bake for 12 minutes. Serve the toasts with the chilled soup.

ALSO TRY...

With basil cream Put 1 oz basil leaves in a blender with ⅔ cup whipping cream, a little salt and white pepper, and 1 small garlic clove, chopped. Blend and taste. You might want to add a good squeeze of lemon juice.

Roast pepper soup with saffron cream Put 8 large red bell peppers in a roasting pan and drizzle with 5 tbsp olive oil. Roast in a preheated oven at 375°F for 50 minutes, or until completely soft and slightly scorched, then discard the stems and seeds and chop. Heat 3 tbsp olive oil in a saucepan and add 2 onions, chopped. Sweat, over a low heat, until soft but not colored. Add the peppers, 2 tsp hot pepper sauce, 4 cups chicken or vegetable stock and seasoning. Simmer for 5 minutes, then cool. Blend, adding 2 tbsp balsamic vinegar and the juice of 1 small lemon. Taste for seasoning and refrigerate. Meanwhile, put a generous pinch of saffron threads in a cup with 2 tbsp just-boiled water and leave to infuse. Add ⅔ cup heavy cream and mix. Serve the soup cold with a swirl of saffron cream.

Ribollita

I never liked the idea of ribollita—it is, after all, cabbage soup, and I've spent too much of my life on the cabbage soup diet—but this is a wonderful, rich, multi-dimensional dish. I learned how to make it (and how important the stock and olive oil are to the final flavour) on a cooking course in Florence. Don't rush it; make it with care and good ingredients and you will be rewarded. Made well, this is one of the world's great soups.

Serves 4

8 oz Savoy cabbage or kale
2 tbsp butter
1 leek, trimmed and chopped
1 celery stalk, finely chopped
1 large carrot, diced
4 oz waxy potatoes, diced
4 cups chicken or beef stock
¼ cup extra-virgin olive oil, plus
  more to serve

2 rosemary sprigs
3 garlic cloves
6 slices coarse white country bread,
  weighing about ¾oz each
¾ cup cooked cannellini beans
2 large plum tomatoes

1 Cut the coarse central core from the cabbage and slice the leaves. Melt the butter in a large, heavy pan and sauté the leeks and celery until pale gold, about 5 minutes. Add the carrots, cabbage or kale, and potatoes and cook for another 12 minutes, turning the vegetables over in the butter every so often. Add the stock, bring to a boil, reduce to a simmer, and cook for 45 minutes.

2 Meanwhile, heat the olive oil in a pan with the rosemary and 2 of the garlic cloves (leave them whole and unpeeled). When the oil starts to shimmer and the ingredients turn light brown, remove from the heat and leave to infuse.

3 Toast the bread and rub each piece with the remaining garlic clove (peeled, this time). Add the beans to the soup and cook for another 10 minutes.

4 Drop the tomatoes into a bowl of boiling water and leave for 10 seconds. Lift them out and rinse in cold water, then slip off the skins. Halve the tomatoes, scoop out the seeds (discard them), and cube the flesh. Add the tomatoes and flavored oil to the soup and taste for seasoning.

5 In another large saucepan, layer up the soup with the bread (break it up to help spread it out) and leave to cool. Put the soup in the refrigerator overnight. The next day, bring it to room temperature, then bring to a boil again. Serve, drizzled lavishly with more extra-virgin olive oil.

Pea and cilantro soup

Frozen peas are a great ingredient to have on hand. This is easy, has a real kick, and you can serve it hot or cold.

Serves 6–8

FOR THE SOUP
2 tbsp olive oil
2 tbsp butter
1 onion, coarsely chopped
1 potato, chopped
1½ tsp ground cumin
large bunch of cilantro
2 lb frozen peas
4 cups chicken stock
lemon juice, to taste

FOR THE CREAM
1½ tsp olive oil
2 fresh red chiles, seeded and sliced
½ cup whipping cream
juice of ½ lemon
salt and pepper
pinch of superfine sugar (optional)

1 Heat the oil and butter in a heavy pan. Add the onion and potato and stir. Add the cumin and stir for a minute to release the aroma. Chop the cilantro stems (reserve the leaves) and add them as well, stir, add a splash of water, and cover. Sweat for about 20 minutes, adding a splash of water every so often to prevent it sticking on the bottom of the pan.

2 Add the peas, stock, cilantro leaves, and seasoning and bring to a boil. Simmer for 3 minutes, then leave to cool. When at room temperature, purée in a blender and add lemon juice to taste.

3 To make the cream, heat the olive oil and sauté the chiles until soft. Put into a blender and add the cream, lemon juice, and a bit of salt. Blend briefly until broken down. Add a little water to thin it out (it should be able to float on the soup but not be in thick blobs). Check the seasoning. You might think it needs the tiniest pinch of sugar. Reheat the soup before serving (or serve cold) and garnish with the cream.

ALSO TRY...

Pea and ham soup Cook the soup as above but use stock made from a ham bone (ensure the stock isn't too salty–dilute with water if it is). Serve with a swirl of cream and flakes of cooked ham on top.

Pea soup with mint oil Make the soup as above, but omit the cumin and the cilantro; this must have a pure pea flavor. To make the oil, put ½ cup mild olive oil, the leaves from 4 large mint sprigs, ¼ tsp superfine sugar, and a good squeeze of lemon juice in a blender and blend. Cover and refrigerate to let the flavors infuse. Strain through a sieve and taste. Serve spoonfuls on top of the soup. Mint oil is also delicious drizzled over seared salmon fillets, or with griddled squid and chorizo. It must be eaten on the day it's made, or it loses its fresh color and flavor.

Cool lettuce and herb soup

Probably, like me, you hate throwing out leftover dressed salad. This is what to do with it.

Serves 4
3 tbsp butter
8 scallions, chopped
about 4 small heads butter lettuce, or
    romaine hearts, plus leftover dressed salad
    (including cucumber and tomato)
small bunch of soft herbs (mint, basil,
    or chervil)

4 cups warm chicken stock
salt and pepper
good squeeze of lemon juice
2 tbsp heavy cream or crème fraîche
    (optional)

1 Melt the butter in a heavy pan and sweat the scallions for 5 minutes, until completely soft. Trim the base of each lettuce, then slice it and add to the onions with the leftover salad (including vinaigrette). Heat until the lettuce wilts.

2 Add the herbs and stock. Season, then blend. Taste, add lemon juice, seasoning, and the cream or crème fraîche, if you want. Chill. This is lovely with a spoonful of vinaigrette on top and a sprinkling of the herb you have used.

ALSO TRY…

With tomato, mint and basil relish Make the lettuce soup as above and chill. Halve 4 oz cherry tomatoes and seed half (I like some seeds, but it shouldn't be too watery). Chop into small chunks. Put in a bowl and add 2 tbsp torn basil, 2 tbsp chopped fresh mint, 3 tbsp extra-virgin olive oil, 1 tsp white wine vinegar, a pinch of sugar, a squeeze of lemon juice, and seasoning. Serve spooned on the lettuce soup.

Hungarian iced cucumber and dill soup Melt 3 tbsp butter in a heavy saucepan and add 1 onion, chopped. Cook gently for 4 minutes, add a splash of water, and sweat over a low heat, covered, for 15 minutes, until soft but not colored. You will need another splash of water. Add 2 cucumbers, peeled and diced, and ⅓ cup diced potato, and cook for a couple of minutes; then stir in 1½ tbsp flour. Cook for 2½ minutes, stirring, then add 1½ cups chicken stock and season. Bring to a boil, reduce to a simmer, and cook for 15 minutes. Cool, then purée with ½ cup fresh dill, a squeeze of lemon juice, and 1 cup milk. Taste. You may want more lemon or seasoning. Add ¼ cup crème fraîche or sour cream and taste again. Chill. Serve garnished with sprigs of dill.

Cucumber, dill, and shrimp soup Make as for Hungarian Iced Cucumber and Dill Soup (see above), but purée some cooked shrimp in the soup and serve more on top, with sour cream and dill.

Cucumber, dill, and smoked trout soup As above, but purée smoked trout, not prawns, in the soup and top with more flakes, the sour cream, and dill to serve.

Soup Savoyarde

There are many versions of this vegetable soup enriched with cheese, which melts into long strings. A great soup for keeping out the cold.

Serves 6–8

3–6 tbsp butter

1 large or 2 medium leeks, cut into rounds

2¾ cups chopped carrots

1½ cups chopped parsnips

1 small potato, cut into chunks

salt and pepper

4 cups chicken stock

1 cup whole milk

6–8 slices rustic country bread

1–1¼ cups grated Gruyère cheese

1 Melt the butter in a large, heavy saucepan and add the vegetables, salt, and pepper. Turn everything around in the butter to coat. Add a good splash of water, cover the pan, and set over a low heat. Sweat the vegetables for 35 minutes to bring out their sweetness, adding a splash of water every so often.

2 Add the stock, season, and bring to a boil. Simmer for about 15 minutes; the vegetables should be completely soft. Leave to cool before pureeing (blending hot soup is very dangerous), then pour into a clean pan. Heat and add milk to taste (you may want to add more, or a little water). Adjust the seasoning.

3 To serve, lightly toast the bread and put a slice in the bottom of each bowl. Put the cheese on top then add the hot soup. Serve immediately.

ALSO TRY...

Soups made with roots and pulses are just about the least expensive you can make and are deeply comforting. Using the recipe above as a blueprint, you can make a soup based only on leeks and potatoes; or on parsnips (good with a little curry powder, which you cook for a minute with the vegetables once they are soft); or with carrot and potato (classically called *potage Crécy*); or Jerusalem artichokes (no need to peel). They are simple soups but, if you sweat the vegetables to bring out their optimum flavor and taste and season well, they can be some of the most satisfying things to eat.

Moroccan lentil soup with yogurt and chile-fried onions

If you don't want to make the chile onions, add 2 chopped, seeded fresh chiles to the soup, or some harissa to taste, instead.

Serves 8

FOR THE SOUP
3 tbsp olive oil
1 onion, finely chopped
2 stalks celery, finely chopped
3 garlic cloves, finely chopped
1 tbsp ground cumin
1½ tsp ground coriander
2 tsp ras al hanout (available online)
1½ cups red lentils
14 oz can chopped tomatoes
4¼ cups chicken stock or water
salt and pepper

6 tbsp fresh cilantro, coarsely chopped,
    plus extra to garnish

FOR THE CHILE-FRIED ONIONS
2 onions, very thinly sliced
2 tbsp olive oil
½ tsp ground cinnamon
2 tsp brown sugar
1 fresh red chile, seeded and finely chopped
juice of ½ small lemon

TO SERVE
Greek yogurt

1 Heat the oil in a heavy pan and sauté the onion and celery until soft but not colored. Add the garlic and spices and cook for 1 minute, then add the remaining soup ingredients apart from the coriander. Bring to a boil, reduce to a simmer, and cook for 30 minutes, or until the lentils become a purée. Season and stir in the chopped cilantro.

2 To make the chilli-fried onions, quickly fry the sliced onions in very hot olive oil until golden brown with crispy bits. Add the cinnamon, sugar, and chile. Stir and, once the sugar has melted, add the lemon juice and season. Serve the soup in hot bowls with a dollop of yogurt and the chilli-fried onions. Garnish with coriander leaves.

ALSO TRY...

Ham and lentil soup with caraway Make following the method above but omit the spices, celery, garlic, tomatoes, and chile-fried onions. Cook 2 onions, 1 potato, 2 carrot (all chopped) and 1 cup lentils in oil. Replace the chicken stock with 6 cups stock made from a ham bone (make sure it isn't too salty; dilute with water if it is). Sauté flakes of ham or chunks of bacon in butter, adding 2 tsp caraway seeds. Sprinkle on top of the soup, with a swirl of cream, if you like.

Lentil and spinach soup Heat 3 tbsp olive oil in a heavy pan and gently cook 1 onion, chopped, and 1 celery stalk, diced, for 8 minutes. Add 2 garlic cloves, chopped, and ½ tsp dried red pepper flakes and cook for 1 minute. Add 1⅛ cups brown lentils, 3 tomatoes, chopped, 2 thyme sprigs, and 4 cups water or chicken stock. Bring to a boil, reduce the heat, cover, and cook until tender—about 45 minutes—topping up if it's too thick. Season well. Shred 10 oz spinach and add to the soup to wilt. Add the juice of ½ lemon and stir in 4 tbsp extra-virgin olive oil. Serves 4.

Ethiopian spiced pumpkin soup (*d'ba zigni*)

This, based on a recipe by food writer Celia Brooks Brown, is a cracking soup: sweet, warming, and great for clearing the sinuses. You will have more spice blend than you need here, but keep it in a screw-top jar and use when you want a bit of heat.

Serves 4

FOR THE BERBERE (Ethiopian hot spice powder)

2 tsp cumin seeds
8 cloves
1 tsp cardamom seeds
½ tsp black peppercorns
1 tsp fenugreek seeds
1 tsp coriander seeds
8 small dried red chiles
½ tsp ground ginger
¼ tsp ground allspice
¼ tsp ground turmeric
1 tsp salt
¼ tsp ground cinnamon
3 tbsp paprika

FOR THE SOUP

2 tbsp sunflower oil
1 large onion, finely chopped
2 in fresh ginger, peeled and
   finely chopped
1½ lb pumpkin or winter squash, peeled,
   seeds and fibers discarded, and cut
   into chunks
3 tbsp tomato paste
1 tsp salt

TO SERVE

Greek yogurt
small bunch of cilantro

1 To make the berbere, toast the cumin, cloves, cardamom, peppercorns, fenugreek, coriander, and chiles in a dry frying pan over a medium heat for about 2 minutes to release the aroma. Shake the pan often. Cool, then grind to a fine powder in a pestle and mortar with the ginger, allspice, turmeric, salt, cinnamon, and paprika.

2 Heat a saucepan over a medium heat and add the oil. Cook the onion until quite soft and pale gold, then stir in the fresh ginger and 2 tsp of the berbere and cook for 2 minutes. Add the pumpkin and coat with the spices. Add the tomato paste, salt, and 2½ cups water. Stir, cover, and bring to a boil.

3 Simmer for 15–20 minutes, or until the pumpkin is soft. If you prefer the soup thicker, remove a few pieces of pumpkin and mash them, then return to the pot. Check for seasoning and serve with Greek yogurt (not authentic but good) and torn cilantro.

ALSO TRY…

Pumpkin, bean, and spinach soup Make as above but omit the berbere and fresh ginger and use 4 cups well-flavored chicken stock instead of water. When the pumpkin is soft, 1¼ cups cooked and rinsed cannellini or borlotti beans or chickpeas. Heat through and add 10oz shredded spinach to wilt. Check the seasoning. If you have used beans, serve with grated Parmesan cheese or Parsley and walnut Pesto (see page 228). Fried chunks of pancetta are good, too. If you have used chickpeas, mix 2 tbsp harissa with boiling water, spoon yogurt on top of the soup, and drizzle with the harissa.

Black bean soup with "pico de gallo"

You can make this warming Mexican soup more of a main course by serving with slices of avocado, sour cream or grated cheese, torn cilantro leaves, and a squeeze of lime.

Serves 6

FOR THE SOUP

1⅓ cups dried black beans
3 tbsp olive oil
4 oz streaky bacon, chopped
1 onion, finely chopped
1 small carrot, chopped
1 celery stalk, plus leaves, finely chopped
stems from ½ oz bunch cilantro
½ small fresh red chile, seeded and
  chopped
2 tsp cumin seeds
3 garlic cloves, chopped
4 cups chicken stock
salt and pepper
juice of ½ lime

FOR THE PICO DE GALLO

2 tbsp finely diced red onion
1 lb tomatoes, chopped
1 fresh red chile, halved, seeded, and
  finely chopped
2 tsp superfine sugar
2 tbsp finely chopped fresh cilantro
juice of 1 lime
2 tbsp lager
salt

TO SERVE

sour cream
grated cheddar or Monterey Jack cheese
  (optional)

1 Cover the beans with water and leave to soak overnight. Drain and rinse. Heat the oil in a heavy pan and cook the bacon for about 5 minutes. Reduce the heat and add the onion, carrot, celery, cilantro stems, and chile. Stir. Add 3 tbsp water and cover the pan. Leave to sweat for about 10 minutes. The vegetables should be quite soft.

2 Toast the cumin in a dry pan, then grind with a pestle and mortar and add to the pan with the garlic. Cook for 2 minutes, then add the beans and stock. Bring to a boil, reduce the heat, and simmer for 1½ hours. The beans should be tender. Season, then cool. Purée in a blender or food processor. Add the lime juice and check the seasoning.

3 To make the pico de gallo, mix everything together. Cover and refrigerate for 30 minutes before serving. Serve the soup hot, with a swirl of sour cream and a spoon of pico de gallo. Add cheese if you like. Serve the remaining pico de gallo on the side.

ALSO TRY...

Black bean soup with avocado salsa Make the soup as above, but without the pico de gallo. Mix the following ingredients together not more than an hour before serving: 8oz tomatoes and 2 avocados, both diced; 1 tsp ground cumin; 2 garlic cloves and 2 scallions, both finely chopped; 2 fresh red chiles, seeded and thinly sliced; the juice of ½ lime; 2 handfuls of chopped cilantro; ¼ cup extra-virgin olive oil; Tabasco to taste; and seasoning. Cover and let the flavors infuse. Serve spooned on the soup with sour cream and chopped cilantro.

Beet soup with goat cheese

Beets are very sweet so they need something tart, hence the apples. The slightly sour, farmyardy flavor of goat cheese is perfect against that sweetness and completely elevates an inexpensive soup (just look at the beauty of it for a start). A swirl of sour cream or Greek yogurt and a scattering of dill is lovely, too. You can also serve this hot.

Serves 8

¼ cup butter
2 onions, chopped
2 carrots, chopped
2 celery stalks, chopped
6 garlic cloves, chopped
1¾ lb beets, trimmed and sliced

1 small tart or Granny Smith apple, peeled, cored and sliced
6 cups chicken stock
salt and pepper

TO SERVE
sour cream
dill sprigs
4 oz mild goat cheese

1 Melt the butter in a large, heavy saucepan and add the onions, carrots, celery, and garlic. Add a splash of water, cover, and sweat for 15 minutes, until the onions are soft. Add the beets (I don't bother to peel them) and apple, cover, and sweat for 15 minutes. Pour on the stock and season. Bring to a boil, then simmer until the beets are completely tender. Leave to cool, then purée.

2 Serve hot or cold with a dollop of sour cream on top and dill sprigs, then crumble the goat cheese and add some to each serving.

ALSO TRY…

Beet soup with salmon Make the soup as above and garnish with sour cream, sprigs of dill, and flaked leftover cooked salmon, or, if you have a piece of raw salmon, cut the flesh into tiny dice, moisten with a little light-tasting olive oil and lemon juice; add salt, pepper, and chopped dill and spoon onto the soup along with sour cream.

Parsnip and smoked haddock soup

The saltiness of the fish is lovely against the sweet parsnips. This is also very good–
and makes a complete meal–with a poached egg on top.

Serves 6

2½ tbsp butter
1 onion, chopped
3 garlic cloves, finely chopped
1¾ lb parsnips, chopped
3 cups light chicken stock or water
1¾ lb smoked, undyed haddock
  fillet, skinned

1 tbsp ground cumin
salt and pepper
⅔ cup milk or heavy cream, plus more
  to serve
1 tbsp chopped chives or fresh
  flat-leaf parsley

1 Melt the butter in a heavy pan and add the onion, garlic, and parsnips. Stir to coat
in butter, then add a splash of water and reduce the heat. Cover and sweat over a very
low heat for 20 minutes. You will need to add a splash of water every so often to keep
the vegetables from sticking.

2 Put half the stock or water into a sauté pan and bring to a boil. Reduce the heat and
poach the fish in this liquid until just cooked (about 5 minutes). Drain off and reserve
the poaching liquor. Break the fish into big flakes, being careful to remove any
remaining bones. Once it is cool, refrigerate.

3 Stir the cumin into the parsnips and cook for 1 minute. Season (go easy on the salt),
add the fish poaching liquor, the remaining stock or water, and bring to a boil. Reduce
to a simmer and cook until the parsnips are completely soft. Leave to cool.

4 Purée the soup, add the milk or cream and fish and check the seasoning. Reheat
gently before serving. Sprinkle with chives or parsley and add a swirl of cream to
each bowl.

ALSO TRY...

Smoked haddock, bacon, and lima bean chowder Melt 2 tbsp butter in a large,
heavy pan and fry 4 oz bacon, chopped, until golden. Add 2 leeks, cut into rings and
well washed, and a splash of water, cover, and sweat over a medium heat until soft
(15 minutes). At the same time put 1 lb smoked haddock into a pan and cover with
1¾ cups milk. Bring to a boil, then reduce the heat immediately and let the fish
poach gently for about 5 minutes. Add 2½ cups chicken stock and ½ cup cooked and
rinsed lima beans to the leeks. Break the fish in the milk into large flakes (remove the
skin if there is any), then add the milk and fish to the leeks and beans. Season with
pepper (you shouldn't need salt), add 2 tbsp cream, if you have it, and heat through.
Serve in warmed bowls with chopped parsley on top. Serves 4.

Chicken, coconut, and ginger soup with lime, basil, and mint

Practically a pantry soup. You can use cold pork instead of chicken and change the herbs, using just basil or mint alone, or cilantro.

Serves 8

1 large onion, sliced into crescent moon-shaped slices
¼ cup peanut oil
1 in square of fresh ginger, peeled and finely chopped
4 fresh red chiles, seeded and finely chopped
4 garlic cloves, finely chopped
4¼ cups chicken stock

2 x 14 oz cans coconut milk
12 oz small waxy potatoes, halved
1 tbsp fish sauce
1 tbsp light brown sugar
juice of 2 limes
1 eggplant, cut into chunks
1¾ cups chunked cooked chicken
¼ cup fresh basil leaves
2½ tbsp fresh mint leaves

1 Sauté the onion in half the oil until just coloring. Add the ginger, chile, and garlic and cook for 1 minute. Add the stock and bring to a boil. Reduce the heat to a simmer and stir in the coconut milk. Add the potatoes, fish sauce, sugar, and half the lime juice. Simmer until the potatoes are just cooked (about 12 minutes).

2 Sauté the eggplant in the remaining oil until golden, then add to the soup while the potatoes are still cooking. Add the chicken and heat thoroughly. Tear in the basil and mint and add the remaining lime juice. Taste—it shouldn't need anything—and serve.

ALSO TRY...

Winter squash and coconut soup Cut 4½ lb peeled winter squash into chunks, and put into a roasting pan. Drizzle with ¼ cup oil and seasoning. Roast in a preheated oven at 400°F for 20–25 minutes, until tender and slightly caramelized. Heat 2 tbsp oil in a large saucepan and gently cook 2 onions and 2 celery stalks, both coarsely chopped, until soft but not colored. Add 2 garlic cloves, crushed; 1 red chile, seeded and finely sliced; ½ in fresh ginger, peeled and chopped; and cook for another 2 minutes. Add the squash, 4 cups chicken stock, seasoning, and 2 x 14 oz cans coconut milk. Bring to a boil and simmer so everything can heat through and the flavors can meld. Leave to cool, then purée. Reheat and add the finely grated zest of 1 lime and the juice of 2, 1½ tsp fish sauce, and 2 tbsp light brown sugar. Taste for seasoning. Stir in torn basil and mint leaves.

Shrimp, winter squash, and coconut soup Make as for Winter Squash and Coconut Soup, but stir in some shrimp—cooked or raw—at the end. Cooked shrimp need only heating through; raw shrimp will cook in 3 minutes or so.

Sweet potato and coconut soup Make Winter Squash and Coconut Soup (above), replacing the winter squash with peeled sweet potato.

Swedish spinach soup with egg butter balls

The egg butter balls melt deliciously into the soup.

Serves 6

FOR THE BUTTER BALLS
½ cup butter
yolks of 3 hard-boiled eggs
salt and pepper

FOR THE SOUP
2 tbsp butter
1 onion, finely chopped

¼ cup long-grain white rice
4 cups chicken stock
1¼ lb spinach
⅔ cup heavy cream
juice of ½ lemon

1 Make the butter balls first. Mash the butter and yolks together (use the egg whites for egg mayonnaise sandwiches) and season. Roll into 1 in balls, put on a plate, cover with plastic wrap, and refrigerate.

2 For the soup, melt the butter in a large saucepan and sweat the onion, covered, over a low heat. Add a splash of water and make sure the pan doesn't get dry. The onions take 10 minutes to become soft but not colored. Add the rice and stock and bring to a boil. Simmer for 15 minutes. Add the spinach, pressing and turning as it wilts. Bring to a boil, season, and cook for 6 minutes, stirring. Cool.

3 Purée in a blender and add the cream. Return to a saucepan to heat, add a squeeze of lemon juice and taste for seasoning. Serve hot with the butter balls on top.

ALSO TRY...

Spinach soup with Thai butter Make the soup as above but use an extra ⅔ cup stock instead of cream. To make the Thai butter, mash ⅓ cup slightly softened butter with 4 heaped tbsp finely chopped fresh cilantro, 1 garlic clove, crushed, the finely grated zest and juice of ½ lime, 2 tsp fish sauce, ½ tsp ground ginger, and pepper. Mix in 1 fresh red chile, seeded and very finely chopped. Chill and serve in melting chunks on the hot soup.

Spring greens and roast garlic soup Preheat the oven to 375°F. Put 3 heads of garlic in a small roasting pan, drizzle with olive oil, and season. Pour in a little water and roast for 40–50 minutes until tender. Melt 2½ tbsp butter in a large heavy saucepan and gently cook 1 onion, 2 bunches scallions, and 8 oz potato, all chopped. Stir to coat in the butter, then add a splash of water, cover, reduce the heat, and sweat for 15 minutes. Remove the tough ribs from 1 lb spring greens and slice the leaves. Add to the pot with a splash of water and seasoning. Stir, cover, and sweat for 10 minutes. When the garlic is cooked, squeeze the soft pulp from each clove. Add this and 4½ cups chicken stock to the soup and bring to a boil. Cool. Purée. Check the seasoning. Serve hot, with a drizzle of cream on top, if you like. Serves 8.

Cold weather soupe au pistou

I often make *soupe au pistou* (see below) in summer. I missed it during autumn and winter, so I adapted it using cold weather vegetables and wintry pesto.

Serves 8

FOR THE SOUP

4 generous tbsp olive oil
1 onion, finely chopped
1 large carrot, chopped
1 celery stalk, finely chopped
1 leek, sliced
8 oz peeled butternut squash, cubed
1 small fennel bulb, sliced
1 potato (about 6 oz), in small chunks
salt and pepper

8 cups chicken or vegetable stock
14 oz can cannellini or borlotti beans

FOR THE PESTO

½ cup walnuts
6 tbsp pine nuts
1 garlic clove, crushed
½ cup fresh flat-leaf parsley leaves
⅔ cup extra-virgin olive oil
⅔ cup grated Parmesan cheese

1 Heat the oil in a large, heavy saucepan. Add the onion and carrot and sauté for 5 minutes. Add the other vegetables, season, and sauté for 10 minutes. Pour in the stock and simmer for 5 minutes. Drain and rinse the beans. Add and cook for 5 minutes.

2 To make the pesto put the nuts, garlic, and parsley into a food processor with seasoning and half the oil. Pulse to blend, then stir in the remaining oil and the Parmesan. Top the soup with spoonfuls of pesto, serving the rest alongside.

LEFTOVERS...

Parsley and walnut pesto is great with spaghetti (add chunks of ricotta salata to make it go further). It's also good with pasta, goat cheese, and fried radicchio.

ALSO TRY...

Summer soupe au pistou Gently cook 1 leek, 1 large potato, and 1 celery stalk, all chopped, in olive oil for 5 minutes, stirring. Add 4½ cups chicken stock, season, and cook for 10 minutes. Add 2 zucchini, chopped; 8 oz green beans, trimmed; 1¼ cups cooked drained navy beans; and 12 cherry tomatoes, quartered. Cook for 5 minutes, uncovered, then add 2 tbsp chopped parsley. Put 2 bunches basil, 3 garlic cloves, salt, and pepper in a blender, process and add ½ cup extra-virgin olive oil. Top the soup with spoonfuls of pistou and grated Parmesan. Serves 4–6.

Hot-and-sour soup Put 2 lemon grass stalks, shredded and 1in fresh ginger, finely chopped; 2 shallots, sliced; 6 scallions, chopped; 3 fresh red chiles, seeded and finely sliced; and 4 kaffir lime leaves into 3 qt chicken stock. Simmer for 10 minutes. Add 4 oz cups oyster mushrooms, sliced; 3½ cups shredded cooked chicken, 2 tbsp fish sauce, and 2 tsp light brown sugar and gently heat for about 3 minutes. Stir in ⅔ cup chopped fresh cilantro and the juice of ½ lime. Taste. Add more lime juice, sugar, fish sauce, or chile, to taste. Serves 6.

Where the wild things are

The idea of wild food has become more appealing over the last few years. It's free, it forms part of our increasing attachment to the countryside and concern for the planet, and it fits in with an idealized, somewhat romantic notion of a rural "lifestyle." There are pluses in the first two parts of that sentence, but a negative in the last. Foraging is the ecologically aware foodie's badge of honor. It is "fashionable," and that's always a worry, as it suggests a fleeting and insincere fad. So listen up. You don't need to take special classes, own a crumbling farmhouse, or tote a gun to enjoy wild food. I have never shot an animal, but I've always eaten "wild food," even though I didn't look at it that way.

Every year I go blackberry picking (one of the greatest seasonal pleasures of my childhood). I track down rosehips to make syrup, and I stand at the bottom of trees while nimbler friends chuck down crab apples. If you live in, or can get to, the countryside, you can pick blackberries, crab apples, rosehips, elderflowers, nettles, sorrel, wild garlic, and arugula, among many other free delights.

Apart from the fact that it's free, why bother with wild food? Well, it seems mad—almost wasteful—not to use a resource that is just sitting there. I find it hard to look at blackberries that have rotted in the hedgerow. Nettles and wild garlic are abundant. Why leave those crab apples on the branch when they can be turned into a jelly to accompany six months' worth of roast pork? But the most compelling reason is that it's a huge pleasure—a thrill, in fact—to gather wild stuff. You are literally getting your hands dirty, often stained and scratched as well, as you try to reach a particularly hard-to-get-at cluster of blackberries, or another handful of wet, heady garlic leaves. And it feels great to take the lid off some pot-roasted rabbit and know you have cooked meat that is just out there for the taking.

I haven't covered wild mushrooms in this chapter because it takes special knowledge to gather them (and avoid poisoning yourself), and those collected by others are very expensive. Game, on the other hand, if you shoot it yourself or have a friend who does, costs nothing.

The greens—wild garlic leaves, arugula, and sorrel—can be found in April and May and nettles (use only the young shoots) in March and April; fragrant elderflower blossoms are everywhere (once you can identify them you'll realize) for six weeks from the beginning of June; blackberries are around in August and September; crab apples in September and October; and rosehips in October and November. Abundance is yours. Fill your boots.

Wild greens soup

You really need to gather the nettles when they are young, otherwise the leaves are coarse and the flavor much less pleasant. The sting goes out of nettles as soon as they are heated. You can also make this soup partly with lettuce or spinach, but making it with nettles feels, well, as if you are really cooking and getting your hands dirty. It's really good with the addition of butter balls (see page 227).

Serves 6

½ plastic grocery bag of young nettles (about 1½ lb), or nettles with other wild leaves, such as sorrel or wild arugula
¼ cup butter
1 large onion, finely chopped
1 large carrot, diced
2 large garlic cloves, crushed
3½ tbsp long-grain white rice
4 cups well-flavored chicken stock

salt and black pepper
freshly grated nutmeg
juice of ½ lemon
½ cup heavy cream, plus more to serve

TO SERVE
heavy cream and snipped chives or sour cream and goat cheese (optional)

1 Go through the nettles, discarding any really tough stems. Wash the nettles and other leaves thoroughly. Melt the butter in a large pan and sweat the onion and carrot until soft but not colored. Add the garlic and cook for another minute or so, then add the rice and stir around. Add the stock and simmer for 10 minutes to cook the rice; then add the nettles, pushing them down into the pot (they will wilt a lot and reduce). Bring to a boil and simmer for 5–10 minutes, until the nettles are really tender. Season.

2 Allow to cool, then pureé the soup in a blender. Pour back into a saucepan, heat through, and add the nutmeg, lemon, and cream. Stir everything together well and taste for seasoning.

3 Serve with an extra swirl of cream on top and some snipped chives, or a dollop of sour cream and crumbled goat cheese.

Wild garlic and goat cheese omelet

I remember the day I first came across wild garlic. I was visiting a stately old home with huge gardens in Gloucestershire, England, and I couldn't understand what the smell was. Now I make forays to the countryside just to collect it. The leaves have a lovely, subtle garlic flavor which an omelet shows off perfectly. Leave out the goat cheese if you want a pure garlic experience.

Serves 2

good handful of wild garlic leaves (about 2 oz)
salt and pepper

4 large eggs, lightly beaten
2 tbsp butter
2 oz goat cheese, crumbled

1 Shred the garlic leaves finely. Season the eggs. Heat half the butter in a nonstick frying pan. Add half the wild garlic and wilt for about 20 seconds, then add half the eggs. Leave for about 15 seconds, then tilt the pan, gently scraping up the bits of the omelet that have set around the edges into the middle of the pan, allowing the uncooked eggs to run into the spaces left behind.

2 When the omelet is still liquid on top but set underneath, put half the cheese on one half. Fold the other half over the filling, let the cheese melt for 20 seconds or so, then turn the omelet out on to a plate (preferably warmed, but we live in the real world, and not many people heat a plate for an omelet.)

3 Repeat with the rest of the ingredients to make another omelet. Serve immediately.

Pheasant with beer, carrots, and honey

If you hunt yourself, or have friends who do, you have access to delicious food that is also free. Pheasant can either be mildly flavored or pretty strong (depending on how long it has hung) but it is very approachable, even by those who aren't big game lovers. Think in terms of a well-flavored chicken. There is anxiety about cooking it as it tends to be dry, but pot roasting is perfect and very simple. The following recipes go well with something gutsy, like a dish of barley (see page 126). Some recipes suggest that one pheasant feeds four. Not in my house....

Serves 2 greedy people

2 tbsp butter
1 oven-ready pheasant
1 large onion, sliced into thin,
    crescent moon-shaped slices
2 oz bacon, chopped
6 medium carrots

salt and pepper
12 oz bottle beer
1½ tbsp honey
4 thyme sprigs, plus the leaves from 1 more
    to serve

1 Preheat the oven to 375°F. Melt the butter in a heavy flameproof Dutch oven (a small one, that will just fit the bird) and brown the pheasant all over on a medium heat. Lift out and set aside.

2 Add the onion and the bacon to the pot and cook it over a medium heat until the onion is soft and pale gold, about 5 minutes. Add the whole carrots and stir them around in the buttery juices. Put the pheasant back in the pot, with any of the juices that have run out of it. Season; add the beer, honey, and thyme and bring to a boil. Cover the pot tightly and put into the oven for 40 minutes, removing the lid for the last 15 minutes. Baste the bird a few times while cooking (pheasant can dry out very easily, so you need to keep it moist). Push a skewer into the thickest part of the thigh; if there are any pink juices put it back in the oven for a few minutes longer.

3 Sprinkle over some more thyme leaves and serve at the table in its cooking pot.

ALSO TRY...

Pheasant with red wine and sour cherries Boil 2 cups red wine and 1 cup stock, separately, until they are reduced by half. Set aside. As in the main recipe above, brown the pheasant in butter, then remove it and sauté 2 onions. Add 2 garlic cloves, chopped, and sauté for another 2–3 minutes. Put the pheasant back, along with any juices that may have run out of it, and add the wine and stock, 3 thyme sprigs, a bay leaf, a 2 in cinnamon stick, seasoning, and ⅔ cup dried sour cherries. Add a slug of port if you have any lurking. Continue to cook as above. If it looks as if there is too much juice at the end, remove the pheasant, boil the juices so they reduce, then return the pheasant to heat through.

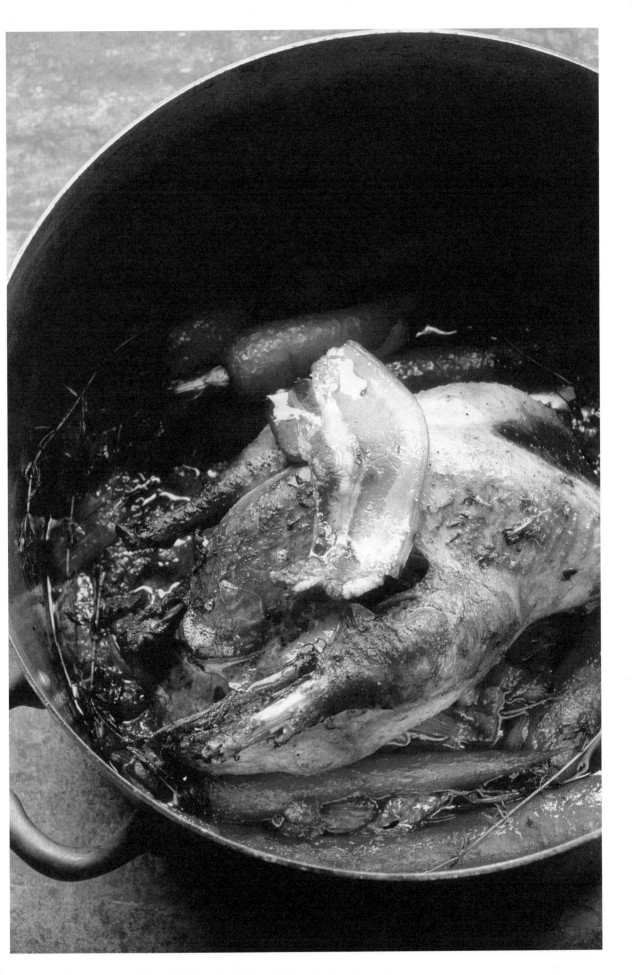

Pheasant with cider and apples As for Pheasant with Beer (see page 234), brown the pheasant, then remove, and sauté 1 onion, sliced, and 3 oz bacon, chopped. Put the pheasant back on top of these and add 1¼ cups dry hard cider. Bring to a boil, season, add 4 thyme sprigs, reduce the heat, and cook as on page 234. While waiting for the pheasant to finish cooking, sauté 2 tart apples (cored and cut into wedges) in 1 tbsp unsalted butter, sprinkling with a little sugar once, until just soft. When the pheasant is cooked, remove it from the pan, cover with foil, and keep warm in a low (300°F) oven. Quickly bring the juices to a boil and add ½ cup heavy cream and 2 tsp Dijon mustard. Boil until the juices coat the back of a spoon. Check the seasoning. Put the apples and pheasant into the sauce and heat through. Serve in the pot.

Pheasant with Savoy cabbage and bacon As for Pheasant with Beer (see page 234), brown the pheasant in butter and set it aside. Add 2 tbsp olive oil to the pan, 6 shallots, peeled and sliced, 1 carrot, and 1 stalk celery, both diced, and 4 oz bacon, chopped. Cook until golden, then add 1 small Savoy cabbage, shredded, 6 juniper berries, crushed, and another 3 tbsp butter. Season and turn the cabbage to get it coated in butter (don't worry if it seems like a lot of cabbage–it shrinks considerably). Add a scant cup chicken stock and 3 thyme sprigs and bring to a boil. Immediately reduce the heat to low, return the pheasant to the casserole, cover, and cook as on page 234.

Georgian pheasant with tea, grapes, and hazelnuts Toast ¼ cup blanched hazelnuts until pale gold, then pound coarsely (use a mortar and pestle or put the nuts in a bag and bash with a rolling pin) so some are ground and others in chunks. Cover ⅔ cup raisins with ¾ cup cold tea and bring to a boil. Remove from the heat and leave to plump up for half an hour. Brown the pheasant in butter, then remove from the pan and sauté 1 onion, finely chopped. Add 2 garlic cloves, crushed, and sauté for another couple of minutes. Return the pheasant to the pan with any juices that have run from it. Add the raisins and tea, ⅔ cup black and green grapes, halved and seeded, most of the nuts, a scant cup port, ¼ cup red grape or orange juice, and a few bay leaves. Bring to a boil, then immediately reduce the heat. Continue to cook as in the main recipe (see page 234). It's traditional, but optional, to add fresh tangerine segments once the pheasant is cooked. If the liquid hasn't thickened enough (though some grapes should burst and thicken the sauce), remove the pheasant, reduce the liquid by boiling, and return the pheasant to heat through. Stir in 1 tbsp finely chopped fresh parsley and sprinkle the remaining nuts on top.

Pigeon, hazelnut, and blackberry salad

Pigeon breasts aren't too gamey and make a grand salad.

Serves 4

FOR THE SALAD

4 pigeon breasts
olive oil
salt and pepper
6 juniper berries, crushed
1 tbsp unsalted butter
1¼ cups blackberries
½ tsp superfine sugar (optional)

8 oz salad greens (baby spinach,
    watercress, or lamb's lettuce)
⅓ cup hazelnuts, halved and toasted

FOR THE DRESSING

smidgen of Dijon mustard
1 tbsp red wine vinegar
1 tsp crème de cassis
2 tbsp olive oil
5 tbsp hazelnut oil

1 Mix the pigeon with 2 tbsp olive oil, salt, pepper, and the juniper berries and allow to marinate for a few hours.

2 To make the dressing, put the mustard and wine vinegar into a cup, season, and whisk in the remaining ingredients. Taste for seasoning.

3 Heat a griddle or frying pan until very hot, then cook the pigeon for 2 minutes on each side in the olive oil clinging to them. They should be rare; cut into one to check. Put on a warmed plate, cover with foil, and leave to rest for 5 minutes.

4 Add the butter to the same pan and heat until foaming. Toss in the blackberries and roll in the warm butter to soften slightly. Add the sugar, if using (I love that sweet-savory thing).

5 Using a thin, very sharp knife, cut the breasts into neat slices. Toss the greens and nuts with most of the dressing, then arrange on four plates. Spoon on the blackberries and lay the pigeon on top. Drizzle with the remaining dressing and serve.

ALSO TRY...

Venison with blackberries Put 1¼ cups blackberries in a pan with 5 tbsp crème de cassis, crème de mûre or chambord and simmer for 10 minutes. Set aside. Heat 2 tbsp butter and sauté 3 shallots, finely chopped, until soft but not colored. Add 1¼ cups red wine and ¾ cup red wine vinegar and cook until reduced to about 5 tbsp. Add 1½ cups well-flavored chicken or game stock and bring to a boil. Reduce until slightly syrupy. Stir in the blackberries and juices and taste for seasoning. Season 6 x ¾ in thick venison steaks. Heat 2½ tbsp unsalted butter and 1 tbsp peanut oil in a frying pan. Sear the steaks on each side over high heat to color, then reduce the heat and cook until rare (about 3 minutes each side). Reheat the sauce and beat in 3½ tbsp very cold unsalted butter, diced; it will become glossy and thicken. Cut each steak into four to reveal the lovely pinkness inside and serve on warmed plates with the sauce.

Rabbit with mustard and tarragon

There isn't masses of meat on a rabbit, but it has much more flavor than chicken, so do try to get hold of it. It delivers a bit of luxury (especially when combined with cream). This recipe is an old-fashioned French classic. The second is very English.

Serves 3–4

salt and pepper

3⅓ lb rabbit parts

2tbsp unsalted butter

1 onion, finely chopped

2 cups chicken stock

½ cup heavy cream

4 tsp Dijon mustard

good squeeze of lemon juice

leaves from 8 tarragon sprigs

1 Season the rabbit. Heat the butter in a sauté pan and brown the parts all over. Remove and set aside. In the same pan, cook the onion until soft and pale gold. Add the stock, bring to a boil, reduce to a gentle simmer, and return the rabbit. Simmer very gently, covered, for 1½–2 hours or until tender, making sure the rabbit is moist.

2 Remove the rabbit from the pan, put in a warm dish and cover. Add the cream to the stock and reduce by about half. Add the mustard, lemon juice, and half the tarragon. Reduce again until it is the consistency of single cream; do taste, though–you don't want the sauce to be thick or over salty. Return the rabbit to heat through and stir in the rest of the tarragon just before serving. Lovely with boiled potatoes or ribbons of egg noodles.

ALSO TRY…

Rabbit with bacon and watercress-and-lemon dumplings Heat 1 tbsp olive oil in a shallow, ovenproof pan and cook 2 small onions, sliced, until soft but not colored. Add 2 garlic cloves, sliced, and cook for 1 minute. Season. Rub 3⅓lb rabbit parts with olive oil, season, and wrap a piece of bacon around each. Set on the onions and drizzle with oil. Tuck in 4 thyme sprigs, pour on 1¼ cup dry white wine or stock, and simmer gently, covered for 1–1½ hours, checking every so often to make sure that the rabbit is moist. Add more wine or stock if you need to. Preheat the oven to 375°F. Make the dumplings by sautéing ½ onion, very finely chopped, and 1 garlic clove, crushed, in 3 tbsp butter. Put in a bowl and add 2 tbsp finely chopped fresh parsley, 3 oz watercress, chopped, 1¾ cups fresh white bread crumbs, the finely grated zest of ½ lemon, plus a good squeeze of juice, the leaves from 4 thyme sprigs, 1 large beaten egg, and seasoning. Bring the mixture together and form about 12 little golf ball–sized dumplings. Tuck the dumplings in around the rabbit. Roast for 20 minutes.

Elderflower and berry jellies

Gelled desserts with fruit suspended in them are quite magical, but one made with the scent of elderflowers is glorious. You can choose just one type of berry for this rather than a mixture if you prefer.

Serves 6

2 x ¼ oz packet plain gelatin
1¾ cups white wine
¼ cup superfine sugar
½ cup elderflower cordial (see page 242)

1 lb berries (raspberries, loganberries, blueberries, redcurrants, whitecurrants, and blackcurrants, all stems removed)

1 Sprinkle the gelatin over ¼ cup wine in a small bowl. Soak for 5 minutes, until completely soft.

2 Meanwhile, heat the remaining wine with the sugar, stirring gently to help the sugar dissolve. The wine shouldn't get any hotter than hand warm. Add the soaked gelatin and stir to dissolve. Add the elderflower cordial and stir.

3 Divide the berries among 6 little glasses and pour over the liquid. Put in the refrigerator to set. There is a lot of fruit here, so it shouldn't bob too much to the top as it is tightly packed into the jelly, but if it does just push it down gently as the jellies are setting. It's best to make these the day before so that they have time to set. Serve with cream on the side.

Raspberry and elderflower sorbet

This has a very intense flavor. It's delicious with vanilla ice cream.

Serves 4
1 lb (3⅔ cups) raspberries
⅔ cup sugar
5 tbsp elderflower cordial (see below)

1 Put the raspberries in a large bowl with 2 tbsp of the sugar. Leave for an hour. Put the remaining sugar in a saucepan with ¼ cup water and heat gently, stirring to help the sugar dissolve. Simmer for 2 minutes. Leave to cool.

2 Put the berries in a food processor and purée, then sieve. Mix the purée with the cooled syrup and the cordial. Cover and chill, then freeze in an ice cream machine according to the manufacturer's instructions, or still-freeze in a shallow container, beating the mixture to break up the crystals three or four times during the freezing process.

ALSO TRY...

Elderflower cordial This is a simple and lovely thing to do. Leave the house with some bags and a pair of scissors and return smelling of heaven. Use only very fresh flowers. Gather 20 heads of elderflower. Shake them gently to get rid of any little insects. Put 4 lb (9 cups) granulated sugar into a pan with 4¼ cups water. Bring to a boil, stirring to help the sugar dissolve. Pare the zest of 3 large unwaxed lemons in wide strips and put into a large bowl with the elderflowers. Slice the lemons and add to the bowl. When the syrup has boiled, pour it over and stir in 6 tbsp citric acid. Cover with a cloth and leave for 24 hours. Next day, preheat the oven to 300°F. Thoroughly wash and rinse some glass screw-top bottles and put them in the oven for 15 minutes to dry. Remove and leave to cool for 15 minutes. Sterilize the lids by boiling in water for a few minutes, and rinse any funnels or bowls with boiling water before you use them. Taste the juice around the flowers and add a little more lemon juice if needed. Strain the cordial through a sieve lined with clean muslin and pour into the sterilized bottles. Cover and keep in the refrigerator for up to 5 weeks. Makes about 2 quarts.

Elderflower and lemon creams This is great with poached rhubarb. Put 2 cups heavy cream and ½ cup sugar into a heavy saucepan and slowly bring to a boil, stirring to dissolve the sugar. Reduce the heat slightly and bubble for 3 minutes, no more, and don't let it boil over. Pour the warm cream into a bowl and whisk in the juice of 2 large lemons. It will thicken; mix to remove any lumps. Stir in ¼ cup elderflower cordial. Pour into a pitcher and cool a little. Divide among six small glasses and leave to cool completely, cover with plastic wrap then refrigerate. It will set in about 3 hours, but it's a good idea to make this the day before it's needed. Serves 6.

Blackberry and nectarine jam

You really need to find a good patch of wild blackberries if you are going to make this, as store-bought ones are just too expensive. If picking your own proves impossible, raspberries are great in this, too, though going to a pick-your-own fruit farm is the only way to make it without breaking the bank. This is good with peaches and apricots, too. Sterilize your jam jars as you would the bottles for my Elderflower Cordial (see page 242). This recipe is for a glut of fruit. If you don't want to make so much, halve the quantities of everything except the lemon juice.

Makes about 10 cups

3⅓ lb nectarines

3⅓ lb blackberries

juice of 1½ lemons

7½ cups preserving sugar

1 Halve and pit the nectarines and cut the flesh into chunks. Pick over the blackberries, removing any stems or withered leaves. Put the fruit into a tall, heavy pan with the juice of 1 of the lemons and 1¼ cups water. Bring to a boil, then reduce to a simmer, and let the fruit cook for about 15 minutes, or until tender.

2 Add the sugar and stir to help it dissolve, then bring to a boil and keep on a steady boil. Skim off any scum that rises to the surface during this time.

3 It's important to test for the gell point about 5 minutes after your sugar has dissolved, as cooking the jam for longer than it needs will impair the flavor. Some jams take as little as 3 minutes to reach the gell point, others can take 15. You can use a candy thermometer (they're not expensive) or–a failsafe low-tech way–put a spoonful of the boiling jam on a plate and then stick it very quickly in the freezer for about 2 minutes. Push the jam lightly with your finger. If it wrinkles slightly, the jam is at the gell point and ready to be removed from the heat. If you have a candy thermometer, the setting point for jam is 220°F, so test on that. Add the remaining lemon juice, pour the jam into warm sterilized jars, and seal. Process in a boiling water bath for 5 minutes or store in the refrigerator.

Blackberry and brown sugar loaf

This is based on a recipe from the inspirational American food writer John Thorne. He uses raspberries, so you can make it with those in the summer. A lovely, no-nonsense teatime cake.

Serves 8–10

¾ cup unsalted butter, softened

1¼ cups light brown sugar

2 large eggs, beaten until frothy

2 heaped tbsp sour cream

1 tbsp grated lemon zest

pinch of ground cinnamon

2 cups all-purpose flour, sifted

1 tsp baking powder

8 oz (1⅔ cups) blackberries

confectioners' sugar, to dust

1 Preheat the oven to 325°F. In an electric mixer beat the butter until light, then add the brown sugar and beat until fluffy. Add the eggs, a little at a time, and beat until creamy. Turn the speed down to low and add the sour cream, zest, cinnamon, and flour. Beat until the mixture just comes together.

2 Sift the baking powder over the top, sprinkle on the blackberries, and gently fold these into the mixture with a metal spoon, breaking them up as little as possible. Spoon into a buttered 9x5in loaf pan, smooth the top, and bake in the oven for 45–50 minutes, or until a fine skewer inserted into the center of the loaf comes out clean.

3 Let the loaf cool in the pan for about 15 minutes, then run a thin knife around the edges and turn it out onto a wire rack. Turn it right side up and leave to cool completely. Sift a light dusting of confectioners' sugar over the top.

ALSO TRY...

Blackberry, apple, and maple brown betty A great, down-home American dessert that's even easier to make than a crisp. Preheat the oven to 350°F. Mix 1 cup light brown sugar with ½ tsp each pumpkin pie spice and ground ginger. Mix 3 tbsp of this with 5½ cups stale cake crumbs and pour over 7 tbsp melted butter. Slice 1 cooking apple thinly and mix with 1 lb blackberries along with the remaining sugar and spice mixture. Butter a gratin or pie dish and put in half the crumbs. Pile the fruit on top and pour over 2 tbsp maple syrup. Put the remaining crumbs on top and bake, loosely covered with foil, for 20 minutes. Remove the foil and bake for another 20 minutes or so, until the fruit is tender and the top golden. Serve with whipped cream or vanilla ice cream. Serves 6.

Blackberry and ricotta hot cakes with honey

An amalgam of an American and an Italian recipe. Great for brunch, and for ekeing out a small stash of blackberries.

Serves 4

FOR THE HOT CAKES
1 cup ricotta cheese
3 eggs, separated
2 tbsp unsalted butter, melted, plus
   more for frying
3 tbsp granulated sugar
½ tsp vanilla extract

finely grated zest of 1 orange
6 tbsp all-purpose flour, sifted
4 oz (1 cup) blackberries

TO SERVE
confectioners' sugar, to dust
honey, to drizzle

1 Mash the ricotta in a bowl with the egg yolks, 1 of the egg whites, the melted butter, sugar, vanilla, and zest. Fold in the flour. Beat the remaining 2 egg whites until stiff, then carefully fold them into the mixture, followed by the blackberries.

2 Melt a little pat of butter in a nonstick frying pan over a medium heat and spoon in enough batter to make a round about the size of your palm. You can do 2 or 3 hot cakes at a time. After a couple of minutes, when you can see the underside is golden (do a bit of gentle levering with a palette knife) and set, carefully turn the cakes over. Cook for 2 minutes on the other side, then remove from the pan and keep them warm.

3 Add more butter to the pan as needed to cook the rest of the hot cakes and try not to let it burn. If it does, discard the burnt butter and start with fresh stuff. Sift confectioners' sugar over the top of each cake before serving and drizzle with a little honey.

Sweet fruitfulness

Fruit is the food that most makes me feel we have been given an embarrassment of riches, and also the one that firmly anchors us to the seasons. A visit to an orchard when the trees are so heavy with fruit that their branches are pulled to the ground can make you gasp at the plenty we enjoy. Even the word "ripe" suggests fullness, perfection, sensual pleasure. Fruits dazzle–the crimson flesh of a plum, or the red blush on the curves of an apricot–and they burst with a taste for which we yearn: sweetness.

I love it when friends who grow fruit bring presents from their gardens: plums in summer, fat golden quinces in November, even huge bags of apples so ripe that they have to be cooked immediately. Gluts of fruit are a challenge. You can initially think, when faced with a large quantity of pears: what on earth will I do with them? But spend a Sunday morning cutting and boiling before ladling pear chutney into clean jars, and it will be worth it. To capture abundance by making preserves gives a special kind of thrill.

Of course, many fruits are now taken for granted and grown for high yield and shelf life, not quality. With so many varieties of apples in the world, supermarkets still fill bays with bland Golden Delicious, and we can eat strawberries in January (jolly red and a perfect shape, but they often taste of turnips). When I was a child I kept an eye on the strawberry patch in our neighbor's garden. The scarlet that suddenly appeared against the green leaves and pale straw was magical, and a sure sign of summer. My children do not enjoy this pleasure–they think strawberries are available year round.

Ensuring that fruit tastes of something requires an almost campaigning zeal on all our parts. Buy it at farmers' markets and produce stands; they aren't as likely to stock varieties just because thay have a long shelf life and they need your support. When you get a chance, visit a pick-your-own farm both to support it and to find bargain loads of fruit. If we accept only what's available in supermarkets, caring growers and flavorful varieties will disappear.

In this chapter, there are recipes for fruits that are cheap only at the height of their season, or if you pick your own. Most stone fruits are expensive, but become plentiful and cheaper in August. Other recipes here offer ways to make more of fruit that's never very cheap, such as cherries, by ekeing it out.

One of the most enjoyable things I do at the height of summer is to slow-bake stone fruits in readiness for breakfast the next morning. When apricots are abundant and on sale, I carry home bag after bag, mix them with sugar and vanilla and look forward to a bowlful of heaven.

It takes very little to make something special out of fruit. Revel in it.

Strawberry and lemon curd cake

This dessert is also delicious as a cake without the fillings (halve the recipe and start checking after 30 minutes). You can make it in the autumn with ground hazelnuts.

Serves 8–10

FOR THE CAKE
11 oz butter
1¾ cup caster sugar
1 tsp vanilla extract
2 tsp almond extract
8 oz plain low-fat yogurt
4 large eggs, at room temperature
1⅛ self-raising flour
7½ oz ground almonds
½ tsp salt

FOR THE TOPPING AND FILLING
1¾ lb strawberries
5 tbsp superfine sugar
finely grated zest and juice of ½ lemon
7 oz mascarpone
1 cup heavy cream
10 heaped tbsp lemon curd
confectioners' sugar, to taste, plus more
   to dust

1 Preheat the oven to 350°F. Cream the butter and sugar together until light and fluffy. Beat in the vanilla and almond extracts. Mix the yogurt with the eggs and beat lightly together.

2 Sift the flour and combine it with the almonds and salt. With an electric mixer on a very low speed add the dry ingredients to the creamed mixture, alternating it with the yoghurt and egg mixture. When all the ingredients are combined continue to beat on a low speed for 1 minute. Split the batter evenly between 3 buttered and base-lined 9 in springform cake pan and bake for 35–40 minutes. A skewer pushed into the centre of each cake should come out clean. Leave to cool in the tin for about 5 minutes then turn the cakes out onto a wire rack and leave to cool completely.

3 Wash and hull the strawberries and cut into halves and quarters (reserve good-looking small berries for decoration). Sprinkle the cut strawberries with the superfine sugar, zest, and juice; stir and leave to macerate for 15 minutes. Beat the mascarpone to loosen it a bit. In a separate bowl, whip the cream until it holds its shape well. Combine the cream, mascarpone, lemon curd, and confectioners' sugar to taste.

4 Assemble immediately before serving. Spread the flattest of the cakes with half the cream, then half the strawberries. Repeat with the next cake then put the top cake on. Arrange a small pile of perfect strawberries in the middle and sift over a light dusting of icing sugar. It's best eaten on the day it's made.

ALSO TRY…

This cake is good with all other berries (blackberry and lemon curd is lovely). Try orange curd or a few spoonfuls of elderflower cordial (see page 242) instead of lemon curd, or make the filling using all cream instead of mascarpone if you prefer.

Strawberry and rose ice cream

Ice creams made with fruit and cream seem purer and more intense than those with a custard base, and are easier to make. If you aren't partial to floral scents in food, leave out the rosewater; you'll still have a lovely ice cream.

Serves 6
1 lb strawberries, hulled
juice of ½ lemon
9 tbsp superfine sugar
5 tbsp rosewater
1 cup whipping cream, chilled

1 Chop the strawberries coarsely and mix with the lemon juice, sugar, and rosewater. Leave to stand for an hour until the sugar has dissolved and the fruit has softened.

2 Whip the cream until it forms soft peaks. Purée the strawberries and all their juices in a blender or food processor. Stir the strawberry purée into the cream, then mix everything together.

3 Churn in an ice cream machine, or pour into a shallow container and still-freeze. If still-freezing, you need to take the ice cream out of the freezer every couple of hours (do this 3 or 4 times) and fork the frozen stuff around the outside into the rest of the mix, to make it smooth.

ALSO TRY...

This is a simple ice cream and therefore very adaptable. You can replace the strawberries with raspberries or blackberries (the blackberry version is better without rosewater), but taste the mixture before freezing; the raspberry version will need a little more sugar as raspberries are a tarter fruit. Raspberry or blackberry purées need to be strained (because they have so many seeds) before being mixed with the cream.

Cherry and almond croûtes

This is just about the easiest dessert in the world, basically baked fruit on toast. You don't have to use brioche—other breads are good, but you just get different results. However, don't cut them too thinly or you'll get charred bread rather than golden croûtes. This is a good way of using up the end of a loaf, and of getting rid of that stash of marzipan (bought only at Christmas) hanging around in the cupboard. Your croûtes don't have to be boozy; use fruit juice to moisten the bread, or spread the bread and dot the fruit with butter. Leave the stems on (and therefore the pits in) a few of the cherries—it looks pretty. But warn your guests, especially those with dentures!

Serves 4

4 slices brioche

⅓ cup kirsch

juice of ½ lemon

5 oz marzipan, broken into chunks

1 lb cherries, pitted

4 tsp superfine sugar

6 tbsp flaked almonds

confectioners' sugar, to dust

TO SERVE

heavy cream

1 Preheat the oven to 350°F. Put the brioche on to a baking tray. Sprinkle half the kirsch and lemon juice over the slices and scatter with the marzipan. Put the cherries on top, sprinkle the rest of the lemon juice and kirsch over, then dust with the superfine sugar and add the almonds.

2 Bake for 30 minutes. The cherries should be tender and the bread and marzipan golden. Leave to cool a little, then sift confectioners' sugar over each piece and serve with heavy cream.

ALSO TRY...

You can make croûtes with apricots, peaches, nectarines, and plums as well, as long as they are ripe (if the fruit is hard, the bread gets too toasted by the time it becomes tender). Plums and apricots should be halved or quartered, depending on ripeness, and peaches should be sliced. Almond liqueur can be used instead of kirsch.

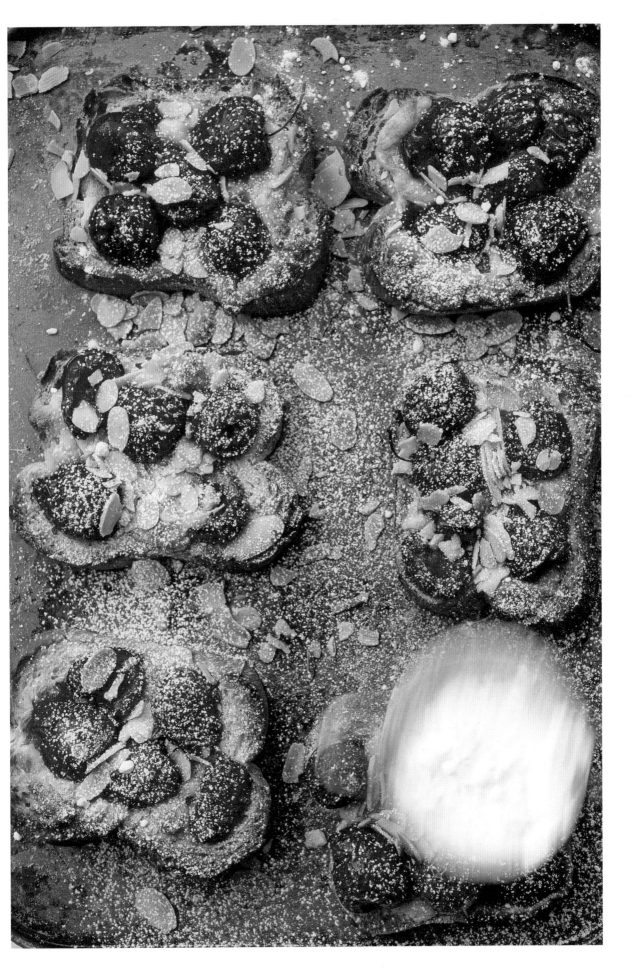

Guignolet, or cherry wine

Fruit liqueurs and "wines" are a wonderful way of capturing summer–doesn't cherry wine seem lovely, even before you've tasted it?–and they are the easiest kind of "preserve" you can make. Cherries are usually expensive, but every so often you come across a mountain being sold cheaply in a market. That's the time to make this. Cherry wine is a French aperitif. Serve it chilled in small glasses (a fresh cherry hanging on the side of the glass doesn't go amiss–it is, after all, a pretty and romantic drink). You can add sparkling white wine to make a sort of cherry kir, or sparkling water to make a spritzer.

Makes about 1 quart

1 lb unblemished pitted cherries	**1½ cups sugar**
1 bottle (750ml) light red wine	**6 tbsp kirsch**

1 Heat the cherries in a saucepan with the wine and sugar, stirring to help the sugar dissolve. Bring just up to a boil, then turn down the heat and simmer gently for 5 minutes. Cool, add the kirsch, cover, and leave for 2 days.

2 Strain and pour into sterilized bottles (see page 242) and add a screw top or cork. The boozy cherries left behind are delicious with chilled rice pudding, or used to make a filling for a summer sponge cake (spoon them onto a layer of whipped cream, or a mixture of mascarpone and crème fraîche).

ALSO TRY…

Apricot liqueur Put 1 lb apricots, halved and pitted, into a saucepan with 2¼ cups sugar and 3 cups dry white wine and proceed as above. Take the pan off the heat. Add 5 tbsp kirsch or amaretto and 1¼ cups vodka. Put into a bowl or pitcher, cover, and leave for 6 days. Strain (I filter it twice through cheesecloth as the apricots do disintegrate a bit) and put into clean, sterilized bottles. Add tops and leave for a month before using. The boozy apricots can be used just like the cherries above, and they also make a lovely fool. The liqueur itself should be served in small glasses–I prefer it chilled–or mixed with white wine or sparkling white wine to make an apricot kir.

Dorothy Allhusen's cherry salad

This sounds quite odd but is totally delicious. It's based on a dish from Dorothy Allhusen's lovely tome, *A Book of Scents and Dishes* (1926). She doesn't use balsamic vinegar, but I like the sweetness it imparts. Dorothy suggests serving it with cold roast beef. I also serve it with roast chicken, roast lamb, and grilled goat cheese on toast.

Serves 4

1 lb cherries, pitted
2 tbsp brandy
2 tsp balsamic vinegar
¼ cup olive oil

salt and pepper
juice of ½ lemon
2 tbsp coarsely chopped fresh
  flat-leaf parsley

1 Put the cherries into a shallow bowl and add the other ingredients.

2 Stir everything together gently and leave to macerate for about an hour before serving. These are good the next day, too; the cherries become slightly softer, but the flavors have permeated the flesh. If you do want to serve them next day, don't add the parsley until about an hour before serving, otherwise it loses its bright color.

ALSO TRY...

Chicken and cherry salad with creamy tarragon dressing Mix 1½ tsp white wine vinegar, ½ tsp Dijon mustard, and salt and pepper in a cup. Whisk in ¼ cup light olive oil, 1 tbsp water, and 1 tbsp light cream. Add the leaves from 3 tarragon sprigs, chopped, and about ½ tsp superfine sugar. Mix and taste for seasoning and a good balance of sweet and sour. Toss with about 2½ cups cooked chicken, neatly sliced, 1¾ cups cherries, pitted, 5 oz salad greens (watercress is very good), and ½ cup toasted flaked almonds. Serve straight away. Serves 2.

Gooseberry "pots"

This recipe was sent to me by Margaret Drummond, a reader of my newspaper cooking column. It originally comes from a very old book, where they suggest using it as a filling for a "coffin" of pastry (basically a pie), but I'd rather have it like this. It has the feel of an old-fashioned English nursery dessert and is a great way to use up a horde of gooseberries. If you can't locate gooseberries substitute rhubarb, cut into 2-inch lengths.

Serves 4

1 lb gooseberries, top and bottom removed
½ cup sugar
2 tbsp apple cider, sweet wine, or
   apple juice

1⅔ cup fresh white bread crumbs
  (not too fine)
2 tbsp unsalted butter
2 large egg yolks

1 Put the gooseberries in a pan with the sugar and cider, wine or juice and cook over a low heat until half-stewed (7–10 minutes). Add the bread crumbs and cook for another 3–4 minutes. The mixture should be quite thick.

2 Take the pan off the heat and beat in the butter and yolks. Taste for sweetness. Leave to cool to room temperature, then put into little glasses and chill. Serve topped with whipped cream, or cold custard sauce.

ALSO TRY...

Stewed gooseberries Lovely to have in the refrigerator. You can eat them for breakfast (that tang is great first thing in the morning), or serve as an easy dessert with rice pudding (perhaps flavored with elderflower cordial, see page 242) or with good, thick, heavy cream and shortbread or a big, blousy meringue. Don't forget their potential in trifle (see page 261). They also make a great fruit fool: combine them with custard and whipped cream or Greek yogurt and a couple of tablespoons of elderflower cordial.

Gooseberry and elderflower mess A play on the traditional British Eton mess, but even better as gooseberries are so much tarter than the traditional strawberries. Don't stir in your crushed meringues until just before serving, or they will become soggy. Poach 1 lb gooseberries in ½ cup water and 6 tbsp sugar. When they are tender, remove the gooseberries with a slotted spoon. Roughly smash up 4 oz meringues (about ten 2½ in cookies) and gently combine them with 1 cup heavy cream, whipped, ½ cup Greek yogurt, the gooseberries, 2 tbsp lemon curd, and 3 tbsp elderflower cordial (see page 242). Pile into glasses and garnish with mint leaves.

Scottish pear and raspberry trifle

I had this in a small hotel in Westray, the island just next to Orkney off the coast of Scotland. Sharp raspberries are lovely with the sweet muskiness of pears.

Serves 6

6 tbsp sugar

strip of lemon zest

2 pears, peeled, halved, and cored

3½ tbsp whiskey

sponge cake or lady fingers

¾ cup whipping cream

2 tbsp confectioners' sugar

seeds from ½ vanilla pod, or ½ tsp pure
   vanilla extract

8 oz (1⅔ cups) raspberries

1 Put ½ cup water and the sugar in a saucepan and gently heat, stirring to help the sugar dissolve. Add the zest and pear halves and poach until just tender. How long this takes will depend on the pears, but start checking after 12 minutes.

2 Drain the pears and leave them and their liquid to cool. Add the whiskey to the liquid. Break the sponge cake into chunks, spread on a plate, and spoon over about three-quarters of the poaching liquid. Leave to soak in really well.

3 Assemble the trifles in individual glasses at the last minute. Whip the cream lightly, adding the confectioners' sugar and vanilla. Cut the pears lengthwise into slices. Add a layer of cake to each glass, then sliced pears, raspberries, a trickle of the remaining poaching syrup, and a good spoon of cream. Repeat, finishing with fruit on top, and serve.

ALSO TRY…

There is nothing trifling about trifles. They are one of the glories of British cooking, far greater than the sum of their parts. The basic idea of a trifle is so good that it's a shame to be restricted by rules. I make trifles without custard (as above), with crushed gingersnaps or amaretti cookies instead of cake, with cooked fruit and fresh fruit. Curds and marmalade can be used instead of jam, and indeed there is not always the need for jam at all. When it comes to alcohol, I have used Muscat, sherry, calvados, and rum. These are all riffs on the basic idea. Go where you will….

Plum and ginger trifle Make with crushed ginger cookies or gingerbread (whiskey or brandy is good as the moistening agent here), poached plums, cream, and custard.

Apple and calvados trifle Make with stewed apples, cream, custard, and calvados-soaked cake.

Caramelized orange trifle Make with cake spread with marmalade and soaked in whisky or cointreau, custard, cream, and segments of orange in caramel.

Gooseberry meringue pie

This has more tang than lemon meringue pie and a good substantial filling (making it more satisfying). If you can't locate gooseberries substitute rhubarb, cut into 2-inch lengths.

Serves 8

FOR THE PASTRY

2¼ cup all-purpose flour, plus more to dust
11 tbsp butter, cubed
pinch of salt
2 tbsp superfine sugar
1 egg yolk, mixed with 1 tbsp very
  cold water

FOR THE FILLING

2 lb gooseberries, top and bottom removed
1 cup superfine sugar
5 tbsp cornstarch
4 large egg yolks

FOR THE MERINGUE

3 egg whites
1⅓ cups superfine sugar, plus more
  to sprinkle

1 To make the pastry, put the flour, butter, and salt into a food processor and process until the mixture resembles bread crumbs. Add the sugar and process again; then gradually add just enough egg and water to bring it together into a ball. Wrap in plastic wrap and refrigerate for an hour or so.

2 Preheat the oven to 375°F. Roll the pastry out on a floured surface and use to line a 9½–10 in and 1½ in deep, metal tart pan with a removable base. Prick the pastry with a fork, and line with greaseproof paper and baking beans. Bake for 15 minutes; then remove the paper and beans and bake for another 10 minutes. It should be a pale biscuit color.

3 Meanwhile, put the gooseberries in a pan with 2 tbsp water and the sugar. Cover and gently heat, stirring to help break the gooseberries down and coax out the juice. Cook over a medium heat until tender. Some will stay whole, some will become mushy. Strain through a sieve into a bowl and put the liquid back into the saucepan. Simmer until it has reduced to about 1 cup.

4 Mix 5 tbsp of the reduced gooseberry liquor with the cornstarch, stirring until really smooth. Pour this back into the liquor in the saucepan and return the drained gooseberries. Bring to a boil and stir vigorously while the mixture is thickening. Add the egg yolks and stir well to combine. It will be thick but still just pourable. Pour into the pastry shell and leave to cool.

5 Put the egg whites in a large, clean bowl and beat until you have medium peaks (when you hold up the beaters, the peaks just slightly droop). Beat in 1 tbsp of the sugar at a time until you have a stiff, glossy mixture. Spoon this over the tart, making sure you don't leave any gaps and being careful to cover the rim of pastry. Bake for 25 minutes, until golden brown on top.

Early autumn salad of blackberries, raspberries, melon, and lemon thyme

A lovely dessert. If you can't find lemon thyme, use ordinary thyme.

Serves 6

2½ cups mixed white wine and
   water, or just water
1 cup sugar
3 lemon thyme sprigs, plus more to serve
juice of 1 lemon

1 strip of lemon zest
5 oz (1¼ cups) blackberries, stems removed
   (though some left on looks very pretty)
5 oz (1¼ cups) raspberries
½ melon (honeydew or cantaloupe)

1 Put the wine and water mix, sugar, lemon thyme, lemon juice, and zest into a pan. Bring slowly to a boil, stirring to help the sugar dissolve. Boil for 4 minutes, or until syrupy; it will thicken as it cools. Leave to cool completely, then strain.

2 Put the berries in a broad, shallow bowl. Cut the melon into slices, remove the skin, and cut the flesh into cubes. Add these to the bowl and pour the syrup over. Add a few sprigs of lemon thyme. You can either chill this before serving (though the raspberries will soften), or serve at room temperature.

ALSO TRY...

Strawberries in Beaujolais Slice 1 lb hulled strawberries and put them into a bowl. Sprinkle with ¼ cup superfine sugar, then add enough Beaujolais just to cover. Leave to macerate for 30 minutes to 1 hour; no longer, as the strawberries get too flaccid. Serve, since this is the French way, with crème fraîche.

Peaches in Marsala Slice perfectly ripe peaches into a bowl and add enough sweet Marsala to cover. Cover and refrigerate for about half an hour. Eat.

Sweet ricotta with berries This is simple but looks spectacular. Beat ricotta with a fork, add confectioners' or superfine sugar to taste and put in a mound in the center of a plate. Surround with red berries and let everyone help themselves. If you have cherry or other berry liqueur, drizzle a little over before serving.

Strawberry, clotted cream, and rose petal sandwiches Spread brioche slices with clotted cream and slice strawberries thinly. Cover half the brioche slices with these, sprinkling with a little caster sugar. Put rose petals–torn if they're big–on top, then make into sandwiches with the remaining brioche slices. Cut each into 3 fingers and dust with confectioners' sugar. Pile on to a plate and sprinkle with rose petals.

Moroccan peaches with cinnamon and orange flower water Lay peach slices on a platter and squeeze over lemon or lime juice. Sprinkle with superfine sugar and add 1–2 tbsp orange flower water (different brands vary in strength; don't make it too perfumed). Sprinkle on a little ground cinnamon and chopped pistachios or toasted almonds. Chill before serving.

Apricot, peach, and blackberry crumble

This is the quintessential British, never-fails-to-please dessert. It's also sensible, by which I mean that it isn't expensive and it is a great vehicle for celebrating gluts of fruit. The only thing to remember is that your fruit must cook to tenderness in the time it takes the crumble to become golden. So, when your fruit is particularly unripe, it's a good idea to cook it slightly in advance.

Serves 8

1⅓ lb apricots, quartered and pitted	¾ cup sugar
3 peaches, pitted and sliced	1¼ cups all-purpose flour
1 lb blackberries	¾ cup almonds, ground
finely grated zest of ½ and juice of 1 lemon	¾ cup butter, chopped
	6 tbsp flaked almonds
	crème fraîche or whipped cream, to serve

1 Preheat the oven to 350°F. Put the fruit and lemon juice and zest into an ovenproof dish and stir in 3 tbsp of the sugar. To make the crumble, mix the flour, remaining sugar, and the ground almonds together and rub in the butter with your fingers until the mixture turns crumbly.

2 Put the crumble on top of the fruit, sprinkle the flaked almonds on top, and bake for 40 minutes. The top of the crumble should be golden and the fruit tender (insert a small, sharp knife to test for this). If your fruit is still a bit hard but your crumble is already golden, cover the top with some foil to keep it from getting too dark and bake a little longer.

3 Leave to cool a little and serve with crème fraîche or whipped cream.

ALSO TRY…

Other fruits: You can fall back on good old cooking apples to extend a meager amount of expensive fruit–raspberry and apple is lovely at the end of the summer, for example–then there is plum or greengage and almond, pear or apple and rhubarb (rhubarb crumbles are good with chopped preserved ginger or grated orange rind) and pear and cherry.

Other toppings: The nuts and sugars can be changed too. Brown sugars are lovely in autumn (a little molasses sugar–available online– makes a particularly fudgy, dark crumble), and honey or maple syrup can replace some of the sugar in the fruit. Nuts can be quite chunky. You can also replace some of the all-purpose flour with whole-wheat, or bread crumbs, in autumn and winter.

Dried fruits: Dried apples, cranberries, sour cherries, and apricots (soaked and drained) are all good when mixed with fresh apples and pears.

Apricot and almond upside-down cake

One of my favorite cakes, with a good balance of sweet and tart, that really makes the best of apricots, especially those that are lacking in flavor or are underripe.

Serves 8

FOR THE APRICOTS

3½ tbsp butter, plus more for the pan

⅔ cup sugar

7–8 fresh apricots (not too ripe) halved
  and pitted

1 tbsp honey

FOR THE CAKE

⅔ cup unsalted butter

¾ cup sugar

2 eggs, beaten

¾ cup all-purpose flour

1½ tsp baking powder

¾ cup ground almonds

1 tsp vanilla extract

½ cup whole milk

1 Butter an 8–9 in cake pan and prepare the apricots. Put the sugar and ⅛ cup water into a small saucepan. Heat slowly until the sugar has dissolved. When the sugar has completely melted bring to the boil and watch until the syrup starts to turn to caramel (it will turn golden first). Swish the pan a bit. Once it becomes caramel (you will know by the smell and color) take immediately off the heat and add the butter. Stir once the butter has melted. Pour into the pan and place the apricots, close together and cut-side-down, on top. Preheat the oven to 350°F.

2 To make the cake, cream the butter and sugar until pale and fluffy, then add the eggs a little at a time, beating well after each addition (add a couple of spoonfuls of flour to the mixture if it starts to curdle). Sift together the flour and baking powder and stir in the almonds. Add the vanilla, then the dry ingredients, alternating with the milk. Spoon this batter over the apricots and bake for 50 minutes. When the cake is cooked, a skewer inserted into the center should come out clean.

3 Run a thin knife between the cake and the pan and invert onto a plate. If some apricots have stuck to the pan, carefully replace them on the cake.

4 Gently heat the honey. Using a pastry brush or spoon, glaze the top of the cake. The honey will run down the sides to give a lush, homemade look. Leave to cool completely. The cake is lovely with crème fraîche (you can sweeten it slightly) or a mixture of sweetened Greek yogurt and heavy cream (no need to whip).

ALSO TRY...

Making this with plums: Red-fleshed ones are particularly good for their great color, or try greengages. You will need to use more or less of these depending on the size of the fruit. If you use red-fleshed plums, make a glaze with melted redcurrant jelly mixed with a little water for a nice shine, instead of honey.

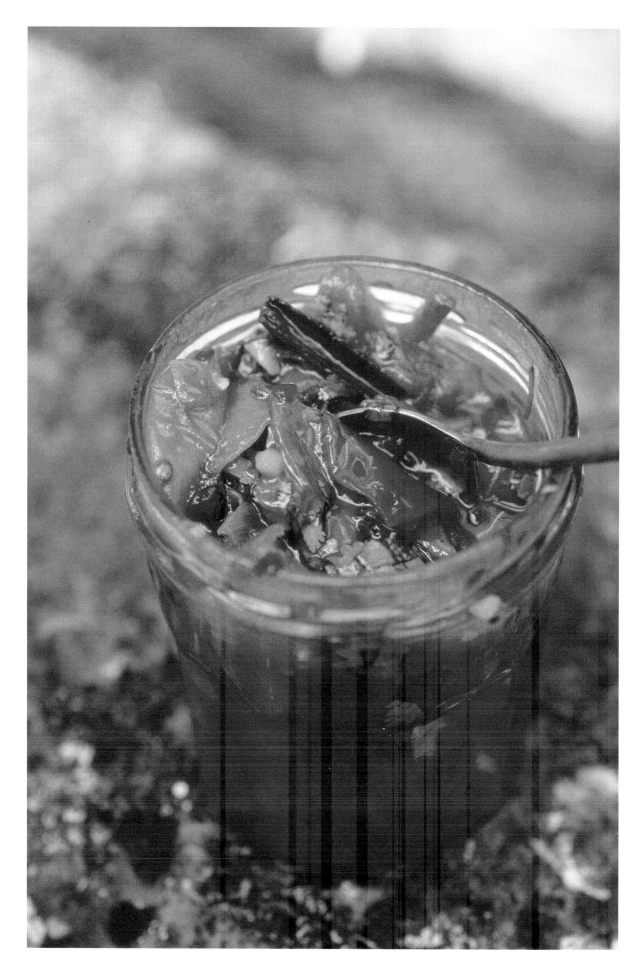

Salsa mish mish

Mish mish is the Arabic for apricot, and the fruit is adored in the Middle East and North Africa. You will see it not only in desserts, but in sweet-and-sour meat and poultry stews, such as the tajines of Morocco or the khoresht of Iran. Sometimes an apricot sauce is served alongside lamb or chicken, and I so like the combination that I wanted to make the sauce into a preserve. This is what I came up with, a kind of Middle Eastern–flavored relish. It is particularly lovely with a leg of lamb that you have marinated in yogurt and crushed garlic for 24 hours before roasting.

Makes 2 x 1 lb jars

2 tbsp olive oil
1 large onion, coarsely chopped
4 garlic cloves, crushed
2 fresh red chiles, seeded and cut into slivers
1½ in cube of fresh ginger, peeled and finely chopped
1½ tsp crushed coriander seeds
seeds from 10 cardamom pods, crushed
2 in cinnamon stick

1¼ cups dried apricots, coarsely chopped
12 oz fresh apricots, halved, pitted, and chopped
1¼ cups white wine vinegar or cider vinegar
1¼ cups granulated sugar
¼ cup fresh cilantro leaves, coarsely chopped (optional)

1 Heat the oil in a heavy pan and sauté the onion over a medium heat until soft and pale gold. Add the garlic and all the fresh and dried spices and cook for another 2 minutes, until the spices release their fragrance. Now add all the other ingredients, except the sugar and cilantro leaves, and bring to a boil. Reduce to a simmer and cook for 15–20 minutes, until the fruit is soft.

2 Now add the sugar and stir from time to time to help it dissolve. Continue to cook until the mixture is thick. It has cooked enough when you can pull a wooden spoon across the bottom of the pan and it leaves a channel before closing again. Discard the cinnamon stick.

3 Stir in the chopped cilantro if you want to use it (it does discolor slightly over time, but it tastes great). Spoon the relish into hot sterilized jars (see page 242) and seal. Store in the refrigerator. I find this relish is better when it's relatively fresh, so I generally use it up within about 3 months.

Plums with red wine and rosemary

Based on an idea from the wonderful Italian food writer Anna del Conte in her book *Food From an Italian Kitchen.* Rosemary in plum compote is fabulous, and it's good with poached pears, too.

Serves 6

1¾ cups red wine

1 cup sugar

1 strip of lemon zest

1 in cinnamon stick

6 black peppercorns, lightly bruised

3 rosemary sprigs

2 lb plums (just under-ripe)

1 Put the wine, sugar, lemon zest, cinnamon, and peppercorns in a saucepan; add 1 cup water and heat gently until the sugar dissolves, stirring. Bring to a boil and cook for 2 minutes.

2 Reduce to a simmer and add the plums. Cook very gently until the plums are just soft. (Be careful; they fall apart easily.) How long it takes depends on the size and ripeness of the plums. Carefully remove the fruit with a slotted spoon to a serving dish.

3 Strain the juices (reserve the cinnamon) and pour into a clean saucepan. Boil until syrupy. Leave until cold, then pour over the plums. Add the remaining rosemary and reserved cinnamon. Cover and refrigerate. Serve with yogurt, or sweetened yogurt mixed with heavy cream.

ALSO TRY...

Wine-poached apples Once I'd made this—when there was nothing much else in the house—I wondered why it wasn't a classic. Put a bottle of red wine in a saucepan with 1¼ cup sugar and 1 in cinnamon stick. Heat slowly, stirring. Cut 6 peeled, cored apples into wedges. Put these into the wine, increase the heat until simmering, then place a circle of parchment paper on top and cover. Poach until tender but not falling apart, about 25 minutes. Remove the apples to a dish and boil the wine until you have 1 cup left. Cool, then pour over the apples. They'll be a fantastic deep red but get even darker as they sit in the syrup. Serve chilled, or at room temperature.

Rose-scented apples Make as for Wine-poached Apples (above) but replace the red wine with white (or mixed apple juice and water) and the cinnamon with 8 crushed cardamom pods. Add rosewater to taste—about 2 tsp—and a squeeze of lemon to the reduced syrup and sprinkle with chopped pistachio nuts (unsalted) and rose petals.

Garnet quinces Prepare the poaching liquid as for Wine-poached Apples (see above). Peel 6 quinces, halve, core, and put them in the wine. Simmer until tender, turning. It could take as much as 1 hour. Remove the cinnamon and let the quinces cool in their liquid (you shouldn't need to reduce it as the pectin in quinces makes the liquor syrupy). Serve with crème fraîche or whipped cream.

Plum jumby tart

Cute name, easy as pie.

Serves 6–8

1¾ cups self-rising floure

7 tbsp butter, plus more for the pan

5 tbsp superfine sugar, plus more
  to sprinkle

1 egg, beaten

1 tbsp vanilla extract

about 10 large or 18 small plums, quartered
  if large, halved if small, and pitted

½ cup firmly packed marzipan

2½ tbsp flaked almonds

confectioners' sugar, to dust

1 Preheat the oven to 375°F. Put the flour, butter, and superfine sugar into a food processor and using the pastry blade, process until you have the texture of bread crumbs. Add the egg and vanilla and blend again until the pastry comes together. If it doesn't come together, take the pastry out and make it into a smooth ball with floured hands.

2 Butter an 11x15 in jelly-roll pan and press in the pastry. You can do this in chunks; it doesn't have to be particularly even. Put the plums on top, cut side up, packed really closely together. Take the marzipan and break off little chunks. Stick a chunk in the cavity of each plum (this is harder with quartered than with halved plums, but it doesn't have to be neat or exact). Sprinkle 2 tbsp superfine sugar over the tart and bake for 30 minutes. About 5 minutes before the end of the baking time, sprinkle with the flaked almonds.

3 Allow to cool a little. Dust with confectioners' sugar and serve either warm or at room temperature. Whipped cream or crème fraîche is good on the side.

ALSO TRY…

Other fruits: You can make this with fresh apricots and sliced peaches or nectarines. Apples take longer to soften so, if you want to use those, slice them quite thinly.

Other glazes: If you want a glossy tart, leave off the almonds and confectioners' sugar and glaze the top thickly with strained warmed apricot jam or redcurrant jelly, then leave it to set.

Free-form autumn fruit tart with cinnamon sugar

"Free-form" tarts remove the need to fit pastry into a pan, so are much quicker. They're brilliant for less confident pastry cooks, and their appearance suggests plenty and simplicity. The nuts soak up the juices, but you can use bread crumbs instead.

Serves 8

FOR THE PASTRY

2 cups all-purpose flour, plus more to dust
11 tbsp butter, in rough cubes
9 tbsp confectioners' sugar, plus more to dust
1 egg yolk

FOR THE FILLING

10 oz plums, halved and pitted
10 oz apples, halved and cored
   (no need to peel)

juice of ½ lemon
⅓ cup ground hazelnuts
¼ cup light brown sugar
8 figs, halved
6 oz (1 cup) blackberries
3 tbsp granulated sugar

TO SERVE

½ tsp ground cinnamon, or to taste

1 To make the pastry, put the flour, butter, and confectioners' sugar into a food processor. Using the pastry blade, blend until it has a texture like bread crumbs. Mix the egg yolk with 1 tbsp cold water and add that. Process again; the pastry should come together to form a ball, though you may need more water. Wrap in plastic and refrigerate for an hour.

2 Slice the plums and cut the apples into thinner slices. Toss with the lemon juice to prevent discoloration. Preheat the oven to 375°F.

3 Roll the pastry on a floured surface into a rough circle, about ¹⁄₁₆ in thick. Put onto a baking sheet lined with parchment paper. Mix the nuts and brown sugar and sprinkle on top, leaving a 1½ in rim. Put all the fruit on top in a higgledy-piggledy way. Sprinkle over the granulated sugar. Pull the pastry up over the fruit all the way around. Bake for 45 minutes, or until the fruit is tender. The tart should be golden and the fruit soft and slightly caramelized. If the pastry gets too dark before the fruit is cooked, cover with foil.

4 Leave to cool slightly. This tart is better at room temperature as the sugar, nuts, and juices under the fruit firm up. Mix a little confectioners' sugar with the cinnamon and dust the top. Lever the tart off the paper with a palette knife, then slide it onto a plate.

ALSO TRY...

Free-form nectarine tart Halve and pit 1¾ lb nectarines and thinly slice. Roll out and assemble the tart as above, but use ¾ cup ground almonds instead of hazelnuts. Bake as above. Melt 1½ tbsp apricot jam in a small pan with 1 tbsp water. Paint the warm jam glaze thickly all over the fruit.

Try this tart with apricots, peaches, or plums. Plums and apricots require more sugar.

Butter and brown sugar roasted apples

If you thought a pan of baked apples was the easiest dessert ever, think again. The apples for this aren't even cored. Instead they are simply halved, so retain those lovely plump appley curves, and there is no filling. But this dish is somehow grand in its simplicity; it will really make you appreciate the beauty of apples. A mixture of apple varieties looks very good and, if you can find any with some leaves still attached to the stems (cultivate friends with apple trees, or look for some at farmers' markets), even better.

Serves 6

6 apples

2½ tbsp unsalted butter

2 tbsp granulated sugar

2 tbsp light brown sugar

¼ tsp ground cinnamon (optional)

generous grating of nutmeg (optional)

¼ tsp salt

1 Preheat the oven to 350°F. Halve the apples. You don't need to core them and you should leave the stems intact if you can; it looks pretty. Put them into a small roasting pan.

2 Heat the butter in a frying pan until it turns light brown and smells nutty. Don't let it burn. Stir in the sugars, spices (if using), and salt; then pour this over the apples. Turn the apples around to make sure they get well coated.

3 Arrange the apples cut side up and bake in the oven for 30–40 minutes, until tender and slightly caramelized in places.

ALSO TRY…

Honey roasted pears with gorgonzola Halve the pears as in the apple recipe above. Put 1 tbsp butter in a pan, add ¼ cup honey, and a pinch of salt and heat until the mixture is melted. Add 2 tbsp granulated sugar. Proceed as above, baking the pears until they are completely tender and golden. Serve each person with two pear halves and about 1 oz gorgonzola (or other blue cheese) alongside. Sprinkle on some very coarsely chopped hazelnuts (lightly toasted).

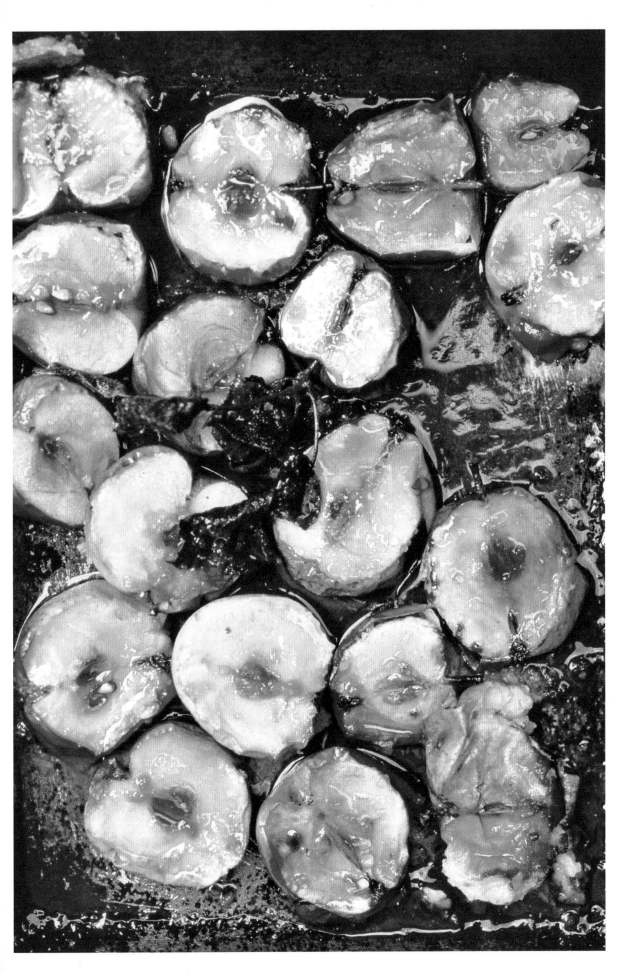

Pear, almond, and red wine cake

If you can, poach the pears the day before, then leave them to get a good dark color while sitting in the wine syrup.

Serves 6–8

FOR THE PEARS

1½ cups fruity red wine

1 cup granulated sugar

2 strips of lemon zest and juice of ½ lemon

6 pears, peeled, halved and cored

1 tbsp redcurrant jelly (optional)

FOR THE CAKE

14 tbsp butter

1⅓ cups light brown sugar

⅔ cup ground almonds

1½ tsp baking powder

2½ cups all-purpose flour, sifted

4 eggs, lightly beaten

2 tsp vanilla extract

½ cup buttermilk

1 To cook the pears, put the wine, granulated sugar, zest, and juice into a saucepan and bring slowly to a boil, stirring to help the sugar dissolve. Reduce to a simmer, add the pears (they should lie in a single layer) and cook until tender (about 20 minutes). Turn them halfway through.

2 Butter a springform cake tin 9 in in diameter and 3½ in deep. Preheat the oven to 350°F. Lift the pears from the syrup with a slotted spoon and carefully arrange them, cut side down, on the bottom of the pan, in a circle like the spokes of a wheel. Alternate the bottoms and tops of each pear half. Reserve the cooking liquid.

3 Cream the butter and brown sugar until pale and fluffy. Mix the almonds and baking powder with the flour. Gradually add the eggs to the creamed butter and sugar, beating well after each addition. Sprinkle on a little flour if the mixture looks as though it is curdling. Mix in the vanilla and buttermilk; then fold in the combined flour, baking powder, and almonds. Spoon this on top of the pears and bake for 45–50 minutes. A skewer inserted in the centre should come out clean when the cake is cooked.

4 Run a knife between cake and pan and turn the cake out. If any pears stick to the pan, carefully ease them off and replace on the cake.

5 The reserved pear cooking liquid should be quite thick and syrupy. If it isn't, boil a little to reduce. It should also be a good red colour; if not, add 1 tbsp redcurrant jelly and a squeeze of lemon juice and heat to melt the jelly.

6 Pierce the sponge of the cake peeking out between the pears with a skewer. Slowly pour the syrup all over. Most of it will glaze the pears, but some will run down into the cake. Leave to cool. Serve with thick cream, crème fraîche, or a mixture of cream and yogurt.

Cardamom, honey, and orange roasted apricots

When stone fruits are abundant I am always looking for different things to do with them. Although almonds (as a stuffing, or in the form of a slug of amaretto poured over before baking) are a classic European pairing, Asian flavors also work very well.

Serves 6

about 30 apricots, halved and pitted

crushed seeds from 10 cardamom pods

⅔ cup light brown sugar

¼ cup honey (preferably orange blossom)

½ cup orange juice

juice of ½ lemon

1 Preheat the oven to 350°F. Put the apricots into an ovenproof dish, cut side up, so they lie snugly in a single layer. Sprinkle on the cardamom and sugar. Drizzle on the honey. Pour the orange and lemon juice around the apricots and bake for 20–25 minutes (depending on how ripe your apricots are), or until the apricots are tender and the sugar is slightly caramelized.

2 Serve warm, at room temperature, or chilled with whipped cream (a little orange flower water can be added to the cream).

ALSO TRY…

Lime and ginger roasted nectarines Put 6 halved, pitted nectarines in an ovenproof dish with a 1in square of fresh ginger, peeled and grated; 1¼ cups dark brown sugar; the juice of 2 limes; and ½ cup water. Mix everything together, then lay the fruit cut side up in a single layer. Bake as above for about 45 minutes (it could take longer, depending on the ripeness of the fruit). If it looks as though your nectarines are a bit pale, put some more sugar on them for the last 10 minutes or so of the baking time. I like these at room temperature or chilled. Serve with crème fraîche or whipped cream.

Roasted plums with brown sugar cream Put 16 plums–halved and pitted–into an ovenproof dish with ¾ cup sugar; a 1 in square of fresh ginger, peeled and grated; and a sprinkling of ground cinnamon. Add ½ cup orange juice and mix everything together. Lay the plums in a single layer, cut side up. Bake as above for 20–25 minutes (though it depends how ripe your plums are; they need to be tender). Serve warm, at room temperature, or chilled. Mix about ¼ cup cream with 1¼ cups Greek yogurt and sprinkle the top with 6 tbsp dark brown sugar. Leave the sugar to form a kind of gooey crust (it takes about half an hour). You can stir this to "marble" the sugar through the cream or leave as it is. Serve with the plums.

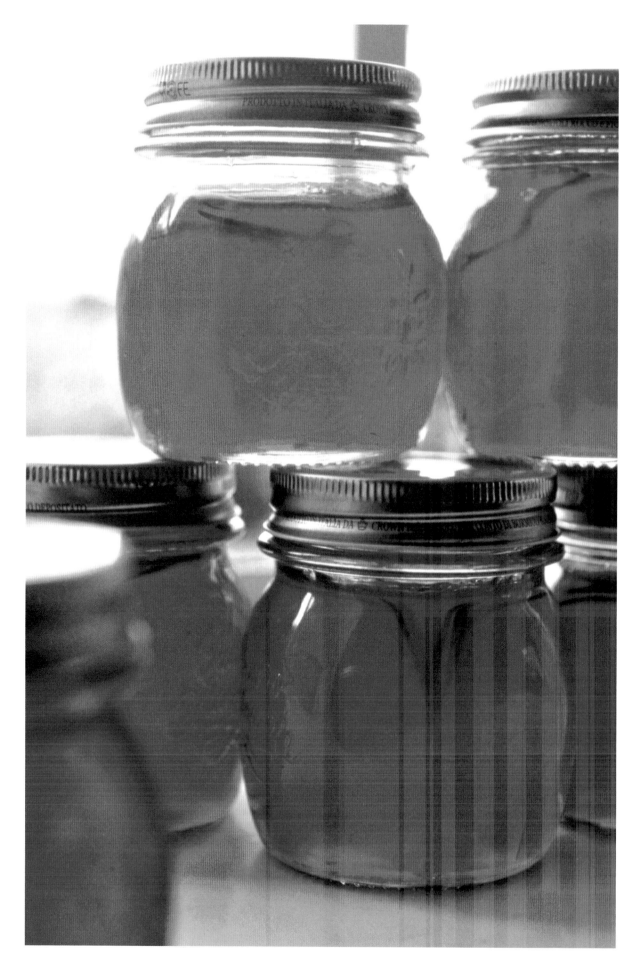

Paradise jelly

I found this recipe in an ancient book, *The Old Yankee Cookbook*, which I picked up in a second-hand store. The jelly is a beautiful red-amber color and is very good with turkey, chicken, and pork. If you can't get hold of any quinces, you can use apples and cranberries, instead.

Makes about 6½ lb
4 large quinces
3⅓ lb apples
1½ lb cranberries
granulated sugar (you'll need about 4½ lb, or 9 cups)

1 Chop the quinces and apples into big chunks. There is no need to peel or core them. Put in a large pan with the cranberries and cover with water. Bring to a boil, then reduce the heat and cook until soft. It will take about an hour.

2 Hang a jelly bag over another large pan and put the fruity mush into the bag. Let the juice drip from the suspended bag overnight.

3 Measure the juice that you have collected. Add 2½ cups sugar for every 2 cups of liquid. Bring to a boil slowly, stirring every so often to help the sugar dissolve and skimming any scum that rises to the surface. Once the jelly is boiling test for the setting point: put a teaspoon of the juices onto a saucer. If, once cold, the liquid sets and wrinkles when pushed with a finger, it is ready. You can check for the setting point using a candy thermometer too. (The setting point for jam and jelly is 220°F.)

4 Ladle the jelly into hot, sterilized jars (see page 242) and seal. You will find a funnel handy here. Process in boiling water bath for 5 minutes or store in the refrigerator.

Les Jacques

From the Périgord region of France, these are thin, like crêpes, but have apples cooked inside. They are lovely with pitted cherries, too: sauté them briefly in butter and a bit of sugar, then spoon them over each crêpe.

Serves 4

1 cup all-purpose plain flour

2 tbsp superfine sugar, plus more to dust

pinch of salt

2 large eggs

½ tbsp eau de vie or brandy (optional)

¾ cup milk

3½ tbsp unsalted butter

4 apples, peeled, cored, and cut into
 wedges

juice of ½ lemon

confectioners' sugar, to dust

1 Put the flour, superfine sugar, and salt into a bowl and make a well in the center. Beat the eggs lightly with a fork and put into a pitcher with the alcohol (if using), ¾ cup water, and the milk. Gradually pour the liquid into the well, beating in the dry ingredients. Mix thoroughly so there are no lumps. Leave to rest for at least 30 minutes (1½ hours is ideal) for a lighter batter.

2 Melt half the butter in a frying pan and sauté the apples in batches until just tender, but not completely soft. Be careful not to burn the butter; if you do, throw it out and use more fresh butter. Sprinkle with superfine sugar as you go to get bits of caramelization. When they are done, squeeze the lemon juice over them.

3 Melt a knob of butter in a nonstick frying pan (ideally 6–8 in across). Ladle in a very thin layer of batter, swirling so it goes to the edges. Put slices of apple on top, then cover with another really thin layer of batter. Once that starts to set, turn over carefully. Dust confectioners' sugar over each pancake as it is cooked. Serve with crème fraîche.

ALSO TRY...

Russian apple pancakes Mix 1¼ cups sifted all-purpose flour with 3½ tbsp light brown sugar, ½ tsp salt, and 1 tsp baking powder. Beat 2 eggs with 1 cup whole milk and ½ cup yogurt in a bowl. Gradually mix the liquid ingredients into the dry. Coarsely grate 3 tart apples, peeled and cored. Stir these into the batter along with the finely grated zest of 1 lemon. Heat a pat of unsalted butter and 1½ tsp sunflower oil in a nonstick frying pan. Add a couple of tablespoons of batter (the pancakes should be about 3 in across). Cook over medium heat until set on one side. You should see little holes forming. You can cook several pancakes at a time, depending on the size of your pan. Flip each over and cook the other side. Add more butter and oil as you go. Serve dusted with confectioners' sugar, with sour cream and honey on the side. Serves 6.

Chilled apple and rice pudding

This is adapted from a recipe by Claire Clarke, pastry chef at The French Laundry in California. It's hard to believe humble ingredients can be taken to these heights.

Serves 6

FOR THE RICE

¾ cup short-grain rice

3 cups whole milk, plus more if needed

3 tbsp sugar

5 tbsp heavy cream

grated nutmeg or ground cinnamon

FOR THE APPLES

3 tart apples, peeled, cored, and sliced

½ cup hard or sweet cider

superfine sugar, to taste

FOR THE SYRUP

¾ cup granulated sugar

TO SERVE

½ cup heavy cream, lightly whipped
  and sweetened to taste

1 Cover the rice with water in a saucepan and bring to a boil. Boil for 4 minutes, drain, and rinse. Return the rice to the pan and add the milk and sugar. Bring to a boil, then reduce the heat and cook for about 25 minutes, stirring from time to time. You may need more milk. You should end up with a sloppy mixture that still holds its shape, with soft grains. Remember, it will firm up as it cools. Leave until cold.

2 Put the apples in a pan with the cider and set over medium-low heat. Cover and cook until completely soft, stirring to break them down every so often. Make sure they don't boil dry. Once they're cooked, add superfine sugar to taste (they should still be on the tart side, but not unpalatably so).

3 To make the syrup, put the granulated sugar into a pan with ½ cup water. Heat slowly until the sugar has dissolved. When the sugar has completely melted bring to the boil and watch until the syrup turns to caramel (it will turn golden first). Swish the pan a bit. Once it becomes caramel (you will know by the smell and color) immediately add about ½ cup water and swish around. It will splutter. Stir so the caramelized sugar dissolves in the water.

4 Leave everything to cool, then stir the cream into the rice. If the mixture still seems rather stiff, add more cream or milk. Season with nutmeg or cinnamon.

5 Layer the components up in glasses. Start with some apple, then add caramel, then rice pudding, then caramel. Repeat. Spoon whipped cream on top and drizzle with caramel. Refrigerate until serving.

ALSO TRY...

Make this in the summer with apricots—they are nice and tart—using white wine and perhaps a little almond liqueur to cook the fruit, rather than cider.

Blood orange and cardamom jellies

Blood oranges are available only for a short time; at other times of the year make this with ordinary oranges. Serve in pretty glasses (Moroccan tea glasses are lovely).

Serves 8

FOR THE JELLIES
4 blood oranges
3¾ cups blood orange juice
juice of ½ lemon
ground seeds from 10 cardamom pods
6 tbsp sugar
2 x ¼ oz packets plain gelatin

FOR THE CANDIED PEEL
2 oranges (preferably blood oranges)
1 cup blood orange juice
½ cup superfine sugar

TO SERVE
sweetened whipped cream

1 To make the jellies, cut a thin slice off the top and bottom of each orange. Set on its base and, with a very sharp knife, remove the peel and pith in strips, working from top to bottom. To remove the segments, cut between membrane and flesh with a thin, sharp knife and carefully slide each segment out.

2 To make the jelly, sprinkle the gelatin over ¼ cup water in a small bowl and let soak for 5 minutes to soften. Put the orange and lemon juices, cardamom, and sugar in a saucepan and heat gently, stirring to help the sugar dissolve. Add the softened gelatin to the warm juice, stirring to dissolve. Divide the orange segments among eight glasses, then pour in the jelly. Leave to cool, then refrigerate.

3 For the candied peel, finely pare the zest of the oranges (avoid the white pith) and cut into fine julienne strips. Put in a saucepan with the orange juice and sugar. Heat gently until the sugar has dissolved, then simmer until the liquid has almost evaporated (about 30 minutes). Scoop the zest out with a fork, gently separate, and lay on parchment paper. Put somewhere warm to dry. Top the jellies with whipped cream and the candied peel.

ALSO TRY...

All you have to remember is that it takes one ¼ oz packet gelatin to set 2 cups of liquid and any juice can be turned into jelly. The only thing that mucks up this ratio is alcohol (it inhibits gelatin's setting properties), so closely follow any jelly recipes you see that include alcohol.

Orange and rosemary jellies Citrus juice with rosemary is deliciously fresh and herby. Make as above but, instead of cardamom, add 2 rosemary sprigs to the juice before heating. Discard these before you add the gelatin. You can use grapefruit or pink grapefruit juice instead, but you will need more sugar.

Apple and blackberry jellies Make as above but use clear apple juice, the juice of a whole lemon and, instead of cardamom, a cinnamon stick (discard it before adding the gelatin). Add whole blackberries before the jelly sets.

Sugar-crusted lemon loaf cake

Classic lemon loaf cake and you don't even need an electric mixer to make it. This is good in the dark wintry months when citrus fruits are at their best and you need something sharp to prick your tastebuds. Any stale cake—hard to believe that is possible but it does sometimes happen—is great in a trifle.

Serves 8

FOR THE CAKE

9 tbsp butter, diced, plus more for
  the pan
1¾ cups self-rising flour, sifted
a pinch of salt
⅔ cup granulated sugar

2 large eggs, beaten
2 unwaxed lemons

FOR THE TOPPING

juice of 2 lemons
½ cup superfine sugar

1 Preheat the oven to 350°F. Butter a 9 x 5 in loaf tin and line with waxed paper. Mix the flour and salt together in a large bowl and rub in the butter with your fingers until the mixture resembles bread crumbs, then stir in the granulated sugar. Add the eggs and the grated zest and juice of the lemons. Mix together until you have a soft batter, but don't overwork the mixture.

2 Spoon the batter into the loaf pan and bake for 45–55 minutes, or until golden and well risen and a skewer inserted in the centre comes out clean. Leave to cool for 10 minutes in the pan. Meanwhile, stir together the lemon juice and sugar for the topping. Prick the cake surface with a skewer or fork, then slowly pour the superfine sugar and lemon mix over it. This will sink in, but some of the sugar will settle to make a nice, crunchy, sugary crust on the surface.

ALSO TRY...

You can make the same kind of cake with limes; just use twice the amount of fruit.

Rhubarb and lemon curd bread and butter pudding

This does work—and is delicious because of the contrast of sweet and tart—as long as you cook the rhubarb very carefully. It must still hold its shape. Don't throw away the rhubarb syrup; instead, keep it and use like a cordial, topping it up with sparkling water.

Serves 6–8

1 lb rhubarb
1 cup granulated sugar
1¼ cups whole milk
1¼ cups heavy cream
pinch of salt
½ tsp vanilla extract

3 eggs, plus 1 egg yolk
3 tbsp butter
about 9 oz bread (soft white rolls, sliced,
  are particularly good)
about ½ cup lemon curd
confectioners' sugar, to dust

1 Trim the rhubarb and cut it into 1¼in lengths. Heat ½ cup water in a pan with ¼ cup of the granulated sugar. Bring to a boil and add the rhubarb. Simmer for 1½ minutes, then carefully drain the rhubarb, and reserve the syrup for another use (see recipe introduction). Set the rhubarb aside to cool.

2 Bring the milk, cream, and salt to a boil in a heavy pan. Add the vanilla. Beat the eggs, extra yolk, and the remaining granulated sugar together. Pour the warm milk and cream into this, stirring all the time.

3 Slice the bread, butter it and spread with lemon curd, then layer it, buttered side up, in an ovenproof dish. Put the rhubarb on top of the bread as you go. Pour on the egg and cream mixture through a sieve and leave to sit for half an hour—this just makes the pudding lighter. Meanwhile, preheat the oven to 350°F.

4 Put the dish into a roasting pan and add enough boiling water to the pan to come halfway up the sides of the dish. Bake for 40–45 minutes, or until the pudding is puffy and set on the top and golden in color. Leave to cool slightly, dust with confectioners' sugar, and serve with crème fraîche, or cream mixed with Greek yogurt.

Crusts and crumbs

I hate throwing bread away. There seems such potential in it, and I'm very aware what a fundamental foodstuff it is: the staff of life. In North Africa it's the one food that will be eagerly retrieved if dropped, then wiped and kissed–it is so prized–yet most of us chuck out the end of a loaf without a second thought. But it's worth considering what you can do with that bit.

Using bread well means you can afford to pay a little more for better-quality loaves. I used to balk at the price of good sourdough, but if you use it all you've had the pleasure of bread worth eating and that also makes you feel fuller. If you don't believe me, compare how you feel after eating a bit of good coarse country bread from a bakery to how you feel after a slice of the sorry processed stuff sold in supermarkets.

Once bread has lost its soft freshness, it passes through different phases. It can be toasted–good toast is a glorious edible platter–but it doesn't end there. A stuffing made from bread crumbs is the most obvious way to use old bread, and sage and onion is just the start. Go Caribbean and mix bread crumbs with lime zest, thyme, scallion, chile, and rum and use it to stuff a chicken, or toss bread crumbs with sautéed eggplant, dates, and cilantro for a Middle Eastern–inspired filling for lamb. You just need enough fat (butter or oil) to bind and keep the bread moist. And you don't have to stop at stuffing meat. Roasted tomatoes, eggplants, peppers, and mushrooms can all be enhanced by flavorful crumbs.

Think beyond stuffing and you'll hit on some of the chicest platefuls around. The trendiness of "peasant cooking" has seen us exalt dishes that were created specifically to use up leftover bread. There's the Italian bread salad, panzanella (the Italians are good at counting every crumb), bread and butter pudding, pain perdu, summer pudding, and spaghetti with fried crumbs. Bread's ability to soak up other flavors, to be soft or crispy, to thicken without altering the character of a dish, make it one of the most useful leftovers. See that sausage and bean casserole that isn't rib-sticking enough, or that puréed mushroom soup that is a bit thin? Throw in a handful of bread crumbs and watch these dishes come together.

I have included only one recipe for making your own bread. There are many other books, from writers more qualified than me, about how to make bread at home. I urge you to consult those and try it. But I wanted to include a recipe for pizza, partly because it is more than just bread, but also because making your own pizza saves you masses of money.

Beyond that, you just need to try to make every loaf earn its keep. It's a simple message: buy good bread and use it well.

Southern Italian cauliflower with fried bread crumbs, capers, and anchovies

Much of Italian food has to do with making the best of very little, or using up what is past its peak. Italians transform the old into the new by using hunger, ingenuity, and their palates. Bread is one of the things they deal with very well. Stale bread crumbs–toasted, or fried in olive oil–are common in southern Italy and are often used instead of Parmesan to top pasta or vegetables. I particularly love the Sicilian way here, which teams bread crumbs with the island's trademark sweet-savoury ingredients: raisins, capers, and nuts. Cauliflower has never tasted so good. A cracking dish can be made by tossing the cauliflower into pasta (add olive oil, salt, and pepper) before sprinkling with the flavored bread crumbs. You won't miss the Parmesan.

serves 4 as a side dish

1 cauliflower, broken into florets
1 slice stale ciabatta or focaccia
2 tbsp olive oil
4 garlic cloves, very thinly sliced
1 tbsp capers, rinsed
½–1 tsp dried red pepper flakes, to taste
8 salt-cured anchovies, drained and
   coarsely chopped

¼ cup raisins or currants, or both, soaked
   in just-boiled water for 15 minutes
   and drained
3 tbsp chopped fresh flat-leaf parsley
2 tbsp pine nuts, toasted
salt and pepper
squeeze of lemon juice
¼ cup extra-virgin olive oil

1 Cook the cauliflower in lightly salted boiling water until just tender. Prepare the topping while it's cooking.

2 Make the bread into coarse crumbs; I use the pulse button of the food processor. Heat the oil in a large frying pan and fry the bread crumbs until golden. Add the garlic and cook for another minute; then add the capers, red pepper flakes, anchovies, dried fruit, parsley, and pine nuts. Drain the cauliflower well (if it's wet it ruins the bread crumbs).

3 You can now either put the cauliflower in a serving dish and sprinkle with the bread crumb mix, or add the cauliflower to the pan, toss with the crumbs, and heat for a couple of minutes to give the cauliflower a bit of color. Season (easy on the salt because of the anchovies), squeeze some lemon juice over, and drizzle with the extra-virgin oil. Serve immediately.

ALSO TRY...

Plain bread crumbs fried in olive oil–without any additions–on pasta. It's particularly good tossed with garlic and chiles.

Using the fried bread crumb mix above to sprinkle on broccoli, cabbage, green beans, roasted tomatoes, or peppers and roasted fish.

Adding chopped green olives to the bread crumbs for the main dish.

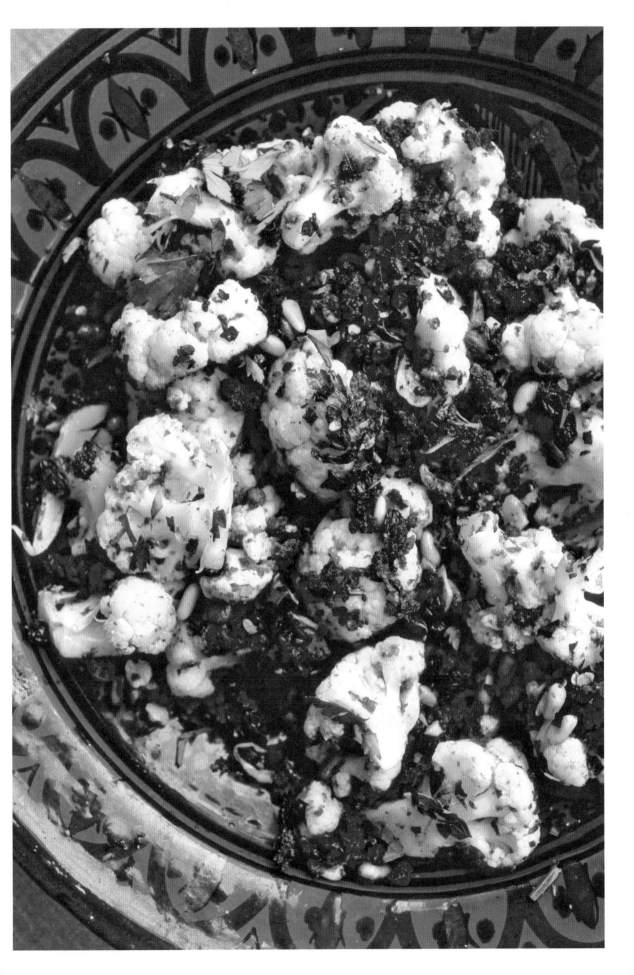

Spring panzanella

A good way not only to use up bread but to extend ingredients that aren't cheap. Chunks of ricotta salata are a very good addition, adding lovely texture, or try finely grated lemon zest.

Serves 6

12 oz ciabatta bread, torn
  into 1 in chunks
1 shallot, chopped
salt and pepper
3 tbsp olive oil
2 cups fresh peas
2 cups fresh fava beans
1 lb asparagus, trimmed

large bunch of basil, leaves only
1 garlic clove, crushed
about 2 tbsp extra-virgin olive oil
3 tbsp balsamic vinegar (white if you can
  get it)
3 oz Pecorino or Parmesan cheese, shaved

1 Preheat the oven to 350°F. Toss the bread in a roasting pan with the shallot, seasoning, and oil. Bake for about 15 minutes, or until the pieces of bread are golden and crunchy.

2 Cook the peas and fava beans in lightly salted boiling water (I do it in separate pans as they cook at slightly different rates) until just tender, then drain. Slip the skins from the beans when cool enough to handle. Meanwhile, cook the asparagus in lightly salted boiling water for 3–4 minutes, or until just tender. Run cold water over it to set the color, but don't make it completely cold. This salad can be served at room temperature, but I like it slightly warmer if I can manage to leave the cooking until the last minute.

3 Put the bread chunks into a large, broad, shallow bowl. Now add the asparagus, peas, fava beans, basil and garlic. Season well. Pour on the extra-virgin olive oil and balsamic vinegar and add the cheese. Toss gently and serve.

Sourdough tartines with labneh and spiced roasted tomatoes

Bread doesn't have to be just a filler. A good sandwich is one of the best things you can eat. But you need great bread with a strong identity and a good flavor, such as sourdough. Most sourdough loaves seem prohibitively expensive, but they have such great keeping qualities that thay are worth buying. The woman who makes the most famous sourdough in the world, Apollonia Poilâne from Poilâne in Paris, told me to keep it under a cloth towel, spraying the towel every so often with water. Like this it is fine for three days, after which it is good for toasting for another two or three. And the sour, tangy flavor is incomparable. A small café beside the Poilâne bakery got me hooked on sourdough "tartines" (basically open sandwiches). You can have diet-friendly versions spread with low-fat cream cheese topped with thinly sliced raw salmon with lemon and dill, or more indulgent blue cheese with toasted walnuts and slices of sautéed pear. Tartines are also a great way to use up leftovers: try flaked salmon and crushed fava beans with olive oil and lemon juice; chicken with mango, watercress, and curry mayo; pork with spinach and sautéed apples. Tartines are certainly grand enough to give friends for lunch (and perfect if there's only two of you).

Serves 4

1¼ cups Greek yogurt
1 garlic clove, crushed
a little salt
12 plum tomatoes
¼ cup olive oil
2 tbsp balsamic vinegar

1½ tsp harissa
2 tsp dark brown sugar
4 slices of sourdough bread
cilantro leaves and extra-virgin olive oil,
  to serve

1 Make the labneh the day before you want to use it. Line a sieve with clean muslin and set it over a bowl. Mix the yogurt with the garlic and salt and put it into the cloth. Tie the cloth up and refrigerate the whole thing. The yogurt will lose moisture over the next 24 hours, gaining a firmer texture, but help it along by giving it a good squeeze once or twice.

2 Preheat the oven to 350°F. Halve the tomatoes lengthwise and put them in a small roasting pan. Mix together the olive oil, balsamic vinegar, and harissa, season and pour over the tomatoes. Turn them over to coat, ending with them cut-side up. Sprinkle with the sugar and roast for 40–45 minutes, until slightly shrunken. You can serve them warm or at room temperature.

3 Toast the sourdough. Unwrap the labneh, spread it onto each slice of bread and top with the roasted tomatoes (and any of their juices). Sprinkle with the cilantro and drizzle with extra-virgin olive oil before serving.

Yoghurtlu kofta kebab

I can't say I first ate this Turkish classic overlooking the Bosporus. It was actually in an inexpensive restaurant in north London, but I immediately tracked down several recipes for it. A great mix of temperatures and textures, it's one of the best meals you can make and for less than the price of a Chinese take-out.

Serves 4

FOR THE KEBAB

1¾ lb ground lamb

1 onion, grated

2 garlic cloves, crushed

4 tsp ground cumin

leaves from 1 small bunch fresh parsley, very finely chopped

2 tbsp olive oil

2–3 white pita breads

1¾ cups plain Greek yogurt

1 tbsp unsalted butter

1½ tbsp pine nuts

pinch of cayenne, paprika, or sumac

coarsely chopped fresh cilantro or mint (optional)

FOR THE TOMATO SAUCE

14 oz can tomatoes in thick juice

1 small onion, finely chopped

2 garlic cloves, crushed

1 fresh red chile, seeded and chopped

2 tsp light brown sugar

2 tbsp olive oil

salt and pepper

1 Put the lamb in a bowl and pummel it. Add the onion, garlic, cumin, and parsley. Season and mix really well. With wet hands, form into rounds slightly smaller than golf balls. Set on a plate, cover, and firm up in the refrigerator.

2 Put everything for the sauce in a pan, add ¼ cup water and bring to a boil. Reduce to a simmer and cook for 20–30 minutes, stirring. It should be thick, but not like chutney. If it's too thick, add more water. Bring the meatballs to room temperature.

3 Heat the oil in a frying pan and fry the meatballs over high heat, in batches to get a good brown color. Reduce the heat and cook through (though they're nice rare).

4 Meanwhile, tear your pita into triangles and toast. Put in a broad, shallow bowl and pour the sauce on. Traditionally yogurt goes next, then the kofta. I prefer yogurt on top, but take your pick. Sizzle the butter and fry the pine nuts for a few seconds, then pour over. Sprinkle with the spice and herbs, if you want.

ALSO TRY...

Middle Eastern Chicken fatteh Fry 1 large onion, chopped, in 1½ tbsp olive oil until soft and golden. Add ½ tsp ground cinnamon, ½ tsp ground allspice, ground seeds from 5 cardamom pods and a pinch of ground chile. Cook for 2–3 minutes, then mix in 2¾ cups cooked chicken. Season really well and add a squeeze of lemon juice. Toast 4 pita breads, cut into triangles, and put half in a dish. Moisten with warm chicken stock and extra-virgin olive oil. Lay the chicken on, then the remaining crunchy pitas. Add 3 garlic cloves, crushed, to 1 cup Greek yogurt and spread over. Sprinkle with toasted pine nuts, chopped fresh cilantro and extra-virgin olive oil.

Le bettelman

An Alsace recipe, in which the broken bread creates something almost like a sponge. Make in a dish with lots of surface area as the toasted top is delicious.

Serves 6

12 oz white bread
1 cup whole milk
1 cup heavy cream
¾ cup granulated sugar
finely grated zest of 1 and juice of ½ lemon
1 lb tart apples

¼ cup butter
4 eggs, lightly beaten
2 tsp vanilla extract
3 tbsp calvados or brandy (optional)
confectioners' sugar, to dust

1 Break the bread into irregular hazelnut-sized chunks and put them into a baking dish. Heat the milk, cream, granulated sugar (reserve 2 tbsp sugar) and zest, stirring to dissolve the sugar. When just under a boil, pour over the bread. Mash, then soak for 15 minutes. Preheat the oven to 350°F.

2 Core the apples and cut into chunks. Melt 2 tbsp of the butter in a large frying pan. Cook the apples over medium-high heat until golden. Toss in the reserved sugar and cook until almost caramelized.

3 Mix the eggs with the vanilla and alcohol, if using. Mix into the bread with the lemon juice and apples and dot with the remaining butter. Bake for 45 minutes. The top should be golden and souffléd. Leave to cool and set for 10 minutes. Sift over confectioners' sugar and serve with crème fraîche.

ALSO TRY...

Cherry, apricot, or peach bettelman Make as above, slicing peaches or quartering apricots before sautéing. If you're using cherries, don't cook them much before adding. Use kirsch or amaretto instead of calvados.

Ham and cheese pain perdu Butter two slices of white bread. Sprinkle 3 tbsp grated Gruyère on one piece, top with a slice of ham and sprinkle on another 3 tbsp Gruyère. Top with the other bread slice and cut in half. Put 2 beaten eggs in a broad dish with 2 tbsp milk and seasoning. Leave the sandwich to soak in the egg mixture for 5 minutes, turning. Melt a pat of butter in a nonstick pan and fry the sandwich on both sides over a medium heat until golden, then reduce the heat and allow the cheese to melt. Serves 1.

"Sicilian" pain perdu with toasted peaches Make as above without the ham and cheese, adding 1 tbsp heavy cream, 1½ tsp Marsala, and 1½ tsp sugar to the eggs. While the bread's soaking, fry a ripe peach, quartered, in butter until toasted. Throw in 1½ tsp sugar and cook until caramelized in places. Slosh in some Marsala and bubble to a syrup. Serve with the pain perdu. Sift confectioners' sugar over before serving. If you prefer, serve with roasted or baked stone fruits instead (see page 279). Serves 2.

Canederli

I first had these in a very humble roadside restaurant in northern Italy. I had never heard of "canederli" and was surprised to learn they were just made with bread, as they were so delicious. They are made the way we would make stuffing for a chicken, but the mixture is rolled into little dumplings and poached. You can also treat them like dumplings and serve them in soup.

Serves 4

FOR THE CANEDERLI
8 oz white bread
½ cup milk
3 tbsp butter
1 onion, very finely chopped
4 oz pancetta, in small chunks
2 eggs, lightly beaten
generous grating of nutmeg
leaves from 4 thyme sprigs

⅔ cup fresh flat-leaf parsley, very
   finely chopped
salt and pepper
chicken stock or water, for poaching
all-purpose flour, to dust

TO SERVE
melted butter or chicken stock
shaved Parmesan cheese

1 Break the bread up into various-sized little chunks and crumbs with your fingers—the food processor does it too finely. Sprinkle with the milk, mix with your hands, and leave for 15 minutes or so.

2 Melt the butter in a frying pan and sauté the onion and pancetta until the onion is completely soft. Mix gently with all the other ingredients except the stock and flour, using your hands. Don't overwork the mixture. Season really well; this is very important.

3 Bring a large pan of chicken stock or water to a boil. Meanwhile, wet your hands and shape the bread mixture into balls the size of walnuts. Roll very lightly in the flour and shake off excess. Once the stock is boiling, reduce to a steady simmer. (If using water, salt it.) Drop in half the canederli, then cook very gently for about 7–10 minutes. If the stock boils, it will break them up. They will rise to the top when they are done. Scoop out with a slotted spoon and drain well on paper towels to soak up excess water.

4 Serve in soup plates with melted butter (you can flavour it by frying rosemary or sage in it) or in hot chicken stock, with Parmesan sprinkled over.

ALSO TRY...

Serving canederli with the same topping as used for Viennese Potatoes (see page 92). Hardly surprising that this works, given that canederli are made in an area of Italy that borders Austria. They are also good with a sour cream and cucumber sauce: sauté chopped cucumber in butter, add sour cream, and heat through. Spoon over the canederli then scatter with ground paprika or poppy seeds. Chunks of both roasted beets and roasted squash are lovely dotted among the canederli.

Beet, goat cheese, and caper pizza

The mark-up on pizza is astounding. Make your own and you won't look back. I learned this recipe on a course at River Cottage in England, and the dough is the best I've tried. Get the oven as hot as possible well before cooking.

makes 2 x 12 in pizzas

FOR THE DOUGH
1¼ tsp dried yeast
1½ cups lukewarm water
1¾ cups bread flour
2 cups all-purpose flour, plus more to dust
1½ tsp salt
slug of olive oil

FOR THE TOPPING
¼ cup olive oil, plus more to drizzle
4 large red onions, very thinly sliced
about 10 thyme sprigs
9 oz goat cheese, in chunks
6 medium roasted beets, chopped
salt and pepper
3 tbsp capers, rinsed

1 Dissolve the yeast in 1½ tbsp of the water and mix in 2 tbsp flour. Stir to make a smooth paste and leave under a cloth, somewhere warm, for 30 minutes to form a "sponge".

2 Put the flours in a bowl and make a well in the center. Pour in the sponge, salt, oil, and remaining water and mix, gradually bringing in the dry ingredients, to form a wet dough (don't be tempted to add too much flour). Knead for 10 minutes until satiny and elastic. Put in a clean bowl, cover with a cloth, and leave somewhere warm for 1½ hours, or until doubled in size. Preheat the oven to 500°F and put in pizza stones, unglazed terracota tiles, or baking sheets.

3 Meanwhile, for the topping, heat the oil in a saucepan and add the onions. Turn them in the fat, add 1 tbsp water, cover, place over very low heat, and sweat for 15 minutes. Add the thyme and set aside.

4 Plop the dough onto a lightly floured work surface and knead for 2 minutes. Divide into two and roll each piece into a 12 in round. Put on well-floured baking sheets or large pieces of cardboard to support them while you add the topping.

5 Top with the onions, cheese and beets. Season and drizzle with oil. Slide on to the hot stones or baking sheets (oil baking sheets at the last minute). Bake for 15 minutes, sprinkling with capers 5 minutes before the end. Serve immediately.

ALSO TRY…

Pizzas can go anywhere. Just remember your topping has to cook, without burning, in 15 minutes. Try…

Fried onions, oregano, and mozzarella cheese (for purists)
Potato, onion, and taleggio cheese (partially cook and thinly slice the potatoes)
Spinach, zucchini, ricotta, and Parmesan cheese
Roasted pumpkin, spinach, and fontina cheese
Prosciutto, goat cheese, and figs

Brown bread and whiskey ice cream

I just love this brown bread ice cream (laced with a bit of whiskey) with raspberries. A coarse-textured brown bread with seeds and grains is particularly good with it.

Serves 4–6

1½ tbsp unsalted butter

⅔ cup whole-wheat bread crumbs

⅓ cup dark brown sugar

1⅔ cups heavy cream

½ cup light brown sugar

1½ tsp vanilla extract

5 tbsp whiskey

1 Melt the butter in a frying pan and add the bread crumbs. Sauté until golden, stirring often; then add the dark brown sugar, pressing with the back of a wooden spoon to break up any lumps. Continue to sauté, stirring, until the sugar has caramelized the bread crumbs. Be very careful not to burn the bread crumbs or sugar. Pour onto a plate and leave to cool.

2 Whip the cream until loose peaks form, adding the light brown sugar as you go. Add the vanilla and whiskey and stir in the caramelized bread crumbs.

3 Put into a broad, shallow container and freeze, beating the mixture about 3 times during the freezing process to break down the small crystals and make the ice cream smooth (some people throw it into the food processor to blend it up, but that would ruin the bread crumbs in this recipe). If you have an ice cream machine then churn it in that.

ALSO TRY...

Brown bread and coffee ice cream Make exactly as the recipe above, but add 2 tsp instant coffee granules dissolved in 1 tbsp boiling water (and left to cool) along with the whiskey.

Wine-soaked autumn pudding

Even better, to my mind, than the summer version. I love the texture of dried apples, but you don't have to use them. If you don't have a source for blackberries—they're so expensive you really have to go blackberrying for them—increase the quantity of plums. It may seem extravagant to make this with wine but you don't need a fantastic bottle. A passable Chilean merlot (or similar) or something leftover from the night before is perfectly good enough.

Serves 8

⅔ cup dried cranberries

8 dried apple slices

1 lb apples, peeled, cored, and sliced

1 lb plums, halved, pitted, and sliced

2½ cups red wine

1 cup caster sugar

1 in cinnamon stick

1 cup blackberries

⅓ cup crème de cassis (optional)

1 lb white bread, sliced ¾ in thick, crusts removed

1 Put the dried fruit into a bowl and add just enough boiling water to cover. Leave to plump up for about 15 minutes, then drain. Put the fresh apples and plums, the wine, sugar, and cinnamon into a saucepan. Heat gently, stirring to help the sugar dissolve, and simmer until almost tender. Add the blackberries (keep some back for the top) and dried fruit and cook for another 5 minutes. Strain through a sieve (reserving the cooking syrup) and add the cassis to the syrup.

2 Cut 1 bread slice in a circle to fit the bottom of a pudding bowl with a 6-cup capacity, and cut the rest into broad fingers. Line the pudding bowl with the bread, dipping it in the reserved syrup before you lay in each one. Fill in any little gaps by tearing off smaller bits of bread to fit.

3 Now spoon half the fruit into the bowl (discard the cinnamon stick when you find it). Put another layer of bread, again dipping it, halfway up the pudding, then add the remaining fruit and finish with a layer of bread on top. If any syrup remains, pour it over the pudding.

4 Put a plate on top and weight it down (use cans or a heavy bottle), then refrigerate for 24 hours (I've sometimes made this in the morning for that evening, but it tastes better the next day). To unmould, run a very thin knife around the edge and invert onto a plate.

5 Decorate with a small cluster of berries. Pour some more cassis over if you're feeling flush; it gives a nice gloss and tastes good. Serve with whipped cream or crème fraîche.

Eggs is eggs

Eggs must be one of the most beautiful ingredients: those lovely porous shells, that rich interior (I often think eggs and lemons are all you need to furnish a kitchen). They are perfectly packaged yet very cheap, and perhaps that's why we take them for granted. We turn to eggs when we can't think what else to make—I bet your heart sinks when someone says, "Not much food in the house, I'm afraid. Could always scramble you a couple of eggs"—and we usually cook them badly. But many of our greatest dishes wouldn't be possible without eggs. They perform so much culinary magic. Their yolks provide the base for rich unguents, such as mayonnaise and hollandaise and their various offshoots. They can hold onto air as they set in a hot oven, giving clouds of meringue and light-as-a-feather cakes. The eggy filling of a properly cooked quiche can be so delicate it trembles, and a teetering soufflé is a thrill.

Eggs mostly provide humble treats, though. When I was ill, my mother used to ask me if I wanted "a nice boiled egg." That phrase still fills me with warmth. A perfectly boiled egg—white set, yolk soft and running down the side of its cup—is a joy. Give me a boiled egg when I'm in the right mood and I'll enjoy it as much as any fancier dish. But eggs require careful cooking. I always think it's funny that the egg is how we judge someone's culinary competence. "She can't boil an egg" is not the worst thing you could say of a cook. You have to be gentle with eggs. Attention must be paid, for example, to the point at which you stop cooking an omelet. It should never be cooked all the way through, but left *baveuse*, as the French call it, slightly uncooked in the center.

I have to confess to problems with poached eggs. I always lost half the white in the saucepan as it disappeared in little strands. It wasn't until I was taught to poach eggs in a frying pan (where the water is shallower, so there is less room for your egg to splay out) that I got it right. Thank goodness for the *oeuf mollet*, or soft-boiled egg, the treat on many a homely French salad. Once it is broken and its warm yolk runs over warm lentils or hot bacon and bitter salad greens, you're in bliss.

Just a word on what to buy. Please go for free-range. Eggs are a really cheap source of protein, so buying free-range or free-range *and* organic eggs isn't going to break the bank, and caged hens have a miserable life. Free-range eggs from farmer's markets don't cost much more than caged eggs from supermarkets.

There are recipes in this chapter that should give you an appetite for these everyday staples. Think all you can do with an egg is scramble it? That's just the beginning….

Eggs and vegetables with two mayonnaises

When I was an au-pair in Bordeaux I went to the same café each Wednesday evening for *oeufs mayo*. It was all I could afford, but I loved its richness and simplicity and looked forward to it every week. Saffron isn't cheap, but you only need a smidgen.

Serves 6

FOR THE MAYONNAISES
2 large egg yolks
½ tsp Dijon mustard
1 small garlic clove, crushed
½ cup olive oil
½ cup sunflower oil
2 tbsp white wine vinegar
salt and pepper
good squeeze of lemon juice
good pinch of saffron threads
¾ cup sorrel leaves

FOR THE EGGS AND VEGETABLES
2 heads Belgian endive (red or white or
   one of each)
about 30 French breakfast radishes
spare 1 oz watercress or lamb's lettuce
12 broccolini spears
9 eggs
cooked ham or poached trout or salmon
   (only if you have some leftover), to serve

1 To make the mayonnaises, put the egg yolks in a bowl with the mustard and garlic and mix well. Start beating with an electric beater or wooden spoon, then gradually add a few drops of the oils. Increase the stream of oil as you are whisking, making sure the mixture is thickening. If it separates, put a new yolk in another bowl and start again, adding the curdled mixture to the fresh egg. (You'll need to double the quantity of other ingredients.) Add the vinegar, seasoning, and lemon juice, then taste; you may want more vinegar, salt, pepper, or lemon. Divide between two bowls.

2 Put the saffron in a glass with 1 tbsp just-boiled water. Stir to dissolve, then slowly add it to half the mayonnaise. Put the sorrel into a food processor and add the other half. Process. Taste each mayonnaise for seasoning. Cover and refrigerate until needed.

3 Divide the endive leaves, radishes, and watercress or lamb's lettuce among plates. Prepare the broccolini and eggs at the last minute so they're bright and fresh and your guests can have both hot and cold elements. Boil the broccolini in water for about 3 minutes and the eggs for about 8 minutes.

4 Put the warm broccolini and eggs on the plates with ham, trout, or salmon (if using) and add a pool of each mayonnaise. Serve with bread.

ALSO TRY...

The Provençal olive paste, tapenade, is a knockout with hard-boiled eggs, French breakfast radishes, unsalted butter, and French bread. Or try salt-cured anchovies and black olives with hard-boiled eggs, bread, and olive oil. Try other mayonnaises such as basil and sun-dried tomato—purée basil leaves with the mayonnaise and add sun-dried tomatoes, chopped—or black olive and anchovy (chop and add to plain mayonnaise).

Buckingham eggs

I have long since forgotten where I read about this dish. I fancy Buckingham is a reference to Buckingham Palace, as this contains a few key ingredients beloved of the British aristocracy, but I don't know for sure. Anyway, they are amazingly good. Scrambled eggs should be cooked over a medium to low heat until creamy and just set, not cooked to rubber over your highest setting. That's really all you need to know.

Serves 1

1 slice of bread
1 tsp anchovy paste
smidgen of English mustard (available
    online or reconstitute using dry
    mustard powder)

pat of butter
2 eggs, lightly beaten
salt and pepper
2 tbsp grated aged Cheddar cheese
Worcestershire sauce

1 Toast the bread on both sides, then spread it with the anchovy paste and mustard. Melt the butter in a nonstick pan and add the eggs and a little seasoning.

2 Stir over medium-low heat until the eggs are just holding their shape (don't over-scramble or they'll be like rubber once you broil them). Pile the eggs on the toast, then sprinkle on the cheese and a little Worcestershire sauce. Put under a *very* hot broiler until pale gold and just bubbling. Eat immediately.

ALSO TRY...

With smoked haddock and Parmesan Cook 3 in piece smoked haddock (see page 225). Leave it in big flakes. Scramble 2 eggs as above (a slug of cream doesn't go amiss with smoked haddock) and gently stir in the fish and 3 tbsp finely grated Parmesan cheese towards the end of the cooking time. Sprinkle fresh parsley, finely chopped, on top, grind on some black pepper, and serve immediately.

With chorizo and wilted spinach Cook 3 oz Spanish chorizo, sliced, in the fat that runs from it as it cooks. Scramble a couple of lightly beaten eggs as in the main recipe and, at the same time, quickly wilt 3 oz baby spinach leaves in a frying pan with 1 tbsp olive oil. Put the spinach on a plate, the scrambled eggs on top, and sprinkle over the chorizo.

Alpine soufflés

There's no mystery to soufflés. Just remember these key points: dust the dishes with bread crumbs so the soufflé has something to cling to as it rises; make sure your cheese sauce is thick, add the egg whites to it while it's warm, season well, beat the egg whites until stiff but not dry, place the soufflé on a heated baking sheet so it starts rising immediately, and don't open the oven before a soufflé has cooked for 20 minutes. Finally, soufflés should be slightly soft within, so don't cook them until they are totally set. They continue to cook once they're out of the oven.

Serves 6

¼ cup butter
dry white bread crumbs, to dust
6 tbsp flour
1 tsp dry mustard powder
good pinch of cayenne
1¾ cups whole milk

1⅓ cups grated Beaufort or Gruyère cheese
6 heaped tbsp grated Parmesan cheese
6 eggs, separated
salt and pepper

1 Preheat the oven to 400°F and put in a metal baking sheet. Melt a good pat of the butter and use it to brush six ramekins. Dust lightly with bread crumbs. It isn't absolutely necessary, but you can make little collars of parchment paper, which should rise 2 in above the rim of each ramekin, and tie them with kitchen string. They just look nice.

2 Melt the remaining butter in a heavy pan and stir in the flour, mustard, and cayenne. Cook for 45 seconds. Take off the heat and add the milk, a little at a time, stirring constantly to remove any lumps. Return to the heat, stirring, and bring to a boil. It will thicken. Cook gently for 2 minutes, then remove from the heat. Stir in the cheeses, egg yolks, and plenty of seasoning.

3 Whisk the egg whites until stiff–they should stay in the bowl if you hold it upside down–but not dry, and fold a large spoonful into the warm mixture to loosen it. Fold in the rest of the whites, then divide among the dishes. Run your finger around the inside of each ramekin: this will give each soufflé a "top hat" look when it puffs up.

4 Put the ramekins on the baking sheet and bake for 25 minutes until risen and golden brown. Don't open the door until they've cooked for 20 minutes or they will fall. Then just open the door wide enough to give the soufflés a shake. If they wobble a lot, cook for another 5 minutes. Serve immediately.

ALSO TRY...

Once you've mastered the technique you can turn almost anything–spinach, potato and anchovy, zucchini, roasted red bell peppers, mushrooms, leeks, fish–into a soufflé. Try making the soufflé above with blue cheese and walnuts (use half cheddar and half blue cheese), goat cheese, or smoked cheddar.

Menemen

A Turkish dish and a fantastic supper (great for when you have a mate over and don't think scrambled eggs quite cuts it). It's spicy-hot but you have cool yogurt and emollient egg yolk to offset it. Great with very cold beer.

Serves 4

FOR THE EGGS
¼ cup olive oil
1 large onion, quite thickly sliced
4 red, yellow, and green bell peppers, seeded and quite thickly sliced
2 green chiles, seeded and finely chopped
14 oz can tomatoes in thick juice
salt and pepper

2 tbsp chopped fresh cilantro, flat-leaf parsley, or mint
4 eggs
extra-virgin olive oil
ground chile or cayenne
crumbled feta cheese (optional)
flatbread, to serve

FOR THE YOGURT SAUCE
½ cup Greek yogurt
2 garlic cloves, crushed

1 Heat the oil in a large frying pan and cook the onion, peppers, and chiles over medium-high heat until the onion is golden. Add the tomatoes, season, and cook until the peppers are soft and the mixture not too runny, though still like a sauce. Stir in the herbs. Break the eggs on top and cook over medium heat until they are set but the yolks are still runny (15–20 minutes). The mixture underneath will become thicker.

2 Sprinkle the eggs with salt and pepper, add a drizzle of extra-virgin olive oil, and the ground chile or cayenne. Sprinkle with feta, if using. Stir the ingredients for the yogurt sauce together and serve on the side with flatbread.

ALSO TRY...

Oven-roasted ratatouille with baked eggs Preheat the oven to 400°F. Thickly slice and deseed 1 red and 1 yellow bell pepper. Cut 4 zucchini into ¼ in slices, and 1 eggplant into chunks. Cut 2 red onions into wedges. Halve 1½ lb plum tomatoes. Put the vegetables, 2 garlic cloves, crushed, ½ cup olive oil, the leaves from 3 thyme sprigs, and salt and pepper into a large roasting pan or wide cast-iron sauté pan. Toss everything around and roast for 45 minutes. When the vegetables have 15 minutes to go, stir in 1¾ cups strained tomatoes, mixing well and seasoning. Five minutes before the end of cooking, reduce the oven temperature to 350°F and break 4 eggs into the vegetables. Drizzle 2 tbsp olive oil and sprinkle seasoning over the eggs and cook until they have set but the yolks are runny (this should take the remaining 5 minutes, but do check as ovens vary).

Smoked cheddar and apple omelet

Cook omelets in butter and serve as the center is just setting (*baveuse* as they say in France), not cooked to rubber. Make sure your filling is properly cooked before adding it. Mushrooms, for example, need to have exuded all their liquid–and that liquid needs to have evaporated–or your omelet will leak pale gray water. Cheese should be added in time to allow it to melt.

Serves 2

2 tbsp butter

1 apple, cored and cut into thin wedges (no need to peel)

leaves from 2 thyme sprigs

4 eggs, beaten and seasoned

⅔ cup grated smoked cheddar

1 Melt half the butter in a small frying pan and sauté the apple over medium heat until golden on both sides and tender. Set aside. Add most of the thyme to the eggs.

2 Heat the remaining butter in a frying pan and, once it is foaming, add the eggs. Tilt the pan, gently scraping up the bits of omelet which set in the middle and allowing the uncooked eggs to run into the spaces left behind. When the omelet is still soft on top but set underneath, put the apples and cheese on one half. Fold the other half over the filling, let the cheese melt for 20 seconds or so, then turn the omelet onto a warmed plate. Sprinkle with the remaining thyme and serve.

ALSO TRY...

Fill your omelet with the lovely, nutty-tasting Alpine cheese Beaufort or, if you can't find that, Gruyère, and shreds of ham. Goat cheese and finely chopped soft herbs–chervil or basil, for example–make another good cheesey omelet. Flaked smoked haddock with grated cheddar is delicious, or add chopped dill to the eggs and fill the omelet with flakes of hot smoked salmon or off-cuts of smoked salmon (you can get these in packages and they are always inexpensive).

Leek vinaigrette with bacon and poached egg

Poaching eggs well is a skill that eluded me for years, so here's how. Put about 2 in water in a frying pan and bring to a boil. Use really fresh eggs (or the white will spread out like a disintegrating octopus) and have a tea cup handy. Reduce the heat so the water is just shuddering. Crack the egg into the cup and slide it into the water as gently as you can. Cook for about 4 minutes. Remove with a slotted spoon and let the egg drain really well, without allowing it to become stone cold. If you're having trouble with poaching, for this recipe try soft-boiling the eggs for 4½ minutes, then carefully shell them, without breaking into the yolk, set them on top of the leeks, and gently break so the yolk runs out.

Serves 6

FOR THE LEEKS AND EGGS
1⅓ lb thin young leeks, or
    medium-sized leeks
6 bacon or pancetta slices
olive oil
6 eggs
balsamic vinegar (optional)

FOR THE VINAIGRETTE
1½ tsp white wine vinegar
salt and pepper
½ tsp Dijon mustard
½ cup extra-virgin olive oil
¾ tsp superfine sugar, or to taste
1 tbsp finely chopped fresh parsley

1 Trim the leeks, removing the dark green bits and any tough outer leaves if you are using larger leeks. Wash thoroughly. If you are using small leeks, simply trim the ends; if using larger leeks, trim the ends and cut the leeks into 3½ in lengths. Steam or boil the leeks until tender. The length of time this takes depends on the thickness of the leeks you are using. If you boil them, make sure you drain them really well.

2 Make the vinaigrette by whisking all the ingredients together. As soon as the leeks are cooked, put them into a dish and cover with the vinaigrette.

3 Cook the bacon or pancetta in a little olive oil. Divide the leeks among six plates, put a rasher of bacon or pancetta on each serving and keep them warm while you quickly poach the eggs. Make sure each egg is well drained, then set on top of each serving. Grind on some black pepper, drizzle a little balsamic vinegar over, if using, and serve immediately.

ALSO TRY...

You can top the leeks with a slice of cured ham (such as prosciutto) or cooked ham, or replace the leeks with purple-sprouting broccolini, when in season. If you use broccolini, you can sprinkle shavings of Parmesan on top and omit the bacon.

Peach and lavender honey clafoutis

Clafoutis is a batter pudding in which the fruit really shines. It's also inexpensive—especially when summer fruit gets plentiful and you can pick up peaches or apricots for a song. Cherry is the classic, but go where you will...plums, nectarines, and greengages are all good, though soft berries are best avoided as they collapse.

Serves 4–6

FOR THE PEACHES
1¾ lb peaches, halved and pitted
¼ cup superfine sugar
juice of ½ lemon

FOR THE BATTER
⅓ cup heavy cream
⅓ cup milk
2 big tbsp lavender honey (available online)

2 sprigs fresh lavender, if in season
3 eggs
½ cup granulated sugar
pinch of salt
3 tbsp all-purpose flour
toasted almonds (optional)
confectioners' sugar, to dust

1 Put the peaches, superfine sugar, and lemon juice into a frying or sauté pan and heat gently. You want to soften the fruit slightly; it should be tender but not collapsing. Cool.

2 To make the batter, mix the cream, milk, honey, and lavender in a saucepan. Bring to just under a boil, then leave to infuse for 20 minutes or so. Preheat the oven to 350°F. Whisk the eggs, granulated sugar, and salt together until the mixture triples in volume and is pale and fluffy. Fold in the flour, then the milk mixture.

3 Arrange the fruit in a gratin dish and pour over the batter. Bake for 30 minutes, or until set. Sprinkle on the toasted almonds, and sift over a little confectioners' sugar.

ALSO TRY...

Apricot and orange blossom Make as above, but replace the peaches with the same quantity of quartered apricots, replace the honey with 2 more tbsp granulated sugar, omit the lavender and add 1 tbsp orange flower water to the cream.

Cherry and almond Make as in the main recipe, but replace the honey with another 2 tbsp granulated sugar, omit the lavender and add 1–2 tbsp kirsch or amaretto liqueur (if you have it) to the batter. You'll need 1⅓ lb cherries, pitted.

Apple, honey, and rosemary Make as in the main recipe, but heat the milk and cream with 3 tbsp plain honey and a rosemary sprig. Leave to infuse for 20 minutes. Remove the rosemary and make the batter with the milk mixture, 5 tbsp all-purpose flour, and ⅓ cup sugar. Peel and core 1⅓ lb apples and thinly slice. Toss with 2 tbsp sugar. Put in a gratin dish, pour over the batter, and bake for 30–40 minutes or until set. Sprinkle on toasted hazelnuts or walnuts and sift a little confectioners' sugar over.

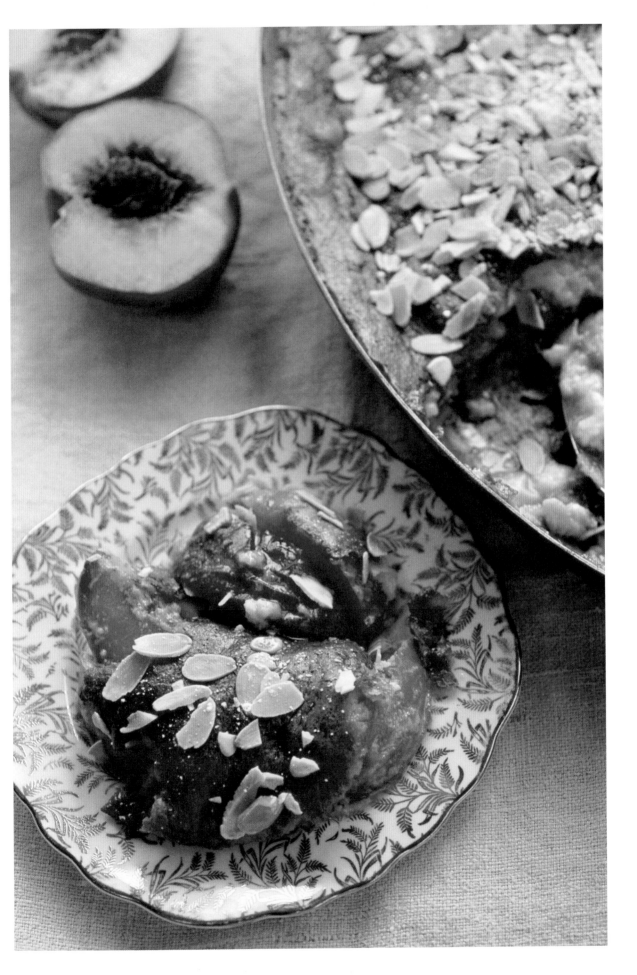

Index

For Ben, with love

Plenty
by Diana Henry

An Hachette UK Company
www.hachette.co.uk

First published in Great Britain in 2010 by
Mitchell Beazley, a division of
Octopus Publishing Group Ltd,
Carmelite House, 50 Victoria Embankment,
London EC4Y 0DZ
www.octopusbooksusa.com

This edition published in 2017

ISBN 978 1 78472 300 2

Commissioning Editor: Rebecca Spry
Art Director: Pene Parker
Designer: Miranda Harvey
Photographer: Jonathan Lovekin
Project Editor: Georgina Atsiaris
Copy Editor: Lucy Bannell
Proofreader: Ruth Baldwin
Home Economist: Sonja Edridge
Stylist: Sarah O'Keefe
Production Manager: Pete Hunt
Index: Hilary Bird

Typeset in Baskerville
Printed and bound in China

**All 'also try' recipes serve the same
number as the main recipe, unless
otherwise stated.**